NO
FA

—

LATE FLOWERING

A Yorkshire Lad's Quest to Find What He Needs to Grow Up

Graham Clift

Quantum Dot Press

First published in 2021 by Quantum Dot Press

ISBN: 978-1-912882-53-3

Cover design by Edwin Rydberg (LightSpeedDreams.net)

For all my fathers

CONTENTS

INTRODUCTION

'Write down those stories from school and work,' my daughter said in 2008, but it wasn't enough; the stories needed a context. In a world full of injustice, social immobility and discrimination of too many kinds my historical teenage problems seemed so small.

Instead I researched people, school and workplaces in local archives and on websites. I found birth, marriage and death records — the only evidence some people left behind. I read deferential profiles and smarmy promotional articles. I was dismayed, but then I realised I *had* discovered something important; there's a *gap* between the official records of people and places, and the reality of what it was like to live and work with those people in those places.

It is a gap down which working class lives are lost to history. They're left off the corporate web pages, they've slipped down between the archived minutes, newspaper clippings and old photographs. The kind of lives rarely represented in the biography shelves of libraries and bookshops, the lives I wanted my book to be about.

Because I set out to tell the truth I have had to change the identities of people and places to respect privacy. In only one case have I created an amalgamated character, and also taken some minor liberties with the facts as I recall them to make for a better story. I know my memory is fallible, but this is my attempt at an honest account of my life from the age of 12 to 20, at school, on the farm and in the garden, as it seemed to me at the time.

I finish my book in a time when even more difficulties face young people of all races, classes and abilities. Writing it has reminded me of the prejudice, control and greed I witnessed in my own young life, and what these vices cost all of us. But shining high above all the troubles is a renewed appreciation of the innate kindness of people, and how the right words at the right time can make such a difference to someone's life.

SCHOOL

ROUND HERE 1968

I want to know stuff. I'm not sure what yet, but I know I like it, knowing. Right now I know I can smell that stinky waterway, even before I turn off the pavement after the scrapyard. That's the scrapyard next to the gas works, by the double railway bridge. That quiet path could be the path of my life so far. It starts next to the grey lattice hoarding with its huge adverts of smiling women, all thrilled with their Daz and Windolene and Omo.

Hoardings carry only lies. The hacked silver birches, with their roots in the railway ballast, trying to grow up in front of the ads say something more truthful about what life is really like round here, I know that, but I can't quite put my finger on what that is yet either. It's so hard to label things sometimes.

I'm twelve years old, and I live in the rumbling bowels of Yorkshire down here at the bottom end. Piles of coal, pit spoil and scrap metal are excreted daily to form the landscape and to stop anybody being too cheerful, as well as giving the traffic something to run around.

I don't actually know what I'm looking for in life yet. I'll tell you what I do know though, without really having a word for it, a creepy feeling I have every time I walk to Pete's house alone on the quiet canal towpath.

Walking gives you space to think about anything you want. I swing my arms and keep going forward, forward, but my mind often drifts backwards. I like that about walking. Last year, in history, at school they said we would look back and learn about Britain. Well, we did loads about Vikings, Romans, Saxons and Normans and a third former told me that later we have to do about German and Dutch kings too. What about Britain? I thought. In the same way, although this book is meant to be a kind of history of me, I just have to tell you about some other people. People like Pete, because in a way I already know he is helping me to become me, if that makes sense. Do you ever wonder which of the people around you will really affect your life in some way? I wish they'd wear badges like prefects do. I haven't got life all worked out yet, but there's still time. There's a lot to learn, and I'm still growing up. A girl in my form said, 'There's *personal stuff* to learn about too.' Whatever that is. But give me a chance, I'm only twelve. I can't understand *everything*. Not until I'm sixteen anyway.

I'll tell you what the problem is with this path, it's the canal's dark water. It has oily rainbows and smells of creosote as if it's challenging anything living to fall into it and survive. I would only need to stumble into one of those holes behind the steel pilings, made by the wash from the industrial barges, to die a terrible death before my life has properly started. And then what kind of life story would this be? I'd just be a square inch in the South Yorkshire Times beginning 'Tragic Boy…' and nobody wants that. You see, I am the only kid in my class who can't swim. Of course I don't tell anyone. Pete can swim really well, just like he does everything else. But I go to the pool and join in, playing 'tiggy' by hopping along in the shallow end on one leg, pretending to myself and the boys that I can swim well enough. I expect I will have to do this all my life.

Anyway, I put up with all this because besides going to Pete's house, this path takes me to a different kind of place. Quieter, with twigs and grass and hills that aren't made of pit waste or broken cars. It's altogether less mucky, greener. Sometimes there's even a kestrel overhead. Countryside I suppose.

Pete is quite a lad; pushy, sporty and bright. I have to run to keep up with him physically and mentally. Having a best friend like him makes you go to the perimeter of yourself, and then try to redraw the line a bit further out. I sometimes wonder what he gets out of being friends with me though.

Hey Pete. Pete.

'Grey.'

Can you say a bit about yourself for this history homework thing I'm doing? And I'll write it down.

'No problemo amigo. I am Peter A. Seacroft, a pretty amazing 12 year old from Upper Finewell. I am going to become a famous polar explorer, and follow in the footsteps of Captain Scott and Shackleton, accomplishing great feats of stamna. Not sure how you spell that Grey. Look it up later. Yeah, so I will get sponsors to back my adventures of course; like Lambretta, Levi Straus, Rolls Royce and Cadburys so I can get the money and equipment. You'll be in the team too Grey because someone has to be in the base camp hut with all the

spare dogs and organising stuff with the walkie-talkies and that. Hey, let's test the walkie-talkies.

'Red Leader to Grey Fox crackle, crackle. We have a white-out. Can you leave more flapjack and Cadburys Fruit and Nut rations at the glacier? Don't forget the Spanish white wine, no ice needed. Over and out.'

He's great isn't he? He's my best friend. Although I know I'm not always his because he has so many other friends.

LIBRARY 1

You'd think school would be good for someone wanting to know things, but apart from History and Maths, where you can't even scratch your lugs without a signed letter from your parents, it's rubbish. Most other lessons follow the same painful pattern. One: 'We are not starting until everyone is quiet.' No chance of that. Teacher gets cross. Two: The yelling starts, 'You are the worst class I have ever had in 'x' years of teaching.' and more stuff that no one can hear. Three: 'Right. Class detention.' Bell goes, move to another classroom. Repeat.

I used to sit upright with my arms folded thinking that if the teacher saw me they'd take pity and teach me something, maybe slip me a note with some facts on. But it doesn't make any difference because at school, I don't exist as an individual, I am just one thirty-sixth of The Worst Class in the School. The French teacher keeps order by using a lot of sarcasm and his board rubber, but not even Margaret Bartle who is the genius of our year can explain why we should learn French at all when most of us don't even get as far as Scarborough, and frankly Scottish or Geordie would be more useful for there. Once, we had another French teacher for a week and he kept saying, 'Don't ask me why, they just do that.' And that's all I can say about the misbehaviour of form 11d, or form 21d as we are now, starting the second year.

I have found a good place to learn once school is over though. I keep it secret. Don't tell anyone will you? Not even Pete Seacroft knows about it. I never see anyone from school there, it's a lot quieter than home, and there are books there about *everything*. It's not very secret really, it's the public library, but hardly anyone seems to know about it. I read 'Jennings goes to School,' by Anthony Buckeridge, and then all the other Jennings books they have. Then I learnt how to play chess from a book, so that I could play for my house. I do my homework first to get it out of the way, so I can read some more. I discovered the Sherlock Holmes books which are all about knowing tons of obscure stuff like; cigar stubs, assailant's footprints and especially, noticing details like the colour of mud or missing fingers. Holmes is great but Dr Watson is my favourite because he gets things wrong, probably as he is not paying attention due to him slyly jotting things down all the time. Thank goodness he did though, as we wouldn't have the books otherwise would we? Anyway, at the moment I'm reading about ways to leave home, like going camping or hitch hiking around the world.

I wonder if it would all have been so different if my dad had allowed me to go to the grammar school after I passed my 11 plus.

But he said, 'I'm not paying t'bus fare for you to go *there* every day.'

I said, 'I'll walk Dad, it's only two miles.'

'No,' he said, 'you're going to the Comprehensive and that's that.'

Mam isn't keen on me reading. If she catches me sitting with a book she says, 'I'll give you a job if you've nowt to do; get them brasses cleaned and sweep them cellar steps.' Our brasses shine like gold, and you could eat your tea off our cellar steps.

When I sit in the library and read about Jennings at his boarding school, I imagine it's like the Grammar, but with gardens and dormitories. Jennings has good pals, and learns a lot and he hardly has to see his parents. Their job is to keep sending cakes, and other things he needs in the post. Now that is what school should be like.

SWISH SWISH 1969

This isn’t the lower school hall I know anymore, it's so dark apart from the coloured lights winking on and off in the corners. My orange Terylene, cord-look shirt with button down collar looks great, but is a bit scratchy without a vest. Shame I haven't got any Wrangler denims to go with it, but maybe, in the dark no one will notice my school trousers, especially with these great looking white socks.

The strong niff, of soap and freshly washed clothes, is almost enough to hide the pong of floor polish and school dinners. I am thirteen, and this is the third years' Christmas party and my first ever disco. It's so ace, and really grown up. I think I should have eaten more buns though to take away the taste of the fish paste sandwiches. In the darkness on the stage Mr Winder is having a crafty fag while he puts on records; he should ask for lessons from the bike shed gang in how to cup a cig in your hand, so no one can see it. The music is just like *Top of the Pops* on telly; 'Flowers in the Rain', 'Ob la di Ob la da', 'Daydream Believer’.

There are lots of girls, and some boys, dancing and jiggling about. It all looks great fun. I *really* want to do that.

‘How do you dance?’ I ask Fordy.

‘I Dunno.’

‘How do you dance, Tim?’

‘I'm not a girl.’

John Perfitt, ace captain of the unbeatable under 14's footy team, and cock of our year is there now. He makes it look so easy. Mind you, he does that with everything. Oh God, he's dancing with Karen Zanner. I *wish* I could do that. But I'm stood here with the quiet boys and we're talking, well shouting over the music actually, about; how unfair class detentions are, about Mrs Gray's dandruff and whether parting your hair down the side or down the middle is best.

'Hey Tingy, how do you dance?'

'Stuff off.'

'Bongo, how do you...'

'Ask Roy.'

The brainy kids get blue enamel merit badges for 'Attainment' every half term. Roy hasn't got one of those, but he had got his first yellow merit badge which they give out for 'Effort.' He has pinned it onto his green sports jacket, it doesn't go with his 'flower power' tie, although it matches his teeth perfectly. His hair is dark, but his face is like a white eggshell. I know it sounds weird but it isn't the special lights or anything, he looks like this all the time. His thin lips look funny and spit at me when he talks, but that might be because Mr Winder has turned the sound up cos he loves the Beatles. Roy is really shouting now, and I think he's saying you can do any movements you like to the music.

'But I need to know some steps or something,' I yell.

He points down to the floor. I want to laugh because his feet are massive. He is wearing some of those zipped boots from Cadley's Shoe Sale. His Mum has bought them big so he can 'grow into them,' or 'get lots of wear out of them,' or one of those other phrases that mothers say when they buy you clothes.

'Watch me' he mouths, jabbing a finger downwards.

Keeping his heel on the floor he wiggles a foot from side to side. I copy him and then he moves both feet together, they look like windscreen wipers. I copy that too. This is easy. Then rocking forward onto his toes he does the wipers thing again, but pivoting on his toes this time. We run through it a few more times, and then we are ready. With knees bent, and elbows by our sides we do the sequence; heel, wipe, toe, wipe, heel, wipe, toe, wipe. Concentrating hard we ease out onto the parquet tiles just as 'Sugar Sugar' starts up.

'Thanks Roy.'

I AM DANCING! Now, where are the girls?

PRINCESS BALLROOM

Poor Devil. You were so busy in 1970. What with the Vietnam War, South African apartheid, and the troubles in Northern Ireland, I was lucky to get any of your time at all.

I was thirteen. Unlucky for some, but not for me. It was the year I told two lies. Pretty immoral I know, but I gained immeasurable benefit from both of them. But before you cast me into your fiery pit Satan, know that it was actually the same lie twice, and once, I didn't even say it.

You'll like this bit Satan. It started in Sunday school when my mate Dave, who was a year older than me, offered to show me his paper round. The newsagent's was a cheaper version of hell; no disrespect intended, but you'd have approved, lots of sulphurous fumes. They were emitted by Albert the owner, who stood there making up paper rounds by scrawling house numbers with a fat pencil on the top of Daily Mirrors, he did this between farting and putting his pencil behind his ear to sell cigarettes to men in caps with tubercular coughs. The walls were lined with the false truths of newspapers and magazines, and a huge display of ways to smoke yourself to death. After I turned up promptly a few times to help Dave, Albert asked me if I'd like my own round for fifteen shillings a week. Actually Albert looked rather like you Satan. He was my gateway to the world of money, your greatest invention.

He even introduced me to the existence of soft pornography by saying, 'There's nothing on the top shelf for you lads.'

He never asked if I was fourteen, he just assumed I was by my association with Dave, and I didn't say anything. Boy did I spend that money *carefully.* Collecting books of two shilling saving stamps got me; a transistor radio, walking boots, records, and for the first time, on credit, my own clothes, bought from my auntie's catalogue.

Money aside I got something much more. For the price of getting up early and lugging a heavy bag of newsprint around the streets, I found something really special: the twilit peace of early morning walking. I soon took on an extra round. The space to think your own thoughts between 6 am and 8am every morning was precious. Not very hellish at all.

But if pop music, sexual awakening and lascivious decor are in your domain Satan, then maybe you brought me to another key place in my life. By putting on my new clothes, and upgrading my personal hygiene to include *twice* weekly baths, I was ready for my second lie. The Princess Ballroom in Brownton was the place to be for the midweek discotheque for 14 to 16 year olds.

'One please.'

'Are you fourteen?'

'Of course.'

Well if you're going to lie, there's no point in being hesitant. I climbed the stairs to the accompaniment of

'Spirit in the Sky' with its mix of old spiritual and totally modern spacey guitar sounds, and walked over the soft carpet between decorated pillars and the pink and crimson drapery while lights flashed. I was entering a dream world. A place populated by friendly faces from school that promised a new wonderfulness from which there would be no way back.

Truth was Satan, or can I call you Lucifer? I was an innocent. I was far from ready for what met me there. I could skim stones, forge my mother's signature for my homework book and make chips, but I could still count the days since I'd had my first ever kiss. While some of the boys in my class talked about masturbation, I was yet to discover how to do it. To see all the dancing and twirling girls in the coloured lights was wonderful. I was fascinated, although puzzled about the strange new feelings. There was only one thing to do, to find my friends.

'Graham, we're all gonna dance. Smithy has asked for 'Woolly Bully', it's after 'Bad Moon Rising'.

'Hey no one is in school uniform!'

'I can't hear you.'

The only mature adult male in the place stood by a column like a lone roman sentry, he was the 'security presence.' A large bouncer with a 1950's greasy quiff and a body squeezed into a maroon jacket a size too small, and neatly creased slacks. He occasionally moved to stop suspected fights but his main forte was pointing to tables if anyone sat on them. Also representing the management was a poised Audrey Hepburn look-alike ballroom dance teacher with 'old fashioned' hair in a beehive. She was probably about 22 but seemed to be from another generation.

And there Lucifer, during a DJ toilet break mix of Motown hits, I think you wandered off. You did pay me a visit at school once when, after being bullied, I desperately lashed out at an innocent boy in order to prove myself to my savage peers, and avoid a bigger fight. It saved my hide, but you have given me years of regret over that.

The Princess was a place to dress up. My orange shirt and cravat with three-button pinky-orange hipsters looked pretty neat. I know because a singer with a very similar look was on *Top of the Pops*. The chunky toecaps of my platform shoes peeped out from the flared bottoms like a pair of irresistible puppies.

We were like the first flocking of juvenile birds: thrilled with our new plumage and restless for something unknown, trying out our wings, exhilarated by our own flapping and smells of sweat and perfume, and the bumping of music.

Familiar girls from school were transformed by bright clothes and Max Factor, without their baggy school blouses, some were seen to have breasts for the first time. Handbags replaced satchels. The haughty, the studious, the shy girls and the stroppy ones had all metamorphosed into new shapes with softer faces. Most looked older than the boys of the same age. It seemed to be perfectly acceptable to stand gawking at the girls but that was the easy bit. Understanding why we were doing this, and what some of the strange sensations this aroused were, proved much more difficult.

One girl, with red hair, moved her body in some way that was unfathomable. Male eyes rolled over her hypnotic contours. The hem of her short dress curled and flicked at her bottom, like a flag signalling excitement and danger. There was something perfect about that fabric, her form and the brown and yellow diagonal stripes of the dress. A pattern that in nature is a hazard warning to say, 'Come any closer and you may get stung.'

Suddenly there you were again Satan, standing in a pool of spilled coke in the shadows. Perhaps you were listening to 'Double Barrel' and hatching the idea of having teenage racists called skinheads dance to the Ska music of the Caribbean? Anyway, look Luce, it's been grand to meet you, but I have my life to get on with and Smithy is heading towards me. Thanks again though for the white lies that brought me here.

The coloured light splashed across the floor and faces and Smithy's voice called out hoarsely, 'Hey Graham. Janet Bennett is looking for you.'

'Shout up.'

'A GIRL IS LOOKING FOR YOU. AND *RIDE A WHITE SWAN* IS ON NEXT, YOU KNOW THE LEG KICK ONE? IT'S EASY.'

'What does she want?'

'I CAN'T HEAR YOU.'

LIBRARY 2

Tonight Miss Evans, the librarian, has shiny red lipstick on, perhaps she is going dancing after work. It makes her little lips look like the plastic ones you get in a lucky bag. Beside the gurgles from the Mini car sized radiators, and the squeak of the book trolley, it's quiet here by the *Real Things and People* section of the children's library. So quiet that you can look up from your homework and think stuff. You can't do that at home with the telly on. Thoughts like; what would life be like if I lived somewhere else, or in another time? Or, what will I be doing, and where will I be in five years' time?

The future is something I don't know about. In the books it's all sci-fi-strange and scary. Mind you so is the past. I suppose all I know is that I'm here now, trying to make a bit of sense of it all and finish my Geography homework. But everything becomes part of the past eventually doesn't it? Even the moon landing. We'll all be in the past soon enough, like our clothes, and even my nylon socks and zip up boots. And speech? Well, look at Shakespeare and Dickens. 'What language is that?' some people say. I've only read *Christmas Carol* right through and browsed *Midsummer Night's Dream,* but you soon realise that people used different words then.

The nearest I ever get to the future is Miss Evans' purple-ink date stamp. It comes down with a soft sticky sound and right there, still wet for a few seconds, is the future. You leave the library and walk home with a 'new' library book. The future is the 2 weeks you've got to read the library book before it becomes overdue. Two weeks where nothing is certain, except that hopefully by the end of it you will have read another book, and maybe you'll know a little more before it becomes an 'old' library book.

The library will always have more 'new' books you haven't read than 'old' books you have. Because there's only the one of us, and thousands of people in the past have written books. Perhaps all books are from the past. When you get lost in a book, it's as if there is no one else in the world. Your body is sat there, but your mind is; in a Victorian Hansom cab smelling horses and leather, or loading a heavy flintlock on a distant battlefield, or macheting your way through a humid jungle. Then a sudden sound startles you; it's Miss Evans shouting, 'Library closes in five minutes.' You stand and stretch before taking your book to her for stamping, so that you can take it home, and resume reading with a torch under the bedclothes.

The dates in the front of the book can go back years. This can make you think about all the people who have read that book before you. I often wish, I could meet them, and talk about the book. We'd say; 'Ooh, couldn't you smell the sawdust in the circus scene?' 'The index was a bit skimpy', '*I* thought the Colonel might have done it', or, 'Sorry about the tea spill I did on page 93.'

This library has been open since 1906. That's the Edwardian period; straw boaters, suffragettes, bathing huts and rickets. Has Miss Evans been here ever since it opened? You can have funny thoughts like this in a quiet library. It would explain why she can take you straight to any book you want, and say, 'have you read…' and, 'I think you might also like…' She has probably read every book in here, and must have a brain that is convoluted and massive inside her skull. In contrast to those ladies at church who have hats that look like they're wearing their brains on the outside of their heads. Gosh, that's another strange thought you could only have in a quiet library too. Anyway I'm not surprised she has to wear glasses with all that reading.

I hope that one day I will meet a girl my age who is like Miss Evans, so that we can talk about Leonardo da Vinci, bicycle maintenance and the best lightweight tents.

TO YVETTE

There are three contacts in the Princess Ballroom Disco beginners' game. Here's the first one, where a girl comes over and puts a hand on my shoulder to shout in my ear.

'Will you go out with my friend Yvette? She's over there in the green skirt.'

'With the glasses on, drinkin a coke?'

'No, next to her.'

'Yeah ok. What do I have to do?'

Soon after, we descend the steps and leave together as Elvis sings, 'The Wahunder of You.' Outside, the night's sooty reality nips me. What am I doing? My ears ring in the relative silence as a breeze, cold and damp like a lost inshore wind, shifts our hair around. If only some words would come, and I could transmit them to you. But instead, I button up my shivering teenage self inside my Levi jacket, and point to say, 'This way?'

You point, in the opposite direction, and we walk.

Under the first street lamp you look at me as if to say, 'Well, what does that look mean?'

'What?' you say, quietly.

'Nothin.' I say.

I'm not clear why we're here. You obviously know already where to go to catch your bus. But your friend told me, 'it's what you do, walk a girl to the bus stop.'

The shops I normally know, are dark and strange. In Kennard's record shop the curved sound booths are undiscernible, Jackson's self-service supermarket is all quiet except for loud pink window 'offers', and the plugs are out in the Rediffusion shop where I'm sent to pay the TV rental. Hardy's butcher's shop is bare except for pink lights on marble fields, and hedges of plastic parsley. We pass them all saying nothing.

I do *think* of things to say. 'It's strange walking along with a girl.' 'You smell nice, like cake.' 'Why do you need make-up around your eyes?' 'Your orangey coat is thick and buttoned right up.' 'You look lovely.' But it's too hard to say any of this out loud.

Oh but it's not as hard as passing Markes's fishing tackle shop, as if it was just the dry cleaners or a bank. Its window lights are on, and I didn't tell you that, in daylight I *always* stop there. I didn't say, 'look at the fluorescent floats, the cone of stacked bait boxes that look like a giant segmented maggot, and the glistening glass fibre rods on the wall. Arranged along the window bottom are swivels and leger weights, spinners and pike lures, brass spring balances and a diminishing line of gilt hooks down to size 24 for match fishing. Which do you like best? Do you like fishing?'

I wish now I had been able to say that, because at least we would have been talking and sharing, warming up some words.

I could have said, 'Look at the wicker baskets with webbing straps - I use a wooden box I made myself, there are bags of ground bait, those are porcupine quills for making floats - I shape mine from firewood that I paint and varnish. Over there are fine monofilament lines that you can hardly see, and a neat plastic lead-shot dispenser - I use a tobacco tin for mine with soldered dividers I made from a bean can. What do you think? Do you make things? What do you like to do?'

But I have learnt that revealed passions are often ridiculed. Being with you is so novel, that I feel weird and I know that, I can't just be my ordinary self.

Contact number two, is made when we pass the closed market hall, and I take hold of your warm hand, and you don't seem to mind. You walk with ceremonial steps. Looking down, but also looking out. There is something about the way you do this that sticks in my mind. You are careful but not fearful. As if you are walking me to somewhere we will never go again.

Oh, if only we had talked. So that when we arrived at your bus stop, we might have really said something. When you said, 'What?' again so gently I might have said, 'I am looking at you this way because, all of this is a new experience, and I'm a bit lost. I know the time for acting cool is over. Catching a fish is special: the float slides, you strike and then marvel at the force pulling from the end of the line; but being with you, walking on the wet pavements of Brownton on this cold April night, beats even that. You are a fish I never caught before, one I've only seen in library books, like a smooth tench.'

I ought to tell you that you are more attractive than all the fishing tackle in Markes's shop, and that being with you is touching something in me that I never knew before. You have such a sense of completeness. At only 14 you have a fully formed strength surrounding you like Stonehill's castle keep. As we stand under the Yorkshire Traction sign you have a way of looking at me and lifting my eyes to yours. I am melting in the presence of your beauty.

I can say none of this to you. I've walked through this place so many times on errands, or for school shoes, but tonight in the dark among the muted shops this is a different place. I have slipped out of my usual world to swim like Cousteau in the ocean. I'm in awe of what I see. You are a, *'new creature never before seen by mankind'*, inspiring a sense of wonder in me that makes me check my air supply. I can't say that I love you because I've no experience of that, but you are making me think about what love might mean. And it is a start. You are from a place where a child has two loving parents, and I cannot comprehend that yet. But I know that you are loved, because everything about you says so, from your steady gaze and air of contentment, to your fearless questions and your substantial well-made clothes.

I watch conscientiously for your bus, because it will signal that contact three may be permitted. When your bus leaves, I will walk back home tasting your lipstick, and noticing the moon and the stars. I'll remember you for all of my lifetime, as the first girl I walked to a bus stop. The orange coated girl who embodied self-esteem, illuminating it for me like a struck match offered to a small pilot light.

In 30 years' time and in another age, I will find myself on another kind of dark street, and I'll remember your beautiful wholeness and confidence and wish it for myself. I will at last find all the words I need to heal and leave the darkness behind. I wish you a long and happy life, with someone who will cherish you as you know to cherish yourself.

But for now I'm back to leaning on the concrete bus stop post, as my underdressed teenage self, and I have thought of something that I *will* say out loud.

'You comin next week?'

'Yeah.'

'Can I walk you to the bus stop then as well?'

'If you want to.'

'OK.'

GYM REFLECTIONS

Pete Seacroft's face reminds me of glaciation. We just did about that in 'O' level Geology. He has watery green eyes and hair prematurely grey like old snow which turns a pale blond in summer. The end of his nose is a truncated spur, and his forehead is slightly flattened as if by the passage of ice.

I suppose he is an extrovert and quite confident, people seemed to strongly like him or dislike him, but he's been my main friend since we started at the Comp. In summer term I'm his chubby non-athletic assistant.

'Here hold me blazer, Grey,' he says, and I do while he makes attempts at school athletics records in his flashy blue spikes.

I don't really like being called 'Grey' but I think sometimes that's how he sees me, his duller companion.

Last summer, when we were fourteen and picked on by Chipton's gang, Pete came up with a solution, and we began weight training here in the Dantley Working Men's Club.

We're in the basement, which has been turned into a gym. We feel tougher after a few months. I think we did right from the start. It's the reek of the sweat, or maybe the act of joining in with the clanging of weights, and the manly huffing and grunting of the regulars. Although the low ceiling probably helps to make us feel bigger too, even before we tighten our little muscles.

Metalwork fills the place. There are benches, forked stands and elaborate bits of home-made engineering with pulleys and cables. Across the black floor, scattered like giant coins and matches, are disc weights and collared bars. All this equipment is arranged, church-like, in a great semi-circle around the altar of The Mirror.

The Mirror is surrounded by magazine pull-out pictures of Reg Park and Sergio Oliva. Perhaps because Pete and I are now body builders, or maybe because Reg and Sergio are naked except for swimming trunks, we feel as if we know them and can call them by their first names. Reg, from Leeds, has won Mr Universe twice, and played Hercules in several 1950's and 60's films. His black and white images make his creased body look like a used napkin forced back into its ring, as if his muscles have expanded in all directions constrained only by his pelvic girdle. Sergio, also an inspiration, is more often in colour. He has won Mr Universe, and other top bodybuilding titles consistently for the last 4 years. His fascinating oiled and depilated body is hard to take your eyes off, like a bull's carcase hanging at the butcher's.

In charge at the gym is a bodybuilder who looks like an inverted pyramid. He's Tich, and he has arms like thighs, and a small head topped with blond curls. He walks with his torso inclined forward from the waist to avoid his head catching on the low ceiling, and he looks like a Commando comic book hero. He uses some of his own training time to help us two scrawny youths get the hang of curls, bench presses, chin-ups and squats. He tells us to always finish our circuit by lying on an inclined plank to work our abdominals, and then to 'warm down' with some stretches. His voice is deep and rich like chutney.

He'll say, 'You could go up to two sets of 12 reps on that one now lads', as we do our circuit, stepping around all the heavy metal that litters the rubber floor made from old pit conveyor belts. The floor is always wet with condensation, and the sweat of us regulars.

Sometimes, Tich talks to us as he sits on a padded bench effortlessly curling a huge dumb-bell, 'Before you lads train for muscle definition, you need to bulk up; eat a high protein diet, no fat, high reps.'

If our adolescent muscles are an unbranded market pack of assorted elastic bands, Tich's are a pack of subcutaneous, hairless, pedigree dogs all known by name; Deltoid, Pectoral, Gluteus.

'Remember lads, there's no shame in starting with small weights when you're beginners. Learn to do the exercises correctly before you increase weight.' He says this while he's sitting there exercising his two Labrador pups, Bicep and Tricep.

He never laughs at us and tell us to, 'bugger off', which seems to be what most adults, except the school teachers, say to us. I think it's unusual at our age to be taken seriously by adults.

Most sessions The Mirror, is in use. There's the miserable weightlifter, Dennis 'Don't Touch My Weights' Kiddleston; he wears a black vest and slacks, fingerless gloves and a deep belt around his back that helps to support his huge paunch. He does these little 'pause-poses' that make him look menacing and also smug. We think he admires mostly the deep wedges of trapezius muscles either side of his neck, he really needs them too, because they act like chocks to stop his big round head rolling off. He does all this posing dead casually while he's just passing the mirror carrying something that could give us amateurs a hernia. Once, Pete said he saw him almost smile as he watched himself.

Sometimes, if no one is around, it's our turn.

'Ey Grey, look at these for biceps. They're definitely bigger.'

'Yeah. Mr Universe 1971, brilliant. You'll be able to open a bottle o' pop on yer own soon.'

'Kin 'ell Grey, look at the definition in Sergio's abdominals. When he lies down to bench press, I bet you could stand beermats up in them creases.'

'Pete. Serious. Will we get all big-headed when we've been coming here for a year or two?'

'No. We don't need to Grey. We are great already.'

HOMETIME HAZARD

This is something I'd rather forget, but if you really must know what started the trips to the gym: here goes.

Twice a day I join the migration of blazered and satchelled wildebeest, walking alongside the concrete fence to the Comp and back. At the edge of the school grounds, the path curves suddenly like a 'U' bend under a kitchen sink, as it passes through a small park. The height of the solid fence prevents sight of any hazards, so there is no warning. And like a drain's 'U' bend, it is a place where scum and detritus gather.

On that particular day as I walked home, a blotchy bunch of a dozen or so teenage rejects had assembled there supervised by Chipton their leader.

He is thin, with big staring eyes and a fringe that, frightened of his stare, curls upwards out of its way. This boy has found a niche in the school savannah as top dog in a handpicked group of greasy inadequates known as 'Chipton's gang.' To be fair though, if you leave school at 15 after years in remedial classes, no one expects you to coin a snappy name for your gang do they? Anyway, they don't go in for a lot of advertising, there's no promotional graffiti. Perhaps that's because, even if you could combine the brain power of the entire gang, they would struggle to operate an aerosol can. Basic intimidation and petty violence are their specialities, but let's give criminals a break, they all have to start somewhere.

The hyena pack waits around until the wildebeest thin out a bit. The stragglers who've been in detention, or school clubs, or just had to stay behind to see a teacher, the ones metaphorically limping at the back of the herd, are their prey. I know two other members of the gang, Ibbotson was in my infant class and probably still writes with blunt pencils and his tongue out; and there's Vernon who lives near me, he gets slapped regularly on the street by his mother. They have a collective ugliness, perhaps from being so unloved. Chipton with his big myxomatosis eyes being the most charismatic.

'Ey, thee. Come 'ere.' is the summons I get from the fearful-fringed one as I'm on my way home after Drama Club. The set behind the gang, like a theatre backcloth, is the glass strewn tennis court and its rusted chain link fence. Behind me, the forlorn park swings and a slide. The gang circle round as I step onto the grass.

'Right Shuggy, 'it 'im.' Commands Chipton.

Shuggy dutifully steps towards me. I glare at him. He is my height and looks unsure of himself. His mouth is small, straight and tight like a used staple, but his nostrils are big and open like two railway tunnels. His hair, just long enough to cover his ears, curls outwards at the ends making a Nazi stahlhelm. His eyes are small and unmemorable, it's the nasal caves that you notice first, like the false eyes on the wings of an Elephant Hawk moth.

Chipton says again, 'Go on 'it im.'

You don't need to be a tactical genius to work out that the best chance of survival is to stand and take what's coming without retaliation. To hit back would invite the others to join in, and if I run away they'll stampede after me.

Shuggy says something like, 'Did you call me fathead?' This is a standard thing that morons set on assaulting you do, as if they seem to need some 'reason' to hit you.

Of course I say, 'Er, no.' and he punches me on the chin. Fresh out of Drama Club, I feign a higher level of pain and shock, and inexplicably, a limp. Shameless overacting really. I can see that now. But nevertheless, I was allowed to flee home for my tea.

Anyway all that is past now. In the fantasy mental replays I respond differently, with a calm forearm block and a kick that leaves him writhing and humiliated in front of his peers before I call, 'Right, who's next?' But, in reality, I know that I did the right thing at the time; no friends of mine saw it, Shuggy got to feel tough, and the gang got to feel menacing.

It was another little taste of injustice that I would never forget. I know many people have had much more to bear than I did. Life just isn't fair sometimes. Forgiveness isn't an easy option. I'll leave it there, so as not to make a school assembly of it.

GLAMOUR INCARNATE

But life isn't all unpleasantness, homework and muscles. Susan is older than me, fifteen years old, and works in a factory. She is a new kind of angel carrying the grown-up perfume of cigarette smoke around her head like an invisible halo. She has a curvy woman's body and a high fringed mod's haircut with curled sideburns. She might be a new Hollywood star on a cig break from the Savoy's silver screen, her long-lashed bright hazel eyes enamoured with all that she sees in this little town.

Despite looking so awake and intelligent she never sullies our perfect three week relationship with too many words. Beautiful, unearthly and enigmatic, she has no plans she is willing to share with *this* mortal.

Her jaw moves as if in deep contemplation while I share my small aspirations then, in response she stops walking, and says, 'Aw.' Occasionally she devastates my fragile intentions with an existential, 'What for?'

Deep in my little brain a voice says, 'Turn and run, lad,' but I am entranced by this Brownton siren. Oh those lips, like two velvet pillows of red blood corpuscles liberated from a vivid biology text book, and moving like restless crimson puppies.

We walk up Fearn Road and to the end of her street. As I turn to her to say goodnight, her tongue seems to be stretching inside her cheek like an athlete warming up. The velvet corpuscle pups roll apart enough to reveal her perfect teeth, and her tongue tip does a victory lap in front of the pearly palisade. She is gorgeous. Time slows.

Her jaw ceases its stirring. I gulp. Her mouth forms a slow pout as our heads move closer. Then she lifts her fingers towards her face, and pushes out her chewing gum before we kiss.

This is a girl with class, or an angel who takes her kissing very seriously.

STAYING TRUE

Pete and I have been coming to the Dantley gym for nearly a year now, on and off, homework permitting. The long conversations we have as we walk cover, well, everything. Often our plans for the future. Pete's plans are always so grand and so certain; he'll play in a band, become a fighter pilot in the RAF, marry a beautiful girl. I still don't know what I'm going to do. Pete says my problem is, that I should be more ambitious and think big.

He also says, 'Don't be talking posh, Grey,' if I voice some thought that isn't like his idea of me, isn't dull and broad Yorkshire. 'Don't be false' is another one. But I'm not false. What Pete means is, 'stay as you are.' It's a phrase that is beginning to echo throughout our chats.

He's always the better dressed one of us, and it's hard to keep up with his changing interests; Spanish guitar, fishing for perch, (last week it was brown trout), motorbikes, dressing as a mod, growing a moustache, being a Led Zeppelin fan or fantasising about grouse shooting in tweeds or the Lambretta scooter he will buy.

'Sometimes Pete I reckon you must believe you're in a story.'

'Yes. James Bond, in his Aston Martin DB5.'

'I was thinking more, Mr Toad in Toad Hall.'

'Well we can't all be heroes, Grey.'

It wouldn't be so bad, but for each interest he learns all about it and sounds so enthusiastic, swearing he is embarking on a lifetime commitment. Then, a few days later, he'll switch, and deny he ever said he wanted to be a Hell's angel or liked David Bowie. I sometimes wonder, if it's not just about trying to impress people with Pete.

The other day we had a walk and Pete was wearing his new trousers.

'What abart these then Grey? Oxford bags. Had 'em made to measure.'

'You mean your britches are meant to billow in the wind like that?'

'Oh, 'billow,' nice one Grey, but don't be false.'

'Are these part of the mod outfit?'

'Fuck no, it's not a uniform y'know, Grey. These are just ace trousers, it's Prince of Wales check is this. I'm gonna get some red socks to wear with em and I'm saving up to get some brogues with leather soles and segs.'

'Ooh, segs. We'll all hear you coming then. As you rattle past fightin to stay on yer feet in a high wind.'

'It's the birds I'll be fightin off. You'll see.'

It is good to learn about keeping fit, and to increase our self-esteem with the weightlifting. But I think that if Sergio and Reg speak to us from their photos by the mirror in the Dantley gym, it is not only to say, 'Look after your body,' and, 'change is possible,' but also to say, 'don't become an obsessive narcissist.'

NETHERGILL CHALLENGE

Pete told me so much about his experience at an outdoor adventure school in the Yorkshire Dales doing gorge-running, potholing and abseiling that I felt maybe I could do it too. So when it was announced in assembly that there were still some places on the last Nethergill course of the year at a cost of £2.20 for ten days, I put my name forward. My course wasn't the rugged adventure one Pete had done, but mostly walking with a bit of climbing and orienteering thrown in. But there was a surprise test.

On day two, I'm naked stepping out of the shower, and there he is; Jud, a prospective new bully. He's wearing his 'bovver boots' and has red braces clipped to his Levi Sta-prest trousers, the braces dangle down by his sides like catapult elastics just where a cowboy would have guns. He is bent over a washbasin lathering his half inch haircut and tight little face.

'Fuck,' he exclaims, 'Av got shampoo in me eyes.'

This is the lad who seemed to push me yesterday, I could've been mistaken, but today he tripped me and grinned, definitely on purpose. We've only been here a day and everyone's been having a good time, laughing at jokes, and getting to know each other. But then I think about it and realise that this lad doesn't really know *me* at all. What if I was someone else? Someone who didn't take that kind of shit. What if, I was Crazy Kev Nuttall, or cock of our school? How would he know?

'Pass me towel mate,' he says, waving his hand.

I tuck my own towel tightly around my waist. I brace myself, and pass him the top half of his 'tough skinhead' uniform; his neatly pressed Ben Sherman shirt from the row of spiky clothes hooks.

'Here you are, Jud,' I say, as he reaches out blindly towards me.

He pushes the checked cotton into his eyes and rubs, before slowly pulling it down his face. He opens his pinky eyes wide, his top lip curls and quivers, showing his teeth like a snarling terrier. 'You…' he says.

'You. What?' I say sounding as threatening as I can. Then I force myself to smile, as if I don't care what he does.

At the far end of the ablutions block, a toilet flushes.

Jud laughs. And for the rest of our nine days together; walking and Youth Hostelling in the summery Dales and in Derbyshire, we get along perfectly ok. In fact he seems to look up to me now.

IMPERFECT FRIENDSHIP

'Hey Grey, Olivia Newton John. She's a beaut.'

'I'll tell you who's a beaut, Mary Mawson.'

'Ha ha ha. No seriously Grey who do you fancy for real?'

'Mary Mawson.'

He throws his head forward and shakes his grey school cleaner's mop of hair, as if he's laughing so much he's losing his mind. It's all put on. Pete Seacroft loves a show. Sometimes I can see why people think he's a twat.

'But seriously Grey, she's got big ears.'

'She bloody 'asn't.'

'They stick out through her hair.'

'It's better than fancying some film star or...Karen Zanner who's swatting 18 year old blokes off like flies every time she goes out. Anyway I've seen Karen's ears stick out too.'

'She's in a different class,' says Pete, scowling at me.

'Well actually she's not. Karen and Mary have been in the same form for years.'

'Ha ha. You know what I mean.'

'You look at Mary's eyes. They're like blue...stars. And they look kindly.'

'Kindly?'

'Yeah don't you understand that?'

'But Grey, if you two have it off your kids could all have 'eads like wing nuts.'

That's one of his standard jokes about ears he re-uses whenever he can. I look down, 'Hang on. What's that?

Oh me sides are splittin. Anyway, some of us are looking for love an' a nice girl not trying to breed the Aryan master race.'

'Been looking ahead in the history textbook again, instead of doing your homework, Grey?'

We carry on walking under the crappy cloud of our conversational skirmish. Nothing is said for fifty yards, a long way for us to remain silent. But as we pass the Dantley sign, Pete taps my arm as if he is going to say something really important: and he is.

'There is more, Grey.'

'Yeah I know. There's always more homework.'

'No. To life.'

'What?'

'There is more to life.' He flips up one hand above his head, as if to point any old where, and it rises across the boarded up cinema, sweeps over the pit buildings and spoil heap, and falls past the yard full of coal wagons. 'Grey, there's more to life than just this shit hole.'

FORM ROOM

Lean on the wall with me, and I'll tell you about the 4th form. Things are different now. Teachers' red ticks have been devalued, and their quirks are no longer worthy of comment, or impersonation. Their dandruff, halitosis and even the whistling dentures of Mr Wigfall, are no more interesting than the P.U.F.F. scratched faintly after the Head's qualifications on the school sign, or the tide marks around the wash hand basins.

School life goes on; bells ding-a-ling us around the place, and most morning's the senior teacher-bats fly to their roost on the assembly hall stage, before pronouncing gravely about toilet paper rationing, loving your neighbour or the evils of chewing gum. Then, they have us sing, 'When a Knight Won his Spurs in the Stories of Old…' But somehow, it's all become less important than they think.

Morning form periods are truly educational though, as like the occasional glimpses of knickers, some of the essential knowledge of life is revealed. As you can see looking around form 4d now, it's a time for standing about, perching on the window sill, or sitting on desks. It *looks* like nothing is happening. Deceptive isn't it? Because it's a crucial opportunity to *learn* if you keep your ears and eyes open. There's stuff about girls (for the boys), about boys (for the girls), music and fashion.

Some girls are whispering, 'She's going out with a 6th former?'

'Lucky her.'

Latest boys' news is; 'Wattsy told Barkin to get his haircut, and it's only an inch below his collar, he says he'll leave first.'

'Unfair. He's only gotta short neck.'

News of forthcoming disco's and parties leaks out to the chosen ones. Pete is telling a few boys about Jimi Hendrix at the Isle of Wight pop festival. He wasn't even there, it was his friend that told him about it.

'He did this ace version of, 'God Save the Queen' *and* he set light to his guitar.'

Only two boys are not agape in wonder, one says, 'But what for?'

The other, 'Fookin' brill,' twice.

Over there, girls are talking about make-up, and trying out different looks they've seen in 'Jackie'. Brenda says, 'I don't want to look like a slag.' Now that's a new one. She's got *green* eye shadow out, and I thought the 'slag look' meant the colour of the bluey-grey slag heaps that are all around us.

Danny Horgan smells funny. And he's telling anyone who will listen the details of his sexual adventures with an older woman. The challenge is to listen to everything that's being said, without showing any interest.

There's someone intent on doing a quick amendment to homework, 'I just want a look at yours that's all.'

There are always two boys talking about football: how Barnsley, Rovers, Blades or Wednesdays are 'going down' or 'going up', and sounding either dejected or ecstatic. In the corner a girl sits holding a throat pastille tin of hair grips while having her hair restyled.

There's Loreta Cartwright with the big blue eyes, don't let her see you looking. Some people call her Hoss after the gap-toothed, loud, burly guy, Hoss Cartwright in *Bonanza*. She is very pretty, quiet and graceful. Nicknames are like that aren't they? She's very smart, but also funny when you get talking to her. She can do Hilda Baker, from the telly, the one who says 'Have you been, Walter?' and, 'You big girl's blouse.' Between you and me I'm thinking of asking her out.

Notice how the school uniform is tweaked to its limits, to allow us to express our individuality. The wealthier boys have smart blazers and bright chrome buttons, and we pull threads from our school ties to make them look different. Flared trousers are aspired to but banned unless of course the widening towards the feet is barely perceptible. Skirts are worn short.

Some girls are wearing white tights and arguing.

'Aw Sandra, they make your legs look thinner.'

'No. I think they look fatter.'

They could just ask the boys, because most of us can identify almost all of the fourth form girls from their legs alone, after hours of dedicated study of course.

Are you looking at my 'new' jacket for the 4th form? My mother got it second hand from God knows where. It has narrow lapels, sloping shoulders and is permanently crumpled. It's a look that was probably dead trendy in skiffle bands about 1960. I will never put a school badge on it because it is such a joke, 'Per Ardua

Ad Astra' - 'Through adversity to the stars.' Dead aspirational eh? The Stars, is the name of a total dump of a night club in Barnsley. I wear a sleeveless cardigan with buttons which I rather like, it is the school grey colour and allows my tie to be 'clearly visible', but it's not the stipulated 'V' neck jumper. I am a wild fourth form rebel.

Oh, there's the bell. Time for History. The formal lessons are another thing. Just as I finally learned to stop taking school so seriously, it all seems to have become very serious with talk of 'O' level and CSE exams, and even 'careers'. There's hardly time for girls at all. The homework has mushroomed and to be honest I'm not really on top of it. It's like trying to get back to the form room at break time when the bell goes, swimming against the current. Still, it's learning about important things that matters most, and it won't be long to break time again.

COMMUNICATION BREAKDOWN 1972

It's been foggy all day. One of those fogs where you can't see anything beyond where you are right now. All the way to Pete's house I'm thinking about my hometown. So many things that are just not right; like the smell from the maggot farm, the chewy yellow-grey air on cool mornings and the oily dark-grey canal water. I seem to live in this lingering smog that obscures, and then, chokes the life out of everything.

Later on, we are sat on the rails by the fishing pond as the fog thickens, and then begins to close in over the still surface. Pete holds forth about the, 'elusive specimen carp' that he will catch here when he gets his new glass fibre rod from Markes tackle shop. 'It's got a Superior Action,' he keeps saying.

I'm getting sick of it, so I say, 'But, it's just another thing. It's more of that idea we talked about ages ago - *buy, buy until you die*. Will it make you happy?'

'What do you mean?'

I flick some small stones that I've lined up on the rail into his precious pond. 'All that glisters is not gold Pete.'

'It bloody is. And, I think you'll find, that it's *glitters,* Grey.'

I flick the last stone further out and it splashes exactly where Pete last saw 'his' carp surface. 'The English teacher said *glisters*.'

Pete scowls. 'Well my mate Dan in the village has got *Led Zeppelin Four*, and they definitely sing, *'all that glitters is gold'*. I heard it last week. We all sat on the floor listening to 'Stairway to Heaven', an I said, It's fuckin' ace that. Dunc said it was a critique of the capitalistic society. And then Edgar got talking about a book by Karl Marx and stuff.'

Another difference between Pete and me, is that I don't apparently have the right friends or people to quote. I climb down to pick up more small stones saying, 'Is it Dan whose parents own Portugal or something?'

'No. That's Edgar, and they only have a villa, on the Algarve.'

As I climb back I mouth, 'villa, on the Algarve.' with him because I've heard it so many times, along with the list of amazing analyses, achievements and acquisitions of his Finewell pals.

'Is it Dan who's rebuilding a motorbike?'

'Yeah, it's a 1950's Aerial twin, with overhead valves.'

'Oh yeah?' I say with mock interest, as if I never heard that before. Pete doesn't always get my brilliant sarcasm.

'Dunc says, Edgar's family speak Portuguese around the dinner table.'

Crikey. My family rarely sit down together for any meals, and don't speak much, in any language. I'm keen to get off the subject, and cheer us up, so I put a reminiscence on the hook, and cast it to him. 'Hey, remember going to the Princess, when we were loads younger, TWO years ago!'

He bites. 'Yeah. They always played Roadrunner by Junior Walker and the Allstars,' and he do-do-doo-doo's the saxophone riff with his thumb to his lip, 'It's ace, still.'

'Remember the bar? Orange, coke or lemonade. Ha!'

He tilts his head back, shakes his hair and declares, 'Oh and what about Denise in that dress?' His eyes widening.

'The diagonal stripy one? How did she...?' I falter. Two years on, and I still don't having the vocabulary to describe the phenomenon of Denise dancing.

Pete is hooked. 'It was her hips. Bloody gorgeous wasn't she? She's still in Dan's class at the Grammar.' He holds his arms out, as if holding a girl.

'Dan in the village says the whole world revolves around a girls hips. Dan says…'

He's heading for the reeds, the hook is out, the nostalgia fish gone. Shit. We're back on the golden boys. I swing both my legs over the rail, and jump down leaving Pete swaying. 'I think it's time I was off home.'

He stands up on the lower rail, drops sideways onto his palm, and vaults off the fence. 'I'll walk with you as far as the canal.'

'No it's ok. Anyway, is that the sound of one of Dan's old bikes starting up?'

'Yeah, that's his D7 1959 Bantam, I'll see you tommoz.'

I walk down the lane into the fog that is now so dense in the dip by the canal, that I can hold out my hands and lose sight of them. So I cross the bridge and walk home by the new road instead. It is not yet open to traffic, and it feels weirdly quiet, but not as gloomy as the canal path. In an eerie sort of way it's comforting. The landmarks of chimneys and scrap heap are invisible, and I'm just here with myself, wrapped inside the pale grey fog on the unopened road. Maybe I'm alright, on my own. I never thought that before. I'm going to treat myself to some chips on the way home.

FIFTH FORM ENDS 1972

The fifth form has been the 4th year speeded up, like a single played at 78 rpm but not as funny. It was quite a memorable last week of summer term. Our form teacher, Mr Wagstaff, is a half-hippy sculptor who plays a Neil Young LP in the art room, and thinks he is, 'so cool, man.' One day he passed my locker and made a big fuss. It was after Pete and I had an argument about breasts, where he said, 'If they're not a big deal then, why don't you put a page three pin-up from the *Daily Mirror* in the back of your locker?'

'That's the point,' I said, 'I don't need to, because they're not a big deal.' He didn't get it. I only did it to shut him up.

'Disgraceful,' said Wagstaff, 'Take this locker to the head of Upper School.'

'The whole locker sir?'

'Yes, Seacroft will give you a hand.'

So we carried the six foot high locker down the long corridor, with stinky plimsolls and footy boots banging about, as they swung from the hooks. We followed Wagstaff, like he was the Pied Piper, with his long hair bouncing up and down and the neon lights reflecting off his massive bald patch. It was like a Monty Python sketch.

'Yes thank you Mr Wagstaff,' said Wattsy, 'I'll deal with this.'

When he'd gone, Wattsy closed the door as if something very serious was about to happen. He waited for a long minute, looking first at the locker, and then us. Next, he smiled, and said quite gently, 'Don't do it again. Take it back.' No detention, lecture, or anything. He's alright Mr Watts.

Anyway all that is past now. 'O' levels are done. Fifth form's over. And, at last, I'm sixteen.

Camping is great. You feel so alive, washing your hair under the standpipe, frying bacon, and lying on the grass watching gulls fly over. You can walk down to the sea whenever you want, and even try smoking. Three of us are in Whitby for 10 days. That's Dean, Ade and me. We have our own tents and equipment, and cook separately because that's part of the fun.

Dean, in the purple silk jacket with the Rod Stewart hair, has the biggest tent. It's blue and orange with a ridge pole, so it looks very smart, if a bit flash, like Dean really. Ade is in the army cadets, and starts his apprenticeship at the pit in two weeks. He keeps singing, 'Girl I'm just a jeepster for your lu- u- u- urve,' to himself all the time, even though he claims not to like Marc Bolan. His tent is a camouflaged ex-army bivouac. At cocoa time when the light fades it disappears in the twilight.

Dean and I make a running joke of it, and pretend we can't see it at all saying to Ade, 'Ooh, you made me jump. Where did you spring from?' and, 'Can we throw toilet rolls over your tent it to mark where it is?'

Ade says, 'You'll not be laughing when the farmer comes round for the rent, and I don't have to pay.'

Apart from when we meet up to natter, it's so peaceful here. Like an outdoor library, with sea sounds.

Dean's dad drove us the 100 miles here in his Ford Escort, gave us a commentary of the sights on the way, and booked us all in at the campsite. I can't imagine my dad ever doing anything like that, even just on the bus. He doesn't say a lot my dad. Mostly, 'Ger out o' me light.' when I watch him making things in his shed. He loves making things. Another thing he says is, 'It's my bloody 'ouse an I'll do as a like.' usually, when I ask him to not knock my bed, as he passes it going to the bathroom in the night. I suppose there isn't much room at home.

My dad spends every evening at The Three Barrels and refers to Jed and Sylvia, the landlord and his wife, as if they're family. Which is understandable, as they see a lot more of Dad than we do. He's decorated our front room to look like a pub; false beams, horse brasses, and a Delft rail full of miniature spirits.

On Saturday nights, when Mam is out dancing, he comes back about half past eight smelling of beer, and says sweetly, 'Ere you are, me old pidge.' He hands over a bottle of lemonade and a bag of crisps each, for my brother and me, as we watch *The Two Ronnies* on the telly. He always asks us, 'Is t'baby alright?' before he goes back to Jed and Sylvia.

Mind you, the next morning he is really grumpy. I'm glad that I'm out of his way, zig-zagging round the streets by half past six, on the first of my paper rounds.

That's how I can afford my tent and the sleeping bag and everything.

My tent is the smallest and least waterproof. When it rained one night, I lay awake feeling the spray on my face. Next day I walked into Whitby and bought polythene to cover it. Dean says I'm, 'double wrapped and snug now, like twenty Silk Cut.'

Our house is pretty small as well: two bedrooms, one for my parents, and three of us in the other; bathroom, kitchen, living room, cellar, outside toilet and not forgetting 'The Front Room.' Mam will be so pleased my 'O' levels are over. She's says every week, 'You're hoggin' that front room you are, with all your books spread out doin that vision.'

I say, 'I'm not Mam, I can soon take my books out. But I need somewhere quiet. And, it's called REVISION.'

I saw a picture of an Indian home in the library. They were very poor, but they still made room for a little shrine to a deity with blue skin and painted toenails, and surrounded it with flowers. In our house the front room is a shrine, to the teak veneered radiogram. Mam loves her front room and likes it to be clean, tidy and people-free. Occasionally she kneels devoutly in front of her hi-fi deity, and sprays it with Lavender Pledge With Real Beeswax. She is very protective of her furniture.

But she really does *not like* being corrected. At 'REVISION' her face screws up like a dish cloth, making her sparkly-topped glasses rise on her nose and with a finger pointing at my face she shouts, 'Don't you get clever wi' me. You ought to be out workin' not 'visin' for bloody 'O' levels.' She is very house-proud. Wait until I get my 'O' level results and then my 'A's and become a doctor or a lawyer or something, she'll be impressed then.

Camping is really good for learning to look after yourself: cooking and washing up, appreciating nature and daydreaming. I love to close up the zip at bedtime and lie there reading with my torch or sometimes, I just think. For example, when I walk into Whitby every day along the clifftops I see a tree close to the edge in a weird shape. It is bent over, and sort of pointing out to sea. I wonder, what made it like that? Why do individuals look the way they do?

PETE MOVES ON

So you've seen how it was with Pete. He was the first person I could really talk to, well that is, when I could get him to shut up. I think we practised expressing our ideas, speaking about the world as we saw it, and began to work out where we might fit into it. I was a good listener for him, as he could be for me. He was also practising impressing people, first me, and then everyone else. I was certainly a good foil for his peacock persona.

He taught me to talk back. Something not allowed at home. And he got me out. He helped me connect with the world of possibilities and imagination. I'm grateful to him for that. At 13 years old we arranged to meet on the bus with packed lunches, and go to an air show. In Doncaster we got on another bus, and had a great day out looking at the Lightnings and Harrier jump jets, that we'd only ever seen as plastic Airfix models before. That was the most exciting day I'd ever had. I never thought of doing anything like that, for myself. Perhaps that's what we need friends for, to do what is good for us, and get us to take that extra bus ride.

But Pete was as cold as glacier ice the day that he announced he was leaving our school, to go to the Grammar school sixth form.

'No offence Grey, but all my mates are there.'

He meant his friends from 'the village' of course. He always called his corner of the conurbation that.

We met up less often, and eventually we both had other things to do. But he never stopped teaching me things. Pete always had this intense sense of himself, as if he was the only person in the world. I think *he was* the only person who really mattered, to him. I don't mean this in a bad way. We all need some of that.

And so it goes on; friends, experiences and acquaintances, that in their time meant a lot, slip behind me into the past. As if I'm a ship passing through broken sea ice.

But you probably want to know how Pete Seacroft turned out. One of our last meetings was my 17th birthday. Where he added so much vodka to my beer that he and Tony had to almost carry me the mile home. Pete scarpered, and left me throwing up into a bucket until the small hours.

As he was always looking for the next 'high' of sorts, he could have become; a hopeless victim of a drug dealer, or a fallen rock star, or been drawn to someone as charismatic as himself - a cult leader becoming a devoted follower of a Brownton Bhagwan. I could also imagine him remaining a dreamer; working as a window cleaner forever smitten by other people's lives and possessions. He might've bought into a franchise, using his magnetism to sell brushes door to door or transform car bodywork, leading a sad life of lost aspiration, a hostage to his dreams.

All these things might well have happened, but I heard he worked hard to pay for nautical school in the USA before working on ships around the world. He took exam after exam, and became a ships officer with P&O, before joining Cunard and working his way up to ship's captain on the cruise ships.

He's the guy who remains charming and polite at all times, while secretly enjoying two things. One; the uneasiness of his overdressed passengers, who fawn before the gold braid on his cap, and are flattered to join his table for the highlight of their holiday experience. And two; when the cruise ends, and he watches you disembark, portlier and poorer, there's a particular second where he gives you that slightly mocking salute, as you leave to queue anxiously for your baggage, and await customs clearance. *These* are his favourite parts of the job.

DEAN 1973

I'm 16 years old, and in a pickle. This time walking the country lanes hasn't helped.

I stop at the garage to see Dean on his Saturday job. The grubby triangles of red, white and blue plastic bunting swing limply in the warm air announcing 'Tarted up cars for sale, some even roadworthy'. Each car has a fluorescent yellow card in the windscreen with a felt-penned price hundreds of times more than my weekly paper round money.

I stamp on the long liquorice sensor cable that runs across the forecourt. The bell normally rings as each car axle drives over it, giving a weedy *tring tring*. I fail to make it work. Dean, in the office, puts his feet down from the desk as I approach, then puts them back again as he recognises me. He ruffles his Rod Stewart hair.

I make a joke because that's what we do. 'How much are yer dead flies in t'window mister?'

'Where've you been?'

'Just round Parwell.'

'Old Round Parwell eh?' Dean puts a thumb into his waistcoat pocket and in one of his old people's voices says, 'Ee that Round Parwell is such a fat sod - too many bloody chips if you ask me.'

He throws a cushion onto a 10 gallon drum of Castrol grease, 'Av a seat.'

I half sing, *'I had nothing to do on this hot afternoon.'*

Dean spots the lyric and sings the rest, *'But to settle down and write you a line, I've been meanin' to phone ya but from Minnesota, hell it's been a very long time.'* Great song.'

I leave a pause, and then continue seriously, 'Do you ever feel Dean, that when you walk in the countryside, it's as if you're not really there?'

'Who said that?'

'Very funny.'

Tring tring.

In my best camp comedy voice I say, 'Looks like it's time to *man the pumps,* Dean.'

'Ooh cheeky!'

A blotchy Cortina in primer-grey and red pulls up, just past the pump. Dean unwinds his feet from the desktop and walks briskly out leaving the door open.

Another visitor, a buzzing bluebottle, enters at top speed as if intoxicated by the petrol fumes. It tours the office, past the new car tyres stacked against the white wall blackened with crescent skid marks. A Champion rack on the wall is filled not with spark plugs, but with Lucas light bulbs in boxes marked with black fingerprints. On the back wall above a grey filing cabinet, a creased and tatty perforated card of fir tree air fresheners hangs, hopelessly overwhelmed by the chewy smell of tyres and petrol fumes.

The fly laps the space again, and again, pausing momentarily on the folding door into the workshop. The front of the office is one large window, against which the fly throws itself repeatedly despite the wide open door onto the forecourt. It is destined it seems, to join all the other dead bluebottles among the imaginative window display: a gallon of Shell 20/50 Multigrade flanked by single tins of Gunk and T-Cut in front of a grubby sky-blue peg board.

I listen to the transaction going on outside.

'What can I get yer?'

'A pounds worth o' two star, an a shot o' Redex, please, lad. An *don't* lean on that wing, av just finished fillin it.'

The pump whirrs, and the spinner in the glass bubble turns, as Dean holds the nozzle in the tank. He stares gravely as the amount cylinders roll.

'That's one pound and five pence then please.'

He returns inside as the car pulls away, opens a drawer, snaps the pound note under a clip, throws the coins in and resumes his position, white brogues up on the desk.

After a short silence I say rather heavily, 'I had to go see Wattsy yesterday in his office, about my essay marks.'

Dean mimics the sixth form's football hooligan, 'Did you kick his 'ead in?'

'Hah. No, he's a good bloke. He said to me, "What do *you* think your options are? What will you do?" '

'What does he mean?'

'I'm not doing very well in the 6th form. Basically, everything depends on my field course write up mark. Then, it's time for a decision.'

'Ooh, University or Teacher Training College? Will he open the box or take the money?'

'No it's more fundamental than that. I don't get it Dean. I'm not stupid. I try my best and at least I'm not a bloody football hooligan. Why aren't I doing better at school?'

'Nay lad, don't worry about it.' This is the best Dean will ever do for serious advice, and even that is delivered in a funny voice. In his 'old-man-without-teeth' voice he continues, 'It's not sho bad round here. There's allush plenty o' work down t' pit lad, we'll shee yer right.'

There's a rare thoughtful pause while he stares at his shoes. Then he looks right at me to say, 'Seriously though, haven't your mam and dad got a career and everything planned out for you then?'

I laugh, perhaps at the gulf that just opened up between us in that moment. A career? His parents speak only of him going to university while mine have been nagging me to leave school and get a job since my 15th birthday.

'Wattsy was trying to give me sensible advice. I told him, Education is really important to me.'

Then he said, "You have all the cards in your hand Graham. It's up to you now." But actually it's like a nightmare, where everyone else is playing poker or something, and my hand is; Mr Bun the Baker, two Lenny the Lion snap cards and a tea card of a Triceratops.'

Dean detects movement on the forecourt and is out like a shot.

Tring tring.

'A gallon o' three star.'

'That's thirty pence please.'

Dean dashes in and flicks change out of the drawer like he's been doing it all his life, and hands it to the customer in the doorway. 'Cheerio.'

Pointing at my jeans he says, 'Hey Graham, you've patched that hole in your Wranglers.'

'Yeah, fine check from a rag I found.'

'Ooh fine check. You smooth little swine! It'll be Pringle vee necks and Levi sta-prest next.'

'But you know Dean, 'I Wear it Well'.'

'A little old fashioned but that's alright,' sings Dean, before digressing as he regularly does, into his knowledge of Rod Stewart and the Faces, his favourite band who he saw at Sheffield City Hall last year, and don't we all know it.

'Do you think Dean that sometimes, it's hard to know what is right? Who we should listen to? What's genuine?'

'Yeah. Remember that first week in the sixth form? It went quiet when Steve Tilson sang 'Maggie May' cos his voice was so like Rod Stewart, it was uncanny.'

'No I missed that.'

'Well, a week later his laryngitis cleared up and he sounded awful. Hey, you should've seen the Faces do 'Maggie May' at Sheffield. Ronnie Lane was laughing when Woody did this improvised guitar solo. So much better than on the single. Rod took the tartan scarf off a fan *just in front of me*. Just in front of me. And put it around Woody's neck. Brill.'

'Dean, did you finish writing up the Field Biology course?'

'Na. Did you?'

'Well almost. I hand it in next week. Funny thing is, I really enjoyed doing it. I think everything is gonna be alright.'

'You bloody puff.'

'I think the teachers and Mr Watts will be reassured of my, er, talent and genius. I did these great drawings, my best ever...'

'Oh yeah, I just remembered something else. When Rod sang 'Maggie May' he was so drunk he kicked a football into an amp instead of into the crowd. It was so funny.'

'It's time I was going Dean. See you Monday.'

'Right. Thanks for helping me pass the time.'

'Passing the time,' is apparently, an important skill in my home town. Finding the right person to pass it with is less easy.

KNOWLEDGE LEGACY

It's all change at school. It's nearly time for the magenta rockets of rosebay willow herb which always mark the start of the summer holidays. The other end of the six weeks will be accompanied by mini-clouds of their fluffy seeds, blowing from the pods of their dying September stems. When I was younger, we made dens with them on the spare ground opposite the end of our street, and went home with the fluff on our clothes. They're going to turn that area into a car park. You don't see so much spare ground now. Things are changing everywhere. By the time the fluff is rising off that patch of rosebay for the last time ever, I will have my exam results in my hand, and I feel scared thinking how life will be. But I know a place that never changes. I'll walk there.

Mam's parents live in a council house two miles away. Mostly I go 'the top way,' past Dean's house then down the hill through some trees. We used to go every week when I was younger, for Sunday tea. I still go and see them. I like to think they have great wisdom because they are old.

The routine doesn't vary. Grandma, wearing a nylon overall, always opens the door and says a really long and high, 'AWWW.' It's always followed by, 'Father, come and see who it is.' I think this is to give her time to remember my name. She does have about 15 grandchildren. If you go, don't have the orange squash as she hardly dilutes it at all, it makes you thirsty. Tea is better and it comes at about twenty minute intervals, not counting the obligatory one as soon as you arrive and the one immediately before departure so you don't collapse with dehydration, or tannin deficiency, on the walk home.

The sideboard clock dings out Westminster chimes every quarter hour, but you can measure the time by the number of mugs you've had. Every one accompanied by compulsory cake, biscuits or buns. She insists on this because, 'you have walked all this way.' This will be her news to tell everyone for the whole week, 'Our Graham WALKED over on Wednesday!' If no one visits to tell, she probably keeps telling Grandad who will say, 'Aye.'

Grandad always says, 'Aye.' He says it as if he is straining to make the utterance travel all the way from the top of his throat to his nose, and afterwards there is a long exhale as if you have put him to a lot of trouble by causing him to speak. I think he is conserving his energy for shaving the hedges and the lawn again, for digging and re-digging his garden, or for more painting. He likes to keep busy since he retired after 52 years on the railway. I don't know anything about railways. Grandad does lots of manual work, but it's speaking that really tires him.

Out of nostalgia for a time when corporal punishment was a part of everyday life, Grandad still wears a belt as well as braces. There's even room for more belts if he wants, because the top of his heavy britches stop just under his armpits. The trousers are thick and woolly as a token kindness to his eight children who were bent over his bony knees to be beaten with his belt. The soft fabric would muffle their cries and absorb their tears. That is tenderness in his family. They don't make trousers like that anymore.

I'm not sure what I learn from them if anything at all. But I seem to hope that one visit they'll say, 'sit down, you're old enough now to be told what you really need to know.' Sometimes I walk up the garden with Grandad. I say, 'Your potatoes look good, Grandad,' or, 'you're well on top of the hedge cutting,' or, 'look at the starlings waiting in the hedge.' But today I say, 'I'm seventeen next week, Grandad.'

His answer to all of my talk is the same. 'Aye.' he says. Obviously this is not the day of the wisdom transfer.

Five teas, two inches of knitting and a round of Grandma's same old stories later, I broach the subject of leaving. She had digressed from the scandal of the starlings taking all the sparrows' bread, to the 'disgusting' articles in her daily paper (The Sun), but as I speak the clacking needles stop, and the knitting is rapidly downed in her lap,

'You're not WALKIN' home? He should wait and get that ten to four bus shouldn't he Father?'

If being cheeky to grandparents was allowed I'd quickly step out the door saying, 'It's alright Grandad, save your strength.' But I daren't.

'He's goin, Father.'

'Aye.' Says Grandad who has barely recovered from the first 'aye' an hour ago, his cheeks swell and he exhales, before the effort causes him to sink back in his chair.

Grandma's on her way to the hob, 'I'll just make you a cup of tea before you go.'

WORK THOUGHTS

If walking the 'top way' reminds me of weekends, Sunday best, and taciturn family teas, walking back the 'bottom way' is about the grimmer prospect of the working week. I'll take us back this way.

Situated between home and my grandparents' house is, according to that esteemed unpublished work - my CSE Geography project - *the largest coking plant in Europe,* and this road will take us through the middle of it. This massive sleepy sci-fi monster *employs 1500 people and supplies coal gas to the East Midlands Gas Board, and ammonia, sulphur and coal tar to the chemicals industry.*

It is ironic that sometimes we can't breathe without coughing, or see to the end of our street, because of the pollution from this place making smokeless fuel.

Overhead soon, passing above the road on stilty legs, an enclosed conveyor belt clatters. As we get near to it, the path narrows and is layered with years of spilt coal slack. Your nose will be smacked by tar, petrol and gassy pongs, but keep walking. It's like the feeling of being by the canal, but without the threat of deep water. Don't be frightened though, the scalding steam is not close to us, and the poisonous whiffs will decline as we move away. That sudden 'chhhhh,' is from vapours escaping from the elaborate, angular pipework. If you look into that opening you can see water running over timber as it splashes down inside the cooling towers.

It's hard to imagine 1500 people, that's more than everyone at my school. But they're somewhere inside, behind and underneath all those buildings, pipes, towers and tanks.

Keep walking. Look at that unreal, bright, green water in the square lagoon. Whiff the mothballs and sulphur. Above us clouds of steam floof out of bulky wooden towers that could be cloud machines. Vapours hiss from black lagged pipes. A row of huge, wheeled gate valves drip, and steam ghosts manifest above shushing leaks and nozzles. But you're right to keep going, it does feel noisy and dangerous, it might mesmerise us and draw us in.

I wonder if any of those 1500 people *like* working here. Does anyone like their work? I never meet anyone around here who does. Don't know if I should feel guilty about this, but I actually like my paper round job. It's harder when the bags are heavy on Fridays, and when it rains, but it's good too.

Keep into the side, coal lorries pass really close here. Look up there, the pit headgear is starting, two huge, spoked wheels side by side spinning in opposite directions, it signals the start and end of shifts. As we turn the corner we might see some of the men captured by this giant industrial plant, as they emerge from their cage. There, see? The miners. They'll walk across the yard to the lamp room, with their faint lamps ready for recharging. And then take their blackened hands and faces, with their dirty orange boiler suits over the road to the pit head baths. When they're all clean, you might pass them on the street and not recognise them as miners, apart from the coal dust around their eyes, as if they're wearing mascara. Best not to tell them that though.

There was a Monty Python sketch about an architect explaining his building. He said something like, 'the people enter here and are moved along the corridor in great comfort on a conveyor belt towards the rotating knives. The last twenty feet of the corridor are heavily sound proofed...' Maybe workplaces are monstrous like that. Is that why no one ever talks much about work? Is it secretly horrible?

I know it's fascinating, but don't stop, keep walking and you won't feel quite so small. We're almost out of it, we'll look as we walk. Behind the chain link fencing is the pit's outdoor stores area, where strange contraptions and machine parts lie on red shale between mats of chickweed, and the odd rocket of rosebay. There are mini tank-like vehicles and rows of hydraulic rams, and all of them painted white like ghostly sci-fi props for an alien world called 'underground'.

Lights flash and the white wooden railway crossing gates are closing, there'll be a long wait while the seemingly endless train of slow coal wagons pass. Wheel flanges are squealing on the curved rails, and the sound rings out, like the noise of the blade on the bacon slicer at the Co-op. At last the gates open and we're free. We can walk up the lane now, under the trees, and then onto the red shale footpath where at last it all quietens down. At last we've left the hell of industry, and we can enjoy the sight of a field of green cereal nodding in the summer breeze, and hear the sparrows cheeping and beeping in the hedge. What am *I* going to do about work?

JULIE 6th FORM

If some friends are not really tuned in properly to what we're trying to say, it was lucky for me that I knew someone who seemed to know what I thought even before I did.

A few days after talking to Dean at the garage, I'm leaning against the coffee bar in the 6th form common room enjoying the smell of coffee and the banter going back and forth, until that is someone asks Kev Deakin, 'Did you put sugar in my coffee?'

Then, he and Baz Miles say together, 'We will ask the questions.' Suddenly they're off into Monty Python's 'Spanish Inquisition' sketch. This will inevitably be followed by more Python; 'Good-day Bruce, let me introduce you, Bruce, this is Bruce,' 'This parrot is dead.' etcetera, etcetera.

I rinse my mug out feeling suddenly inferior at this end of the room. If *I* could recall TV sketches word for word after one viewing, then I could probably also remember my economic geography facts, and get better marks for my 'A' level essays.

I walk self-consciously in my frayed blazer between chatting groups, and then cross the wide expanse of turquoise carpet towards Julie. She is standing with her pale face looking out of the window, her light grey uniform conspicuous against the tangerine wall. A new single clatters down on the record player, some girl's choice probably as it's the O'Jays' 'Love Train', and I have to concentrate so that I am not walking in time to the music. Julie always looks as if she's waiting for someone, always by the radiator, her habitual haunt even in summer.

'Now then, young Julie. No Mary today? Is she alright?'

She turns her gaze to me, 'Oh hiya. She's just feeling a bit under the weather, having a day off. You look a bit the same actually.'

There's a pause, while I mentally discard a sarcastic response. I start to look away, but her concerned gaze pulls me back.

'I'm OK.'

She takes a hand off the radiator, and gently moves her index finger horizontally, as if to underline these words as she speaks them, 'You know, you can tell me anything.'

Thoughts I barely know I am thinking tumble out, 'The Head of Geoger said, in my report, "6%. There can be no possible justification for a mark as low as this."'

Julie scowls, 'Has he met your mum and dad?' She sounds slightly annoyed.

'No, they don't come to parents' evenings,' I say and her face falls like she's watching the Andrex puppy ad on TV, so I quickly continue, 'I'm trying to decide what to do. The council careers man said I should consider some kind of outdoor work, or use my 'O' levels and my "practical inclination" to get something in engineering - maybe a work's clerk. Is it clerk or clark?'

'It's spelt *clerk,* but pronounced *clark.*'

'Right, thanks. I tried to talk to Dean about it but he didn't seem to hear me. I know I have to get away from here, and I can't explain why.'

'Where could you go?'

'Well I gave up thinking about the RAF since we had that talk from the hippy bloke last year. I bought a Farmer's Weekly and I've applied for a job on a farm down south.'

She smiles, and puts both hands on her hips slightly comically, 'On a farm? Down south? By eck lad, as tha lost thi marbles?'

'Hmm.'

'I'm just teasing, sorry.'

'No that's alright. I'm sure there'll be worse to come. It just seems right. Farming is a long way from the pits, and the steelworks and all this, "but thar born and bred in Yorkshire lad" crap. After a year, I can go to an Agricultural college.' I finger the hair from over my eye, and hook it behind my ear.

'It's great that you've decided, but I thought you saw Mr Watts?'

'Oh Julie. Nobody is ever going to believe that my Geoger and Biology Field Course file fell off the back of my bike and the pages blew away in the wind.'

'What?'

'Wattsy was going to let the mark for it decide whether I could stay on. It was like, slow motion, in a film. There was a loud crack, and by the time I looked back, the file was open on the road. Pages scattering, twirling up into the air, like seagulls. Lost in the wind. Hours of work.'

'Oh no.' Her Andrex puppy face returns.

'My chance of getting 'A' levels was gone in seconds, over the waterworks railings and run over by cars on the wet road. It was horrible. I loved doing those periwinkle drawings too. It's the last straw Julie, after all the bad marks.'

'Things will work out.'

'Will they? You can't redo drawings. Is this how life is going to be? Nothing going as you want it?'

'Have a Spangle.'

'Thanks. I've really *got* to leave now and get a job. I might never come back. Will you write to me?'

'Course I will. Anyway I'm off too. I've got an interview in Nottingham for a nurse's job. So we might both be escaping together.' She looks down thoughtfully and I wonder what's coming next. 'What are periwinkles?'

'Molluscs we found at Robin Hood's Bay. Each species has a different shell, and is found at different places between low and high water. It's really interesting the way they all seem to just know where to go, where they belong.'

'Oh, right. What about Mary?'

'She is definitely not a mollusc Julie, she's just a bit shy that's all. You're her best friend you should know that!'

Julie convulses with laughter, bending forward and putting her hand to her face, then lightly stamping her platform shoes as if trying to regain her composure.

'Graham. You know what I mean. Will you keep in touch with her?'

'I really don't know. I just know this place isn't where I want to be.'

'Well we are friends aren't we, whatever happens?'

'Course. Thanks Julie. Gotta go, General Studies.'

'Don't forget the Drifters, Top Rank, Friday.' she shouts after me.

Soon after I cry quietly in bed because, despite all the crappy things about my school, I know something good is over and that my future is uncertain. How am I going to get an education now?

FARM

FIRST DAY

I'm rattling and bumping but holding firm as I sit on the tractor's red mudguard, at each jolt my hands grip more tightly around its cold steel edges, my fingertips pressing into the soft mud underneath.

'Watch. Clertch down then change up into 5th gear.' Perry, the driver, is my instructor and he has a perfect public school accent. And why shouldn't he? I'm in the south now. Here, this is probably normal. I hope this mudguard and I will stay attached to the tractor. The air smells of burning diesel and cows.

'Pick-up coming. I'll pull over. Brake, clertch, gears to neutral, handbrake on.' We pause while Perry exchanges loud pleasantries with the driver who keeps looking at me. We are not introduced.

My lesson resumes. 'Now, clertch down, into 4th gear, handbrake off. Away we go. That was Dave Squeaney he keeps some livestock in the field at the back of the cottage. His daughter is the secretary of the Young Farmers in Dabinton. I'll take you to meet them before too long.'

Perry knows everybody.

'I can change up into 5th gear here…'

I'm trying to concentrate and learn how to drive but Perry is also naming the farm fields as we pass them, 'This is the 50 acre - largest on the farm. Behind the trees is Saltpot, the smallest field, its shape reminds me of a lacrosse stick.'

We pass through a long olive-green puddle and I feel my first cold spatter of cowshit across my fingers.

'Gate coming up. Throttle down, clertch, stamp on the brake - left and right pedals together. Jermp down and open the gate. Over there's George's field with the old ridge and furrow.'

I lift a loop of baler twine over the gate post, and try to ignore my khaki hand as I push the rusty gate. Perry drives smartly through, black smokes rising from the vertical exhaust. He stops with brakes squealing, at just the right distance to allow me to close the gate past the tractor's fat tyre, leaving me the minimum distance to walk. He's good at this. I haul myself up onto the mudguard again and curl my fingers back, now knowingly, into the soft felt of cowshit underneath.

'Hold on tight, I'm putting it straight into 8th gear. On the left, here's the 20 acre, best gra-rss on the farm.'

The track drops down, we are doing *sixteen* miles an hour and I can feel my hair blowing behind me. Wow! And in one year's time I will be like Perry. I will be introducing the new student to the farm and driving, and everything. Probably in a loud and, dare I say, a slightly posh voice.

But now my vision is blurring with the vibration. Will I be able to remember all this lot? My guts feel as if they've been taken out, hit with carpet beaters and thrown back. What kind of a first day at work is this? And we're not even at the farmyard yet.

DEAR JULIE AUGUST 1973

Thanks for your letter, my first bit of post. Sos it has taken so long for me to answer it. Your nursing job sounds interesting. Have you seen anyone else from school? Isn't it weird writing to each other instead of just chatting on a school corridor? Mind you here, in the land of 'Down South,' everything seems weird, or maybe I just mean it's very different to home.

My lodging arrangement is 'living in as family.' Not with the farmer's family though, it's a bit odd. I'm with an American family who have no connection with the farm other than living in one of the farm cottages. I will have my own room soon when the present student leaves. Until then I sleep in the children's bedroom, although I'm so tired after work I could sleep anywhere there's space, if there isn't already a cat asleep there. I've never seen so many cats in a house, but then I never saw a house like this before. I suppose it's country life.

I've had no time off so far as there is so much straw to get in before the wet weather comes. Most days, farm work makes me ache all over, but I do get to drive tractors every day which is a rest from lugging things about.

You know how when you go for a walk in the countryside it's quiet and peaceful? Well the odd thing is that when you work in it, it isn't at all! You are never more than 2 yards away from a running engine with a rattling exhaust pipe. We bring bales back to the farm for stacking and the tractor engines finally stop, but then my job is to load the elevator that sends the bales up into the barn, its lawnmower sized engine bub-bub-bubbing next to my face. In the farmyard there will be an auger motor rattling grain up for milling or storage and then four hours a day the generator for the milking machine blasts out. I sometimes bring a tractor home at night when it's a treat to drive one without a trailer attached. But the best bit is arriving at the cottage at the end of a long noisy day, pulling the stop button and hearing the engine's sound die in the dusk.

Not sure what I learnt in 12 years at school anymore because I am such a dunce on the farm. I have to ask 'where is the filler cap on this tractor?' and when they say 'get a new link pin' I say 'what does it look like and where are they kept?' Everyone is very helpful though, even when I knocked out a gate post with a trailer, no one was cross they just said, 'Don't worry, take it a bit wider next time and, you'll learn. And I know I will. Someone said, 'even Perry made a few mistakes when he started.'

Perry is the 'old' student coming to the end of his year. He has agreed to stay on to 'show me the ropes.' Why do we say that? On a farm, it should be 'show me the grass' because that's what we seem to work with all day whether it's green, turned to silage, dried for hay or straw, or decomposed by digestion. We lift, fork, and shovel the stuff on and off trailers for the cows and then ultimately when they've finished with it back onto the fields again. Have you seen a muck spreader working? I hope you are not reading this over breakfast!

Now, I was telling you about Perry. I should be grateful that he is helping me because in the first few days he was the only person I could actually understand because he talks like a newsreader. Everyone else has an accent from a different part of the country except the family I live with. Being American they speak a different language entirely.

There is something odd about Perry though. Do you remember that time Perfitt was made captain of the school's footy, basketball and rugby teams all in the same term and he was unbearably cocky for a day? Well, Perry is like that, but all the time. He is leaving soon to go to the Duke's College of Agriculture, and

I'm glad. Everyone else seems to like him especially Mr Thurpley who is the farmer. Come to think of it those two even speak a bit like one another.

When Perry and the harvest casuals leave there will be just four of us working on the farm. The farmer tells us what to do but he rarely does any work. Maybe he is busy organising and planning, anyway as long as he brings the wage packets on Fridays I don't think anyone minds. He talks a bit like a Royal, saying 'gosh' and 'jolly good' a lot. The others are; Johnny, the old tractor man from Wales who drives the combine harvester, Henry the cowman from Lancashire, and Victor the assistant cowman from the local village who is on holiday at the moment, and me of course, the farm student.

As posh Perry is away for the weekend I am writing this from his room, soon to be my room. Outside the open window the night is as black as a fireback. There's not a streetlight for

2 miles. In contrast to my day at work there's absolutely no noise at all. It takes a while to get used to this much quiet. When I first noticed the silence it had a strange effect, I thought something had gone horribly wrong, as if I'd gone deaf or the Bomb had been dropped, it seemed so unnatural. Can you imagine a Saturday night at home without the sound of cars or lorries? Without trains tooting, buses' air brakes hissing or drunks calling to each other across the road? That's how it is here, a black blankness outside the cottage. We're down a stony track off the road among the trees, half a mile from the next house, and the nearest town is five miles away. I am wrong about the quiet – a lone owl has started hooting as I write. Perhaps he is telling me I should get to bed as it's late and I have to be at work tomorrow.

I should tell you about the family I'm living with. In the village, the rumour is that they are hippies who take drugs and have wild parties. They are certainly bonkers. Will tell you more next time. If I survive.

All for now.

Graham

VIC 1

Everyone on the farm seems to like Vic. 'Vic's a good old boy,' and, 'you'll like Vic.' people have been saying since I started. Today, Wednesday, he arrives. All and sundry want to talk to him. Someone slaps his back. Even the van driver delivering some parts gets out and shakes his hand. There's lots of jokes and laughing, something to do with him coming back from honeymoon. I just watch while I'm refuelling the two small tractors.

I'm still sounding like a budgie saying, 'Sorry can you repeat that?' 'Sorry can you repeat that?' to most people who speak to me. I haven't been here a week yet and it's more like Babel farm than Bellaby farm with all these different accents along with loads of new agricultural terms. I think the first three days were the worst. The others didn't always understand what I was saying. They must've thought me a bit simple. I have learned to stop using some Yorkshire words. I say 'anything' now instead of 'owt' and 'nothing' for 'nowt.'

All except the boss constantly use the 'f' word in every sentence. It's as common as straw around here. It doesn't mean anything: it's just a habit, I think. Eventually I'll join in too because if you are learning a new language that's what you have to do isn't it? Like shrugging in France.

But then Vic started back at work today and suddenly none of the accents are quite as incomprehensible to me as his. He pronounces 'I' as 'Oi' and 'A' as 'i', it's very confusing. Vic has been put in charge of the bale carting today.

'Cauld mawnin, but oi loike a noice frorst' he says to me while he warms his hands around a tractor's exhaust pipe.

I do a little smile and say 'Yeah' a bit vaguely while I wonder what he means.

Then Dave the casual turns up late. He's had a puncture and Vic sends him off to get it fixed telling him, 'There's a plice if y' turn roight orff the boy- paarss.' I'm not sure I'll ever get the hang of this new language. Am I supposed to try and speak it too?

Vic is changing the hitch on his tractor to fit the special bale trailers and he tells me to watch. His strong chin is blueish as if it has been rubbed in coal dust. He has one of those manly faces with a square, dinted chin and that lurking kind of dark facial hair that threatens to become a doormat unless shaved off twice a day. He's wearing a dark blue, double-breasted military jacket that would look great if it wasn't stained with cowshit from one shoulder down to the wrist and had only three of its shiny buttons left.

'Can you paarss me the draw bar?'

'Where is it?' I say not realising I'm almost standing on it in the crusty mud.

'It's behoind ya.'

I pass it and try to help, as he kneels saying, 'Can you hold it there mite, keep clear of the PTO sharft.'

'What's the PTO shaft?' I say.

'You ain't bin on a farm afore arve yer?'

I take the old hitch to the workshop while he's finishing off. I'm not sure if he intends to make me look foolish. He's one of those people with a ready smile. But it's too early to tell whether it's the smile of a man who knows a hell of a lot, or one who knows nothing at all.

When he's done he looks at me and says, 'Ow's about that then?'

'What?' I say. He repeats it more slowly.

'That's what you say in Yawkshire ain it? Oop Norf?'

'Not really.'

'Not reeelly.' He imitates my voice with a strange twist. He tries again, this time as 'Not reallah.'

He is the only true local person on the farm and I'd been looking forward to meeting him, but I'm not so sure now. Someone said he was going to join the army when he left school but was persuaded by Thurpley to come to Bellaby farm instead.

Soon he's leading our little convoy of tractors and trailers down the Leamington road where we turn off into the first of today's fields of bright yellow stubble. Vic bumps the 165 over the ribbed soil surface without changing gear. He stands up on the footboards and points where we should go. He is tall and maybe he thinks he is John Wayne, missing only the white gauntlets to make him look like a galloping US cavalry lieutenant in a film. Upright in the stirrups he indicates that Perry should round up the stray outlying bales while I should attack the ones on the field's far edge.

'Tyke the headland,' he shouts, whatever that means. Is Tyke me? I can understand his hand signals better than his speech.

All around me is complexity. The language, this new place and all this clever machinery that can do the work of umpteen horses. There's the combine harvester; tractors that tow, lift and spin things, a baler that can pack straw into tight uniform bales *and* tie string around them *with knots*. Even the bale sled that looks like a broken farm gate being dragged around is doing something ingenious because it holds bales and then releases them in clusters to minimise our driving. Amidst all this sophistication is me, stacking bales by hand onto trailers and taking them off again, wondering when I'll get a rest and something to eat.

'Oill give you a haind,' says Vic, joining me in the corner where the bales are heavier than elsewhere. After more 'now then' idiocy, he says something I don't understand I think it's about the weather or similar, 'got bayuwled a bit daimp.'

I nod my head and feel stupid again. He drags a bale in each hand to the trailer. I try that too but all I can manage is one and I feel like a weakling. He pauses, one bale stood on its end spanned by his huge hand. Vic is so big and very strong. The army is missing a good bullet stopper.

BLUSH TESTING

Whoa! 17 is too young to die. Especially on my first day off work. We're on the A45 to Northampton and closer than I'd like to be to the car in front. We seem to have followed its green, rounded form for miles with our engine whining. If petrol rationing comes in, Hank my landlord is going to have to drive more carefully. Maybe his big tan boots are causing the high revs?

'Jeez, at last the fuckin' snail car is moving over. WHAT! Look Gray-ham. He's eating a goddam sandwich at the wheel. Open your window,' Hank commands, before shouting, 'I hope it chokes ya. BA-ERSTERD.'

This is awful. How embarrassed can you be?

Hank's long hair is tied back in a pony tail that curves into the fur collar of his shortie jacket, his eyes are red and veins bulge in his neck. We drive close alongside the Morris Minor for what seems a very long time. I am trying not to think about that scene in gangster films where a car is bumped off the road. Hank glares hatefully across me at the elderly snacking driver and repeatedly mimes stuffing his face. I discretely crank the window back up and simultaneously shrink down in my seat, just as I am doing inside.

That poor innocent old man. I really shouldn't be here. If I were a drawing I'd want to be erased now, rubbed into tiny threads of latex and graphite and fall from the page. I thought hippies wanted peace? There is no escape. All I can do is to continue shrinking as if I've pulled an imaginary cord to deflate myself until my blushing skin slithers down the seat out of sight into the footwell among the crisp packets and Hershey bar wrappers.

The two little girls in the back seat cheerily hit another verse oblivious to my terror in the front…

'You'll have to speak up, I got beans in my ears…

Beans in my ears, beans in my ears

You'll have to speak up, I got beans in my ears Beans in my ears'

Finally, Hank overtakes, and it's as if the incident is completely forgotten. The embarrassment it seems is just mine. Maybe Hank doesn't get to overtake much in this little Renault 4, so when it happens it's a big deal.

'So Gray, whaddya say we hit Sainsbury's and then grab a beer in one o' these cute English pubs on the way home?'

'Hit Sainsbury's? You make it sound like a bank robbery, Hank. No, I think we should just get home safely with the kids and give Susannah time to cook the food.'

'Are we nearly at Sainsbury yet, Poppa?'

'No. How about a game, huh? Gray-ham will think of one.'

We play I-Spy into Northampton.

The shopping is mercifully uneventful, although it's tense when we approached the checkout queue and Hank says, 'Ok Gray-ham, this is what we'll do, you can be the muscle, I'll knock down this old woman and steal her bag while you grab the cash register... say, could we get some handguns?'

On the way home I suggest it is Hank's turn to provide a suitable in-car game.

'OK. A candy bar for the person who spots the most broads on bikes.'

'Ladies', explains the oldest.

The children look out conscientiously for quite a time but eventually get bored and begin singing 'Bananas in Pyjamas.' Hank's 'candy bar' is pretty safe. I haven't seen anyone cycling since I came to Northamptonshire.

We'll be back soon and I can go out for a peaceful walk for the rest of my time off.

Susannah is out to meet us by the time the car reaches the end of the long stony drive.

'Hank, you've been a long time.'

'It's Gray-ham's fault. He was arrested for shoplifting again. We had to go to the precinct. There was bail. I said no, but Dottie and Sophie said they would pay in candy, or sing a song to get him released.'

Susannah laughs.

'Six Swizzels,' I add.

Hank slaps me on the back, and laughs too, 'That's funny, Gray-ham.'

I'm sure I'll get the hang of this soon.

I suppose I left home because I wanted something different. And now, as my new family would say, I goddit.

JOHNNY 1

'You haven't mentioned Johnny before. Is he the one who looks like a wood gnome?' says Susannah, at breakfast.

'How do you mean?'

'His face is kinda brown and gnarled, like it was carved outta wood I guess.'

'But gnome? Do we all look little to you and Hank? Because you are so tall?'

'Don't forget your sandwiches. Shorty.'

I walk to the farm wondering if jokes mean things are going well.

By the diesel tank in the main farm yard, one of the harvest casuals is telling me that Mr Thurpley went to Sandhurst, the army's officer training college, when Mr Thurpley pulls up in the Land Rover. At 'zero eight hundred hours' each morning we all break off from checking tractor engines or sweeping up, to receive our orders for the day.

Mr Thurpley always speaks to Johnny first, and phrases his instructions as a request, using a special high-pitched deferential voice that he keeps solely for Johnny, 'Jorn-eee, would you mind checking the stock in George's field on your way to plough the 25 acre?'

'Right-o.' Johnny says, flatly and deeply, as if he is having none of this flutey nonsense.

Johnny is the oldest and most distant of the farm staff and is often obscured by something. He drives the only tractor on the farm with a cab. I don't know how long you have to work here to get a cab. One way he's distant is by working in his own field ahead of the rest of us. He does the combining in a large cloud of dust and chaff, and then the baling in a haze of flying straw. The rest of us follow, a day or more after, to pick up the bales he makes.

I have worked with him on little jobs while waiting for the dew to lift in the morning. When we levelled barley in the grain dryer he told me, 'Mind your lungs. Have a minute by the door cos this dust is a bugger.' I think it was so he didn't have to talk to me while we had a rest from pushing grain about with large aluminium shovels. We also put stone backfill over some clay drain pipes in the new cow yard together. He doesn't say much, but he is very keen to look after his tractor and the combine very carefully.

One damp day he joined us stacking bales in a barn. The bales have to be secure so they don't fall down in the winter and get wet. This stack, over the top of a sloping silage clamp, was apparently tricky to build. We made a chain, passing the bales man to man. But I was outside, putting bales on the elevator, and he was at the opposite end of the chain, so I couldn't see how he placed the bales to make it so strong. But everyone said the stack could withstand a gale now that Johnny had built the corners up. Does being so old mean you know how to do everything?

When he ploughs there's a flock of gulls around him, and then as he drives to the next field, the gulls are replaced by the three shiny mouldboards of the plough pointing up in the air. As he starts creating brown corduroy furrows in a new field, I drive into his last field with the disc harrows to break down the soil ready for seed sowing. If he passes through the farmyard mid-morning between fields he waves to me from behind the luxurious plastic cladding of his cab. He shook hands when I was first introduced to him but he didn't speak.

As a new person to a place, you can't help but look and listen to the way things are done. Thurpley's morning orders are different for each of us. It's a brief note for Vic; 'Victor. Bale carting between milkings.'

'Roight,' Vic says.

But at least Thurpley uses his name, even if Vic doesn't like being called Victor.

When it's my turn I don't have a name. I just get, 'Go with Perry, or go with Victor.'

I didn't spot it for a while, but Henry is never given any instructions at all in front of the rest of us. Maybe he gets written orders or there's a private chat for him.

When Henry speaks to Johnny, he received a curt 'yes' or 'naw' in reply. But I see that Johnny occasionally jokes with Vic. People laughing together is always a good sign.

DEAR JULIE   SEPTEMBER 1973

Thanks for your letter which I took to work to read at lunchtime in the barn. Lunch is what at home we call dinner and dinner is what we have at night time - like an early supper. Strangeness is everywhere here.

I really like to read your news, it feels like I have home with me if I have a new letter from you in my pocket. But yuck! I couldn't do what you do, I couldn't work in a hospital. The wards sound smelly and chaotic. I'll stick with my farm work. Talking of chaos, the children (aged 3 and 4) are playing a very noisy game that involves shouting and shuffling about on the bare board of the landing outside my room...

'HELP. GRAHAM, GRAHAM.' It's Susannah's voice.

I drop my pen and rush out. Sophie is using the balusters to hold herself upright wearing a pair of baseball sneakers on their sides while Dottie is sitting with both her feet inside one of her poppa's desert boots, both are wearing old lady style hats with artificial flowers.

The call is coming from the kitchen. 'GRAHAM. IT'S THE GODDAM FAUCET.'

I have no idea what she is talking about but it's obviously urgent. Two cats run up the stairs as I go down. All becomes clear as I arrive in the kitchen doorway.

Water is running down the front of the sink unit and pooling on the floor. The tap which has been dripping for attention for some time is now in a huff and refuses to be turned off. I open the cupboard, kneel in the puddle, and begin taking out cleaning products and passing them to Susannah. 'There must be a stop tap somewhere in here.'

I find it and break its stiff seal of limescale to close it off.

'Thank you Graham,' she says dropping tea towels into the puddle. 'Thank goodness you were here.'

'You need a plumber to fix the tap, the er, faucet, but the sink is blocked too. If we can empty this cupboard I can maybe clear it. Is there a bucket or something?'

Soon, over an almost full large saucepan of dirty water I poke out some gunge from the now detached 'U' bend with my finger. 'It's something gritty.'

'Lemme see.' She holds her hair back and bends for a close look. 'Coffee grounds. Fuck!'

'It's choked with them. I need something thin I can poke in.'

I wiggle a delicate paintbrush handle about and bang the bend out over the bin until the blockage is gone.

Soon after tea towels are wrung out into the gratefully gurgling plughole and order is restored.

'I suggest we use the bathroom taps for cold water or turn it on and off with the stop tap until a plumber comes to fix it.'

Susannah lifts the Rayburn lid and slides the kettle into position on the hob. 'Sure. I'll ring Mr Thurpley in the morning. Let's have some tea.'

'Like Dunkirk. Or an air raid?'

'What?'

'In the war, it's what everyone did. Made tea after every disaster. It's like a British thing. Your house might have been bombed but if you could find the kettle you could make tea, and then everything would be alright.'

Susannah shakes her head in disbelief, 'This is one crazy fucking country.'

But the funny thing is Julie some chaos is fine. Dottie and Sophie know how to enjoy themselves and I quite like hearing them laughing and playing. We are all gradually getting to know each other a little better and I'm beginning to feel more useful both here at Fenley and at the farm. Perhaps sometimes life can be strange in a good way.

DAWN THOUGHTS

It's Sunday morning at 5.30 a.m. I close the porch door and set off for my first day working with the cowman. Walking out along the stony drive is like that slightly unreal moment leaving a Youth Hostel in a National Park, where you can't believe you are really there, in the depth of peaceful countryside. A light breeze stirs the leaves of the trees as I pass the broken wooden gate with its peeling 'Woods Cottage' sign. I cross the narrow road to the farm track. It's now weeks since I sat on the mudguard of the 135.

It's good to have some time to myself. Chance to walk and think. I'm in my wellies and oldest jeans looking forward to a day of not bale carting. Over my shoulder is Susannah's canvas donkey nosebag with my food for the day and a flask of tea. I'm humming, 'I am on a lonely road and I am travelling, travelling, travelling,' from a Joni Mitchell song that Susannah plays a lot. She has made me peanut butter sandwiches. There is always something new to try here. There was to be 'jelly' in them too, which is American for jam, but I said no thanks to that. One novel food in a meal is excitement enough.

Mr Thurpley told me I can walk anywhere I like on the farm. So it's as if this entire countryside belongs to me. It's all my new living room. From the party wall of the Leamington road in the east, to the picture window of Fenley lake in the west, and from the tree-framed threshold of the Fenley road behind me to half a mile ahead where the curtains of Oak Ridge and Benby Wood hang on the north wall. The fields of harmonious yellows and green crops are the furniture of the room.

The cuts on my fingers, from the baler twine, have all healed up and my hands have hardened enough so that I don't need the gloves to lift the straw bales anymore.

As if a cellar door has been left ajar, my new living room has a hint of damp coolness in its morning air. Autumn is hovering. I pass an amber coloured field and glimpse, through an elderberried gap in the hedge, a flock of pigeons that have found spilled grain, and I smile at them doing their tick-tock walk among the stubble. Every few feet there are tufts of Italian ryegrass that the cow's tongues haven't reached through the fence, and between them, dark stinging nettles lean into the track. I rise up out of a dip on the grassy track to see a dozen rabbits grazing ahead of me, before they scatter in an instant. Rabbits probably don't score much in the *I-Spy* book of the countryside, but as I never saw any on my early morning paper rounds at home, it's still a novelty to me. Straw is gradually disappearing from the barley and wheat fields into the barns as summer slips away.

The track drops down the short side of the 50 acre, over a stream and past what everyone calls the hovel. It is a dilapidated building of ironstone and brick the size of a large garden shed. Rising up from its earth floor, brambles have grown through the 'V' of its dropped ridge and the ribs of rafters to get to the sky. Mossy and lichened clay pantiles are scattered like dropped playing cards around the ruin. They say someone used live there many years ago.

Bellaby farm is far from the 'home farm' of the children's picture books. No hens cluck in the yard, no hams hang in a cosy kitchen, no red cheeked farmer's wife cooks breakfast for an extensive 'family' of workers. At the centre of this farm are two chilled tanks of milk filled daily from 120 cows, and all farm work revolves around them. The farm might seem big at 500 acres, but it all sits within a thumbprint on the one inch OS map of this bit of England. The cynic might say that money is the stone cold heart of this farm-business; that the milk cheque and the market price of wheat and barley grain are all that matter. But give me a break, it's still early days, and I am enjoying being green and optimistic about my new rural life.

I will not see, for some years, that the real treasure of my farming experience is not the time spent playing with machinery or even these quiet moments of bucolic bliss: but the growing I will do alongside the people I work and live with. I am unaware that they have lessons for me at all. But I am unconsciously absorbing ideas and information, like the cereal seedling taking in nutrients in the autumn sunshine.

FENLEY GARDEN OCTOBER

Susannah, the children and I are in the grassy garden of the cottage in the fading light. Susannah's hands, despite being deep in the pockets of her long droopy fawn cardigan, point outwards and swing parallel like an imitation of flight.

Her head lifts and her frown releases, 'I think a path here. Then we can grow zucchini and lettuce, tomaytoes and maybe try some corn.'

'Corn? Wheat?'

'Maize, you know, sweetcorn? Gawd it's so beautiful, picked in the fall and boiled.' She pauses, to look dreamily into the yellow sky, adding, 'Oh and then you must put a little butter on it. You never had it?'

'Only tinned.'

'You'll love it fresh. It reminds me of my Mom…'

There's a commotion behind us. 'Momma, Sophie has taken the blue chalk and I need it for my dragon.'

'But Dottie…' Sophie's protest quickly ascends to an unintelligible whine, although her sense of outrage is perfectly clear.

'Scuse me, Graham. It's time to be the United Nations.'

I cut out a square of thick turf, and then dig a small pit in the garden to investigate the soil, while truce negotiations take place. The girls' dresses are multi-coloured pastel shades from the chalking, and Susannah crouches carefully alongside their drawings on the clay tiles to discuss the artwork before returning to me.

'You could grow vegetables here, Susannah. It starts getting stony lower down, but I think it should be OK.'

Susannah kneels on the grass and reaches down into the pit, holding her hair back with one hand and tucking it into the neck of her tie-dyed shirt. She doesn't feel the soil as I expect, but pats it. 'Oh Graham, I *love* home grown vegetables. Doesn't the soil smell so nice? It's like it's talking to us.'

I crouch to share something of the experience. Sometimes, it's hard to know what to say.

'Did you say you helped your da-ad with his garden?'

'His allotment, yeah.'

'Do you think you could help me to dig, so I can plant some things in spring? When is the right time?'

'Well now really, autumn. I can dig it for you, when I get some time off.'

'Momma, Dot is taking all of the chalks away…'

'Ok thanks Graham, you're a brick. It looks like the Middle East is kicking off. I need to get these guys to bed. Could you put the keddle on the stove when you've finished? I'll make us some coffee when peace returns. It's getting cold now.'

Half an hour later the smell of coffee fills the kitchen. Susannah makes it easy to talk about anything. I'm always finding myself in conversations I never imagined before.

'So Graham, what did you do with the snotty scrambled egg and the green dog-vomit dessert?'

'Ate it.'

'You ate it?'

'I was hungry. And I thought it was a test. Like the electric fence, where you lay a piece of fresh grass on the wire until you feel a pulse and your fingers start to twitch. It hurts, but you have to do it.'

'But why would the Thurpley's be testing you with that kinda slime food?'

'I thought it was to check if I was a fussy eater or something. Like facing the stampede of young cows earlier, when Thurpley parked the Land Rover in the Coppice field.'

'What?'

'As we got out they ran down the field at us. They were just curious, it was a bit frightening. But I knew I had to stand my ground, or I wouldn't get the job.'

'Wow. That was some interview. What did you say about the slime?'

'Thank you very much.'

There's a pause and then we both laugh.

'Graham, why don't you write a book?'

I couldn't answer this properly either. The distance, between me and the kind of person who might write a book, is unthinkable. It's more than all the curving miles between Yorkshire and Massachusetts. Maybe guys in Boston who empty 'trash cans' for a living can write books, but here in England labourers who shovel shit around on farms, mostly don't.

'People like me don't write books, Susannah.'

She is moving to the door but stops and turns, 'Look at me Graham. This is serious. You should not EVER say that.'

A dog beats his tail against the kitchen shelving. There's a noise in the hall. Hank is back. They hug by the hanging coats and Susannah says excitedly, 'Hank. Graham fixed the faucet on Monday, there was warder pouring all over the floor and he rescued me.'

'Jeez well done Gray. Doozy. You are the New York Fire Department. Sounds like I missed all the excitement by going to London.'

'We're using the bathroom faucet to fill the keddle.'

'It all sounds like a Joni Mitchell song.'

'Hank!'

I take the kettle and go upstairs, so they can have their usual argument about Joni Mitchell's lyrics in private. Hank says they're banal and Susannah adores them. I return to find them kissing, and I hover sheepishly in the door before handing over the kettle. I retire early to my room. What would it be like to live with an ordinary family?

HENRY 1

Henry the cowman has a stillness about him, which I like. The stillness of cows waiting. The cows stand in a collecting yard before entering the parlour for milking, after which, they move ponderously into the other yard to await the rest of the herd. All the while patiently chewing before being slowly walked back to the field. Cows spend a lot of time waiting. I don't know whether the cows acquire their placidity from Henry, or vice versa.

Even Henry's metabolism is different to the rest of us. How else can he wear a blue jumper that he never takes off? It's stayed on throughout the August heat and now it's late September. Perhaps it's cooler in the parlour, where he lives for half of every day. He's warmer than some in other ways though, for example he can understand my speech. He has a Lancashire accent, which sounds so familiar to me, apart from the occasional odd word he uses.

I return from feeding the heifers in the 20 acre field to be beckoned by Henry to stand in a gap at the bottom of the yard. The cows are returning to their grazing after morning milking. As the last one passes I join Henry as he pulls the gate back. I lift and drop the latch, and as the gate's rattling subsides he says, 'Arr you settling in?' He's looking at me searchingly.

'Yes I think so.' I pause like he does. 'I'm getting the hang of it, feeling a bit more useful now.'

If a cow could speak I imagine that they'd sound like Henry, with all the words being very carefully considered. Perhaps, Henry mentally ruminates in the two hour sessions he spends in the parlour with his friends.

'Useful,' he repeats as if noting it down. He turns away for the next question, and watching the herd make for the fresh strip of grass at the far end of the field, he says, 'Different here to where you hale from.'

'Just a bit!' I say not wanting to stir my homesickness up, or give too much away because this sudden interest in me doesn't feel right. 'I've still got a lot to learn. What does a cow weigh?'

We watch stragglers catch the herd up, as the cows move to the newly exposed grass, between the electric fences.

'Why do you ask that?'

'One caught the side of my foot.'

His tongue pushes deep and low inside his face, and he makes a couple of jaw rotations with the newly retrieved gum.

'You'll know if one steps on yurr toes. About horff a ton.'

We walk back up the shit splattered stone slope. Henry is clearly in no hurry at all to give me the next task now that milking is over. 'How are you getting on at Fenley? Susannah giving you enough to eat?'

'Oh yes,' I say without hesitation. But I'm now feeling wary. I don't like him speaking of my landlady in such a familiar way when she has never spoken of him.

He stops by the nettles that fill a wedge of ground by the diesel tank, 'Now if I ask you to take the 165 to Fenley barn for ten bales of hay, you could have your breakfast at home couldn't you?'

'Yes.'

'I'll meet you at the calf pens 'bout horff ten.' Then pointing into the sky, he adds, 'Don't go thur baht yurr coat.'

'Sorry?'

'It doesn't matter to me whether or not. But thurs nawt worse than a soak.'

'Oh right, thanks, Henry.'

I check the tractor has fuel, hitch up a small trailer and drive the two miles to Fenley barn thinking of food and how it's the first time I've heard the use of *baht,* for *without,* apart from the song, 'On Ilkla Moor Baht'at.' Which I sing loudly, accompanied by the rattling and turning exhaust pipe, for the benefit of the listening countryside.

FENLEY PHOTOS

At last Perry has gone, and I'm settling in a bit more. I just got my photos back from the chemist's: they're all of my home town. I know Hank likes to look at photographs so I show them to him. He takes ages to view each one.

'So this is your street right?'

'Yeah. There's the corner shop.'

'Corner shawp?'

'Yeah, bread, cigarettes, and milk if we ran out, penny lollies out of the freezer in summer. I was sent there every day from being a bairn, to get cigs.'

'Bairn?'

'Child.'

'And this is my friend Pete Seacroft, who I told you about, with his Lambretta scooter. He's just had it resprayed.'

'Susannah. Come see this. It's amazing.'

I'm puzzled and I look again, yep, it's just Pete in his Pringle v-neck. The scooter is pulled back onto its stand and he is lying back on his new pillion seat rest on Bessemer Street, with the chewing gum machines of Williamson's corner shop in the background.

Susannah appears wiping her fingers with a rag smelling of turpentine. 'Look Susannah, this is Pete on his Italian scooder.'

She looks intently at my six by four print as if it's a Rembrandt miniature and slowly shakes her head in disbelief. 'Jeez.'

'I know, it's like fucking California.'

'Gawd, he looks so proud.'

'Yeah' I explain, 'He just paid £25 for the custom paintwork to match his helmet colours, he's saving up for some more mirrors.'

'All that chrome. And the clothes.'

Hank turns to me and completely seriously says, 'That's a *great* phodo, Grey-ham.'

'Thanks.'

They were seeing much more than I could see. They saw a window into a working class culture they didn't know, and I was unaware of. They saw pride of ownership and aspiration in the clothes and the transport, in the freshly repainted corner shop, and in the scrubbed steps of red brick terraced houses. I saw only a rare 6am smokeless blue sky with Pete swanking off his scooter when he came to say goodbye. His *Easy Rider* sunglasses mercifully pocketed for this photo.

No one was hurrying off anywhere, so I decided to say more. 'Perry reminded me a bit of Pete.'

'Really?'

'You know, the blond hair, pretty girlfriend, everybody knowing him, not always easy to get along with.'

'You didn't like Perry?'

'Well I'm not saying that, but he could be a bit hoity toity with me.'

'How's that?'

'He made me work late with him, without pay, to finish discing a field because he'd told the boss we'd definitely finish it. Twice when machinery needed repairing he said, "We'll do that Mr Thurpley, we can go at lunch time." Lunch time!'

I slowly realised that we'd moved from the warmth of photo appreciation to a strained silence. It was as if a large cat, carrying cold in its fur from the October night, had entered the room, and I felt suddenly guilty about it. I was tiptoeing around the fact that they'd known Perry for a whole year, forgetting for a moment that *I* was the newcomer. Perry had only been gone a few days. There was a silence that clanged loud in my head, in which time I thought, *Oh no. Why am I saying this?*

Hank speaks first. 'Yeah, Perry could be a bit of a puppy for Thurpley.'

'Sorry?'

'You know,' Hank lifts two eager paws and puts his tongue out panting, "Yes Mr Thurpley, I'll do it Mr Thurpley." He was a *kissass*.'

Susannah seems more reserved and does a sad forced kind of smile. 'Anyways, look, he's outta here now. At agricultural cawledge.'

'No. He's at the *Duke's* agricultural college,' I say. 'He always corrected me.'

They laugh and Susannah says, 'Hank asked him if Duke's college was named after John Wayne, and he didn't like that.'

'A cowboy college,' says Hank, and we all laugh.

We are laughing about Perry and it feels a bit strange, like it is illegal or something. I haven't dared tell anyone before what I thought. I venture a bit more into this new territory, 'He was good to me though. On one of my first night here, Perry took me with him to the local Young Farmers' Club. His girlfriend Vera was there. Did you know her?'

Susannah picks up the kettle, 'We should all have some tea. He always talked about her, but we never met her. She sounded like some kinda exquisite doll.'

'She was very good looking, a blonde from Wakefield, near where I'm from. We got on very well.'

Hank looked even more interested, 'Did Perry mind that?'

'No he was circulating around his young farmer pals. There was one strange thing though.'

'What was that?'

'Perry came back to the table and sat down at the other side of Vera. As they talked I felt a hand on my thigh. It was Vera's.'

'A mistake huh?'

'Just what I thought. I removed her hand. But then, she put it back and looked at me with her blue eyes widening, as if to say, *It's no mistake.*'

Susannah suddenly has a noisy issue from her nose that takes the back of her hand to her face, and Hank throws his head back and seems to shake, before the happy sound of hooting fills the kitchen. I'm not sure this is meant to be funny, but it clearly is. Tears roll down Susannah's face, Hank smacks me lightly on the back. It's lovely.

Susannah explains, 'Perry was always such a stuffed shirt, he talked for months of Vera as some exquisite virginal duchess.'

'I love it,' says Hank, 'that she wasn't the nun that Perry described. She was more like a cock teaser with the hots for the latest bit of ass in town.'

'And I was that *ass*.' I say, as correctly as I can, and we all laugh together.

HENRY 2

The dairy is an island of civilisation and cleanliness, amid the shallow sea of wet dung that the farm becomes in wet weather. The sea levels rise and fall around Dairy Island like a foamless khaki tide, twice a day, as we push and scrape it from the concrete roadways and collecting yards.

I find Henry in the dairy as I slide open the heavy wooden door. He's scrubbing at the milkstone deposit on the walls and paddles of the refrigerated bulk tank with a long-handled brush and bleach solution. A regular task after the milk tanker's been.

He looks up and continues chewing, eventually parking his gum to say, 'How far have you got?'

I step in and look over the tank's edge to watch him brushing the stainless-steel surfaces. My voice, strange and echoey, says, 'Well my career has barely started, ask me in a year's time.'

Henry grins, 'You daft buggur.'

'Well I know how philosophical you are. I've taken up the electric fence, cleaned out the loose boxes, strawed the calves by the workshop, and filled a trailer with silage.'

'Philosophical! Vet's coming later you can give him a hand. He's PD-ing the six cows I've left in the top yorrd.'

'What's PD, Henry?'

'Pregnancy diagnosis. He'll tell you what to do, it's like when you helped the AI man.'

'Right, getting them into the crush or wedged behind a gate, and then holding their tails out of the way while he goes in?'

'That's it. I'll leave his soap, bucket and clean towel ready, run him some hot water off from this pipe here.'

If the farm buildings are the soiled body of the farm, the dairy is the freshly-flannelled clean face, albeit with a chilly demeanour. The spotless, wet, concrete floor is stained by my wellies as I walk back across it, to stand on the high step in the doorway. I look around at the thick, white painted, walls, and the overhead pipes. Pipes that shake every time milk is pumped to the tanks, where warm milk chunders out through the cheesy cotton milk filters into the freezing, paddle-stirred centre of the farm.

It's time to return to the khaki world. 'I'll go and scrape the bottom yard now, Henry.'

'Listen out for the vet, I won't be away long, just taking one of the kids to the doctors. If I'm not back, have your dinner at twelve and, I'll see you at one o'clock.'

The vet arrives minutes after Henry leaves. I assist, doing as the others do, and not talking to the vet unless spoken to. Always the way it's done when serious professionals visit the farm.

Soon it's lunchtime. I take my bag from the dairy and walk to the barn to ascend the giant steps of crackling bales, where my world changes to gold and becomes very calm. I pull out a bale, to give myself an armchair shaped space, and kick off my wellies to sit, and listen. Nothing, but a sweet silence. I'm surrounded by listening straw made of condensed summer. As I eat my jam sandwich light beams through the single plastic corrugated sheet in the roof making the straw glisten around me, as if I'm in noiseless outer space falling into the sun.

My mind is free to float about. I wonder; what's for dinner tonight? When will I get a girlfriend? What kind of farm I will live on when I am qualified? Then I give up all these thoughts as being impossible to resolve, when I'm still so new to this job, and Northamptonshire, and country life.

I am unaware, as the young can be, of family history. I see only my uniqueness. As if I alone have triumphed. I have escaped the polluted air and cloying atmosphere of my home town. I am a rebel, no pit job or shift in the steel works for me. Stuff the factories. I could not feel further away from all that. I am free.

I am completely ignorant of the fact that my great, great grandfather made a similar journey in reverse from this same rural latitude, 120 years ago. From farm labourer to Durham coal hewer.

EVELINE SQUEANEY

The red Morris Minor Post Office van turning down our lane to the cottage is a sight we love. Incoming letters are instant company, something that we crave. Lifebelts of words thrown to us, the overboard, by kindred spirits.

There are other daily vehicles though; Dave Squeaney's battered Ford pick-up, and his daughter Eveline's old Escort. They keep livestock nearby but their main trade is gossip.

As anyone in the village will probably tell you, *'There's a strange hippy family live in the wood at Fenley. You know the sort of thing; drugs, wild parties, orgies and probably naked satanic rituals every full moon. It must be true, the Squeaneys told me, an' they got cattle up there…'*

We live there, but we never see the strange family. Where can these ideas come from?

Eveline is secretary to the local Young Farmers group and passes the cottage most mornings. She always winds her car window down and stops the engine to speak to me, 'Hell-o-o-o.'

The last vowel falls and rises as if it has had to be retrieved from her cleavage. It is drawn out long enough to slide like a hot wet finger, down my chest and stop by the top of my Y-fronts. I know exactly the effect it is meant to have, but my body responds by stepping back out of harm's way.

She often makes clear that she is familiar with all matters agricultural. She can talk horsepower, pig breeding and torque, at the drop of a lady's handkerchief. But she's undoubtedly spent serious time studying femme fatales too; how else could she speak the way she does? With eyes widening, and her mouth making that 'glocking' sound, she ekes out sensual pauses to allow time to lick her bottom lip between words.

'We're having a talk on Zero Grazing…Forage Crops and Silage Additives next Thursday…If you'd like to come.' Her eyes flash with each topic, and the last words are spoken as her right hand slides down the steering wheel.

She is playing a character in her own film; Carry on Farming. And she laughs a little too readily at anything I say. Her laugh is a high pitched release of terrifying energy, like something leaking from a cracked pipeline, which should probably be kept away from sources of ignition.

I might look 17 and sexually mature, but really, I just want a friend, as perhaps she does, behind that siren performance and those blue-lidded, morning mascara'd eyes.

'Ooh! Is that yours?' She says excitedly, pointing up at the high bonnet of the Massey Ferguson 165 that is parked outside the cottage.

And here, I too incline to a stereotype. I'm the cowboy, giving away as little as possible. Keeping it brief and factual, with no room for gossipy interpretations. I stand silently, arms down, legs braced and ready to draw. Until that is, I feel I'm being too rude.

'Yep.' I say, 'Well actually, it's Mr Thurpley's. *One* of Mr Thurpley's.' I am desperate, to prevent any leak of information, but I'm also embarrassed by her. Although not as much as by the sudden awareness, that I am nervously brandishing my boss's name like a big, red fire extinguisher.

HENRY 3

The stone track is strangely silent under our wellies, as if each stone is wrapped in fibrous cow shit. It's late afternoon as Henry and I walk to fetch the cows who are enjoying their last days outside before coming in for the winter. We set the gates as we go and I say, 'Henry, does a farmer own us?'

'Whur d'yer get that idea from?'

'Just wondering. He gives us somewhere to live, and pays us, it seems a bit like that.'

Henry pauses to kick down a spear thistle, 'Yoor a funny 'un. Why d'you think that?'

Well, I've only had one half day off, when it was pouring with rain, I haven't had a proper day off since I started over six weeks ago, and you seem to work every day too. Mr Thurpley provides my lodgings and your house.'

We arrive at the field and Henry lifts the gate's latch, 'I'll have to think about that.'

I'm sent out like a collie to walk round the back of the cows, while Henry stands by the gate and bellows, 'C' MO-UN. C'MO-UN', his voice rising and falling. When I occasionally bring in the cows alone, imitating Henry's call is the secret to getting the cows onto their feet and moving. If I get the impersonation right as I approach, the cows move towards the gate, and save me the long walk to gather them.

Back at the farm buildings, I start my round of strawing and feeding and later report to Henry, now milking, in his green parlour over-trousers with the sleeves of his purple jumper pulled up. He points upwards and says, 'Shovel some more cake into the hoppers above the parlour will you?'

The long loft above the parlour is divided into two parts with separate access. One is the brain of the farm; an office where, above its smart new wooden steps and handrail, a fluorescent light tickers into service, and illuminates the neat logic of farm maps and records on index cards. A white wall is dominated by a large circular planner, with coloured and numbered pins to represent each cow in the herd. Next to it, an angled window looks down into the parlour pit.

But the other part of the loft, where I'm heading, is the torso. It's up worn stone steps, and unlit but for the door opening. My presence disturbs the mice from their dreams and non-stop feasting. Hundreds of them bound and dart over the heap of ground mixed meal, the mouse herd flowing like a shock of grey loosed intestines. They flow into and out of the floor level hoppers as I shovel the meal in, and gradually they become scarce. Eventually, feeling a little more alone, I pause a moment to daydream myself, and listen to the parlour's rhythms.

Under my feet, 12 cows are letting down their milk and munching their most concentrated feed of the day, to keep the milk flowing through vessels and pipes. I'm standing right over the beating heart of the farm. As I finish the job and replace the shovel by the door, the last of the mice, like slippery night thoughts, disappear into the walls.

I return to the parlour to get the next task, and Henry gestures me into the pit. He turns a valve, draws the cluster of units from a cow, and hangs them up while releasing the gate to send the cows out. While six more cows walk in keen to get their heads into the cake feeders, he says, 'What you said earlier, you said "Do farmers own us?" and you looked at me a bit old fashioned. The way I see it is this, when you work, you are selling your *time*. That's all work is.'

I bend down to feel the warmth of the milk in one of the glass collecting vessels, as Henry continues, 'Soon as the straw's in he'll have you just doing a five day week. You'll be missing the overtime then.' He reaches out automatically for one of the iodine warm-water dilutors that hang from hoses, and sprays the first cow's teats while rubbing the cowshit away with his fingers.

'Yeah good point, Henry.'

I don't say, that I'd like some choice in how much time I sell to the farmer, as I'm keen to not have Henry think of me as some kind of mutineer.

Later at ten minutes to six with afternoon milking coming to an end, I finish my jobs, and report to the parlour pit again, knowing that I need to somehow lighten the mood. Henry swings the levers of the feed hoppers as each of the last cows enter their place, and I say, 'How do you know how much feed to give each cow, Henry?'

'Look at their tails.'

I watch silently for a bit, 'You don't half know some stuff.' I watch for a while longer. 'How on earth can you tell? Is it the way it swings or…'

He smiles. 'You daft buggur! It's the coloured tape on thur tails that tells me how far from calving they arr. That's what decides how much cake they get.'

I suspected as much, but it was nice to make Henry smile.

'Did you finish bedding down the last yorrd, and check the water trough?'

'All done, Henry.'

'You can get off home then if you like.'

'Are you sure?'

'Yes.' Henry fingers a cow's teats into each unit, 'but there is one thing, aforre y'ask. Mr Thurpley doesn't want you to take a tractor home anymore.'

'But I thought it was OK?'

Henry stand back as a cow urinates, 'No. It's not.'

'Perry always did.'

'I'm just telling you what he said.'

'But he never said anything to me when he came around earlier.'

'I'm just telling you what he said.'

'Ok. I'll have a walk then. See you tomorrow.'

Sometimes it seems that more than one kind of shit ebbs and flows around Bellaby Farm.

WASHING UP

To my eternal shame I rarely washed up at Fenley. In my teenage arrogance I thought tipping up half my hard earned income to Susannah each week entitled me to be looked after.

Susannah is out for the evening. So here I am, sluicing off the large white dinner plates as Hank reappears in the kitchen after he's put the children to bed.

'Hank, while Susannah is out can I ask you something?'

He picks up a tea towel, 'Hey sure. Kind of man to man, eh? What's this gonna be, Gray-ham? Don't tell me, *you* are the one who damaged Squeaney's pick-up truck, did you hit it with the tractor?'

I pass him a sudsy plate, 'Hank…'

'Did he deny you his daughter's hand, or see you wiping the rain off your tractor seat with her knickers? Did you get Eveline in the family way?'

'It's nothing quite as newsworthy in the village as that, I...'

He hold the ladle he's drying at his waist, 'Wait, I got it. You borrowed Squeaney's 12 bore to gun down the bawss in the farmyard?' He pulls an imaginary trigger, and the ladle recoils. 'Cos Jeez, if you did, I'd understand. In fact, I'm gonna find that box o' Cuban cigars I got, before the cops come for you and we can smoke one each…'

I hold out a bundle of cutlery, 'Hank. Shut up. What are pizzas?'

'WHAT?'

'Pizza, linguini, pastrami, black-eyed beans and pardon my French, but what the hell *is* in salad dressing?'

Hank drawers the knives and forks, then looks at me as if I'm an alien. And I am, but I am serious. Perpetually hungry, I push unfamiliar food around my plate while hearing plans of even stranger meals to come.

'Susannah is a great cook.'

'I know that, but I miss baked beans, on toast. Like you miss pretzels and bagels.'

'You're serious Gray, aren't you? We can get you beans. That's OK.'

I put the heavy casserole dish upside down on the drainer, 'And gravy?'

'Sure.'

There's a pause, in which the weight of a tractor wheel that feels to have been parked on my chest, drives off.

'Hey, maybe if you eat more beans, you will get to home base with Eveline, and really make her squeal huh?'

I take the tea towel off him and place it over his head, 'Hank!'

FARMER THURPLEY

I think Horace Thurpley sees himself as a gentleman farmer. He is addressed by everyone on the farm as 'Mister Thurpley.'

He wears a flat cap now that the weather has turned colder. Not at all though like the old northern blokes. Thurpley is quite a different stereotype. His checked cap is narrow and pulled tight onto his head, so that his bumpy crown pushes up like a stone under a picnic blanket. The peak is down over his eyebrows, guardsman style. The effect is haughty and doubly superior, as if he has two noses. All the better to look down on me, from the small window of his green Land Rover.

He looks the sort of well-to-do chap you see on TV when the Royal family are out shooting, he could be the one passing a 12 bore to Princess Anne. He is probably in his early thirties, but like Prince Charles, looks much older. Imagine Bertie Wooster drained of bonhomie, and with his amicability away at the dry cleaners (against Jeeves' advice).

When not in his vehicle he is easily distinguished from the rest of us by his paler skin and his clothes, which are unsoiled by any physical labour. We manual staff are all wearing old jackets and trousers that look like they've been dipped in mud, or worse, and then had a bit of it brushed off.

Beside his Queenly pronunciation, another difference is the smell he carries. We all smell of silage, grease or cows. In fact, you'd better not to get too close to us at all, and especially if you see thin yellow streaks decorating a jacket because that's scoury calf shit, and it has a smell that can really put you off your sandwiches. His lordship, on the other hand, smells of soap. Now I know that we can all be forgiven for that at times, especially in the morning, but the strange thing is he carries that whiff about with him all day long.

'I dunno Graham, it's nobody's life. Maybe old Thurpley just had a bad start to his day. Maybe his wife didn't kiss him because he had a zit on his face or something. We all say the wrong thing sometimes. He probably didn't mean to upset you...'

I interrupt, 'Susannah, I just saw a mouse. It went from the Rayburn to the cupboard.'

Susannah leans back from the sink, soap suds dripping from the saucepan, and casually shouts up into the hall, 'Do-ttie. Sweedie. Do you think you could bring Norman down to the kitchen for me?'

She rubs at a dripline of chilli sauce on the pan's side, and continues talking to me, 'I know you look up to Thurpley because he's kinda pawsh but you know, maybe…' She pauses with her tongue folded onto her bottom lip while she draws a noisy breath past it. I will learn that this little mouth drama always precedes a carefully considered truth, 'Maybe, he actually isn't such a bright guy.'

I respond, as many of us do to the truth, by not seeing it. 'But Susannah, he has a farm and, he's in charge…'

Four year old Dottie appears in the doorway. She is wearing a cardboard cone as a medieval damsel's hat with a net-curtain veil. A scarlet silky cloak is tied in an elaborate knot around her neck, under which is a large grey cat's head, with very angry looking green eyes, and two immobilised furry legs sticking up. The cats lower limbs and tail dangle to the floor.

'Oh thanks Dot. You are such a good girl.'

Norman, released, takes only a second to assess the situation. He dashes into the darkness under the corner cupboard. There's a crunch. And he leaves along the stone flagged hall with a limp tail swinging from his mouth.

Nothing is said about the killing. Instead Susannah turns and beams, 'You look sensational, Dot.'

'Mom, I am the Queen and Sophie is the King, but *she* wants to wear the crown *all* the time.'

'Aw honey. Some Kings are like that, the power goes to their head. Maybe, Graham could make you a crown too?'

'Yes! Is dinner ready soon, Momma?'

It's time for me to stop grumbling about my day, and do something useful. 'So what do you have to make a crown with Dot, I mean, your Majesty?'

JOHNNY 2

Is history with us wherever we are? Like the farm soil, always right under our feet, stuck permanently in the tread of our boots and staining our clothes?

When I'm discing, I veer to one side as I approach the end of a field to turn around. With older tractor-trailed implements like harrows you have to do this. The results is that you make a long opened out 'S' shape with each trip you make up or down the field. It wasn't just me doing this, but every farm worker for centuries leading oxen or steering horse drawn ploughs. These subtle curves have become fixed into many of the old boundary hedges and fences which form the seams and stitches in the patchwork that is the English countryside.

And here I am on a freezing cold November day, standing in a ditch alongside a leafless thorn hedge, on just such a field boundary. From the top of the ditch a grass pasture white with frost rises and then slopes gently away under the open space of a grey sky. The countryside seems completely lifeless.

I am working alongside the oldest person on the farm, the tractorman Johnny, who usually works alone. I'm a bit wary as he knows everything about farming and I know nothing much at all. Also, he's old enough to have known Thurpley since he was a boy.

We're using tools that look like medieval weapons; a sickle, an axe and ones I don't have names for, like the one Johnny presented me with that has an 18″ long straight blade socketed to a five foot heavy shaft.

'So what is hedgelaying about, Johnny?'

'It's a masterpiece, you know, when you looks at a good laid 'edge. It's stock proof jus on its own see. No need for that bloody barbed wire.'

'So how do you do it?'

'Well you can't make a whossname without crackin eggs see? You av to thin out these little branches, and then cut the other buggers down to make em grow better.'

'Can I have a go?'

'You need to clear about four yards of ditch ahead of me first, otherwise the falling thorn will tangle in the brambles. Then you can have a go and tickle some of these that are hanging out of line.'

'OK.'

'Once we get crackin on a bit I'll show you how we lays em. Ow old are you again boy?'

'Seventeen.'

'I suppose you're old enough to be layin em!'

I don't always understand what the old guy is talking about, but I'm keen to pull my weight as I shuffle along the damp ditch to avoid tripping, and slash at all the scrubby growth attempting to establish itself. It is good work to keep us warm. My blade rattles against bramble stems and tears at long grass, dead hogweed and nettles, while Johnny's thwacks into hawthorn uprights which creak and clatter as they fall. Breathing hard in the icy air, we don't talk very much.

After each bit of progress I reach back for the muck fork to gather the cut stems, and then throw them up and over the ditch side, onto the field's edge. Clambering in and out of the ditch to keep the debris in tidy piles, I make a remark and am slightly surprised by the reaction it gets. 'Hey Johnny, I just saw Mr Thurpley's Land Rover turn into the 12 acre.'

I carry on working, but Johnny stops to pull a sharpening stone from his suit jacket pocket, 'Aw yeah, I seen im. So e's sneakin up behind us eh? He'll probbly be lookin to see how the contractor is getting on, but he's sure to peep in at us too.'

Two fields away from us working our hedge by hand, a JCB is growling and pulling out a hedge to make two ten acre fields into a twenty. I resume work, and smile to myself at the new image of Mr Thurpley sneaking shiftily about his farm and peeping through hedges.

Johnny strokes his tool's straight edge with the stone. There will be no break while 'He' is in the vicinity. Johnny resumes his upcuts at the hawthorn brash, throwing the stems across the ditch.

We are in a ritual as old as time, where the novice tries to learn from the old hand. The youngster thinks he is learning a single task, but actually much more is being taken in. Centuries old perspectives are being assimilated, but it will take the passage of even more years before the young un will see it. That's the way with history.

'So what's that tool called, Johnny?'

'Well, I calls it a billhook see. It's got a chopping blade on one side and a nice little notch yur, an this curved beak that's good for smaller branches and smoothin off the big cuts. I'll show you later when we start laying proper, after we done some thinnin.'

'And this one that I'm using?'

'There's Gwyneth, see.'

I laugh, surprised by the sudden surreal turn, and Johnny laughs too. But not for long, as the Land Rover is approaching on the concrete road on the other side of the hedge. It drops down a gear for the bend, but we are spared a visit for now. Instead a Barbour jacketed arm reaches up and shows a clean palm, before the engine's sound fades away.

'Somebody got *portant things to do,*' says Johnny, in a grave tone I will later recognise as mocking, but for now I'm not sure what he means.

As wintry days pass, and yards of hedge gradually fall, in similar situations I will dare to say, 'Did he do the royal wave?' And Johnny will laugh. Each moment of laughter we create will eventually yield a profit.

Fleeting royal visit over, Johnny declares, 'Baccer time boy.' We make our tools safe, and I follow him to stand behind the rear tractor wheel out of the wind. He takes out a twenty pack of Embassy tipped from the bib pocket of his overall, and lights up, while I have a polo mint. He doesn't say, 'Boy', as Thurpley does, as if it's the name of my species, as you might say 'Rat.' Johnny pronounces it in a way I like, with a kindly Welsh bounce.

'Watch out for drain pipes in that ditch boy. They're about every 10 yards. It used to be a bugger this field.

Always too wet before the drain contractors came. Clay see. We ad it for permanent pasture. Rushes and kingcups it was, at the bottom end. You couldn't put the cows in afore June.' His cigarette smoke loiters in the tractor's lee, as if it too is listening to him.

'You know a lot about the history of the fields, Johnny.'

'Well I bin yur since 1942. Came up from Wales to Bellaby with my old boss. Now 'e was a good man, a good boss e was. It was all sheep an orses then mind. I lived in the farm I did, where the dairy an parlour is now.'

As he says more about leaving Wales, I check with him that it was 30 years ago, because he speaks of it as if it was yesterday.

Johnny decisively pinches out the cigarette stub and throws the past, and the stub, aside. 'Time to start layin' em.' Stepping over the ditch, he begins chopping the remaining tall stems with downward cuts, almost all the way through, and pulling them down close to horizontal. The splinters are trimmed off with the billhook's curve, to leave a smooth surface on the newly exposed wood. 'You gotta leave some livin wood attached see, an then it will grow back.'

I resume my work, and he watches me before saying, 'I f'got to say, just go steady, Graham boy. Only we've got weeks on this. Your arms an shoulders will ache for a couple o' days. No sense in killin yourself.'

Then, taking a big axe with the head upside down, he knocks in the thinned stems to act as stakes along the centre of the hedge, before putting on his thick gloves to roughly weave spiny branch tips down among the stakes. I comment how good it looks, and he says, 'You can use 'azel stakes if you got em. An if you want a top class job you put em in every six foot. Some weave split 'azel or willow wands through the tops to make a neat line too. You'll see that in Warwickshire. They do some good hedges there, they do.'

Lunchtime comes, and Johnny drops me off at the farm at 12 o'clock. We'll meet back up at 1 o' clock and resume our working pattern, including apparently illegal breaks for 'baccer time', until we finish at the farm buildings at 5pm exactly. Unlike cow work, arable work can be rigidly planned, and we follow Johnny's arable timetable as closely as we follow the snaking line of that hedge over the days and weeks ahead, weather, and my cow days permitting.

'Jus' one thing, Graham boy,' Johnny says, as he reaches for the crinkly leather strap to close his van door, at the end of the day, 'Watch what you says to Mister Henry. 'E's got Thurpley's yur, see?' And he touches his ear lobe and nods solemnly, before he reaches for the ignition key.

DEAR JULIE NOVEMBER 1973

Thanks for your lovely letter. I didn't know that you'd lived on a farm once. You might like to know that the dairy cows are all inside now, and the farm plough has been put away for another year. It's on a limestone 'hardstanding' area in front of a nettley wooden fence. Its red frame is greyed with old sump oil and its three curved steel mouldboards are ginger with fresh grease. Winter is coming.

Here at the cottage things are getting better. I'm liking the food more now. It was a shock at first, especially when I found they had no chip pan. I'm trying out new things all the time. I had yoghurt last week have you heard of that? It's like soured milk with fruit bits in it.

We tend to eat late. Sometimes I look around the kitchen for something to eat and can't find anything, because Susannah cooks almost everything from scratch. Once, standing there by the Rayburn after a hard day working in the cold, I longed for the smell of cooking, and even little Sophie's playschool picture made with broken dried pasta shapes, peas and coloured lentils, began to look VERY appealing.

One day I struck lucky. I found a Sainsbury's individual cherry pie in a bag hanging on the back of the larder door, it was delicious. 'Where has my pie gone?' Hank said the next day.

'Oh I had a pie yesterday,' I said. Then he called me some names that I am probably not allowed, by the Post Office, to put in a letter. 'Look,' I said, 'be fair, there was no one's name on it.' (Although technically, it did say Sainsburys). I had unwittingly stumbled upon the secret place where Hank stashed his pies.

He's wrong if he thinks I am going to let it drop too. When Sophie was looking for somewhere to hide from Dottie, I said, 'I know a good hiding place – behind the larder door.' Hank looked over his newspaper and smiled. I think he quite liked me teasing him really. That's how things are done here.

Anyway when dinner is at last ready, and Susannah shouts, 'Time d'eeeat,' I swear it is the sweetest sound in the world.

Yes I miss school too. Not the lessons, but being amongst people my own age. Apart from Dottie and Sophie, I am the youngest person wherever I go. The people at work are all so old. I've recently been working with Johnny, the old quiet one. Remember? He's the chap I spent the long rainy half-day with stone picking, in the field where dead moles hung on the barbed wire. Turns out he's not so bad after all.

Perry is long gone now. I'd almost forgotten about him until you asked. When he spoke his vowel sounds seemed extended, so the letters 'o' or 'a' took him ages to say. Imagine him saying, 'Trebor mints are a minty bit stronger!' Do you remember how the 2nd year kids used to sing that and add on, 'stick em up your arse and they last even longer'? Well I think Perry definitely must have stuck them up there to get those long minty sounds. Anyway, no Trebor mints for me I prefer Polos, cos, as you know, I've got real class. Or 'claarss' as Perry would have said. Actually I'm not sure if you can say 'arse' in a letter. Not something we covered in English was it?

I do get out a bit. On my Friday off, I often go to Northampton to look around. And some nights, one of the young farmers comes to give me a lift whenever there is a disco dance at one of the village halls. There's usually about four of us swaying about, as we sit on old carpet offcuts holding our knees, in the back of his Escort van while it bumps along country lanes. I am the only one wearing a rounded collar and baggy flares, most of the lads dress more like our dads; flat shoes, straight trousers and sometimes those shirts with little patterns that we wore back in the fifth form.

There is no larking about dancing like Mick Jagger, or anything flashy, it's all 'elbows in and shuffle, shuffle.' There are girls too but, well, it's difficult when you're an outsider, so I haven't got a girlfriend yet.

You asked for more about life at the cottage with my landlord and landlady. Well, putting the competition for food aside, the main thing about them is that they are so brainy. The living room is like a library, they even name the dogs and cats after people in English Literature. Even though we are in the same house, they live in a different world to me. Susannah loves to do oil painting on canvases set up in the dining room, and they both seem to get so much more out of life, they talk all the time about every little thing. Even when they argue it's interesting, because it's not 'life or death' like with my parents. Mostly I can understand them, but then, especially if they get talking about 'The States', it can become like Mr Sims reading Shakespeare, where you know that it's English, but it still makes no sense. But you know what? For all their education, they've never heard of mushy peas!

It can get so crazy here. Well, is dancing holding a plant pot on your head normal? Or eating really long spaghetti that's not from a tin? Or reading books about subjects like Ecology that no one has ever heard of?

Ooh gotta go, it's dinner. ('Viddles ready. Come an' geddit!' is the call tonight.) Will resume later...

WHAT'S WRONG SOOTY?

'Jeez Graham, you never saw *Sesame Street* here?' Susannah and I are clearing the dining room table. Hank is putting the kids to bed.

'No I never heard of it. But we didn't get a telly until I was ten.' I pick at bits on the meatloaf plate as we move the last dishes into the kitchen. 'So what was *Sesame Street* about?'

'It was an educational TV puppet show for young children. They had great characters like Big Bird and the Cookie Monster. Do you want coffee?' She moves the enamelled cowboy coffee pot into the middle of the Rayburn hotplate.

'Yes please. You mean like, Sooty and Sweep?'

'What's that? Can you pass me three mugs from the hooks?'

'Glove puppets. A bear who speaks in a tiny whisper and a dog with an irritating squeak for a voice.'

'Did they go out and have adventures and stuff? Can you pass me the milk?'

'Yeah. Well, they never went very far from Harry Corbett.'

'Ah OK, that's some little English village right?'

Hank reappears quietly in the doorway and Susannah reports, 'Graham is just telling me about a strange English TV puppet show set in Harry Corbett.'

'No, no. He was the guy working them. The man with the puppets on his hands was Harry Corbett. He told us what Sooty was whispering, and what Sweep the naughty dog's squeaks meant.'

Hank's eyebrows drop in mild puzzlement, 'OK.'

'They would pack a suitcase to go on holiday, or spray Mr Corbett with a water pistol.'

Susannah pours coffee from the red pot through the tea strainer into each mug in turn, and sets the pot on the back of the stove. 'So they did stuff, but didn't have voices? That seems kinda sad.'

They push for more about Sooty and Sweep, but what else is there to say? A black and white TV show about a mute bear and his depressed looking dog? With a man who looked like a friendlier version of your dad? We sit down around the kitchen table in the orange light. I say, 'Tell me about *Sesame Street*.'

And away they go, talking and talking. Both Hank and Susannah speak with such fondness and enthusiasm for their programme. It had bright colours, fun, spelling, songs and crazy patter. It makes me wish I could see it too.

They break into silly voices together, 'Mmm Cookies!' and then both laugh.

Hank says slowly, 'There was Enzo, Elmo, The Count. And Ernie and Bert.'

At this Susannah's chair screeches back. She bends forward causing her long curly hair to appear suddenly on the grainy wooden table top. Her shoulders shake, and her hair is pushing crumbs onto the floor. She is trying to say something. Her voice is high and squeaky.

Is she choking on something? Or maybe she is someone who has fits like that girl in the fourth form?

I look at Hank, he is grinning. Susannah is shaking at the mention of Ernie and Bert. She is trying to say something like 'When they...' but after the shriek comes a kind of grunt from her throat. 'When they took…' she is impossible to understand.

I look to Hank for enlightenment, but now his head is back, and he's laughing at Susannah laughing. I can't help but join in, even though I have no idea what was funny about Ernie and Bert.

Susannah straightens up eventually. She wipes the tears from her cheeks with the folded teacloth she'd used for the coffee pot handle, and declares, 'I LOVE Ernie and Bert.'

Her depth of feeling is so evident, that I sense an awkwardness, as if I shouldn't be here. But the funny stories resume, and I stay to enjoy them. Underneath the recollections of this children's TV show, I can feel Susannah's longing for the States. It's taken a while to penetrate my teenager's carapace, but I slowly begin to realise that, I am not the only person here who is many miles from home.

JOHNNY 3

The hedging and history job continues. We work and chat. We work and daydream. Time blurs as we work and ruminate on our own thoughts and each other's. Days pass.

One morning between the hacking and forking, I stop to pee. Johnny is lost in his work. He is standing side on to the misty morning light lovingly making a stake out of a piece of felled thorn, hooking off side shoots then turning it in his soiled palm to shave wedges of wood from the tip with his flat blade. He creates a point that, for all its perfect symmetry, will never been seen again once hammered into the wet earth. It could be dawn on the Agincourt battlefield, with Johnny an Owain Glyndwr loyalist joining the English archers. All have forearms thickened by years of land work. They are preparing the inclined pointed stakes they will use to dodge in and out of, for protection against the thundering advances of the mounted French knights. The familiar hedging ritual, a small comfort in a fearful situation.

I'm brought back suddenly as Johnny shouts, 'Land Rover. No time to piss boy, I can hear Thurpley is on his way.'

'Doesn't he ever stop to pee?'

'Probbly got someone to do that for im as well, e as.'

Every week we need a fire, to burn all the thorn brash and the thinnings. November rolls into December, and as the days get colder, we leave the hedge and ditch more often to attend to the fire. Forking the circle of charred twigs into the greying embers, makes the flames and our spirits rise with the light and heat, especially in late afternoon, as sun and temperature drops, and frost begins nipping at our tired limbs.

Standing in the blissful warmth of the ash and listening to the pop and whistle of hot thorns we revive our feet, always cold in our Wellingtons, and Johnny speaks. 'There was a fox in that field last year while I was ploughin.'

'Do you like foxes, Johnny?'

'They make a bloody mess o' young lambs. Sickenin what they do. Like they can't stop killin. They do the same with hens an' all.' He draws deep on his Embassy and the tip glows orange in the grey light. 'Mind you, they're bloody smart too.'

'Smart?'

'While I was ploughing, I seen the hunt was out. They started at Fenley an crossed the fields, following the 'ounds. I was just leavin the 'eadland and he comes out the hedge. I noticed him see cos he was trottin, not runnin mind, just trottin towards me. Allo, Mr Fox is it? I say. An' e says, *Don't mind me*. D'you know what he done?'

Johnny sucks on his cigarette and exhales leisurely. 'The crafty old bugger, he ran in front o' me, straight down the field on the whossname. You know, the edge of the land before the furrow. Like he knew, that his scent was gonna be ploughed nine inch under as I followed im.'

'That's clever.'

'Crafty old sod. He knew those 'ounds were gonna lose his scent right in the middle of the field. An they'd would look silly buggers.'

'And did they?'

'Well they never got im. The light was goin, an they packed up after that.' From talking into the air, as was Johnny's habit from being ever vigilant for Thurpley sightings, he turned to look me in the eye. 'You gotta admire 'im our Mr Fox, he knows what 'e's doin. 'E made up his mind see, and that's it.'

'That's a grand tale Johnny, you see some stuff don't you?'

'You carn elp it see? When you're up the field an down the field, all day long.'

He pulls out his pocket watch and flicks the cig butt into the flames. 'Nother ten minutes boy, an it's 'ome time.'

More days come and go. Besides Thurpley's visits and 'baccer time,' one other event is guaranteed to stop Johnny's work in the hedgerow. The presence, of a robin. And just as for the fox, Johnny is a medium able to express their words for them.

'How aroo, Mr Robin? *Veru wahl* 'e say. *Have a minute, while I spies out some worms 'ereabouts,* e says.'

He addresses the various robins we encounter during our work as if they are all the same individual, 'Get Christmas out the way, an spring'll soon be ere boyo. You got a Mrs Robin picked out avroo?' The robin's head cocked to one side is taken as a sure sign it is talking back. If one squeaks out a call, 'Some bread is it?' crumbs can always be found from the bottom of Johnny's pocket.

The tractor needs moving forward so we can load the heavier branches onto the trailer. 'Draw the horse on, Graham boy.'

It seems that in Johnny's world, where he speaks to robins and respects foxes, horses *transformed* into tractors sometime in the 1950's. He treats them both much the same, never working them too hard and spending a little time refuelling, and fussing over them, at each end of the working day.

Draw the horse on, boy seems like language from past centuries. Wherever people piled stooks of corn onto wooden wagons, gathered turnips, or collected the corpses of plague victims, some lad between ten and twenty would be told to, *draw the horse on, boy*.

If I drive the tractor on too far, giving us an extra two feet to throw the branches, as the engine quietens I'll hear Johnny say, 'Pull er back, you're nearly in Aberavon.'

Between hacking and slashing, chopping and trimming, we break to attend to the fire, again and again, forking the outer ring of twigs into the sleepy orange-grey centre. More of Johnny's life story tumbling out each time. Leaving Wales and the valleys for certain employment on his motorbike, with his wife in the sidecar. Staying loyal to his old boss, 'a good man, good boss.' Living at Bellaby farm; his children climbing the farm track up the hill, to walk through the woods to the village school every day.

Johnny lights up the last Embassy of the afternoon. With another good twenty yards of hedge laid we warm our feet in the ashes of the day and I hear, between the singing of wet wood and the soft falling sound of ashy branches, yet more of Johnny's story.

The Thurpley family take over Bellaby farm, Thurpley Senior first. 'You know boy, you change boss, an you jus never know. I got my name down for a council 'ouse then. I made up my mind see. I says to Missus, "we'll get a council ouse in Benbyshire that's what we'll do." They can't touch you then see. Bloody tied ouses. You can tell the boss as nice as you like that he got something wrong, an next thing, you're off down the road. No job an no home see?'

There's a pause as he adjusts his reduced cigarette, appearing to kiss his fingertips like a French chef before leisurely blowing out smoke, 'No one can throw me out now. That's the bloody thing, they got you by the goolies boy. No more o' this,' and he touches the hair at his forehead. 'S'not fair, when you got kiddies at school an all.'

We stand and stare silently at the fire, in respect of the truths spoken. As the air stirs into a light wind, and the outer embers brighten and then seem to glow just for us, the pocket watch comes out and the last tab is flicked to the low flames. 'Another day done boy, let's load up the trailer and take this 'orse home.'

THE PRINCESS

It's Hank's turn, in our made-up round-the-table story. 'So, the boy from the farm took the princess with her new reading book to the drive-in movie. Her cute pony, with its gingham ribbons came along too, trotting alongside next to the car's rear fender. They stopped in the parking space and climbed into the back seat together. "Hey Not You," said the boy to the pony, "you eat your hay out there on the sidewalk."'

'The princess kicked off her shoes, laid back, and made herself real comfy on the plush seat, and said, "You know, I ain't nairver seen such a *huge* carton o' popcorn like you got there boy. Just hopin' you're a plannin' on giving me some…"'

'Hank!' Susannah glares in horror, and a kick brushes past my denim flares under the table.

'Ouch', says Hank, beaming broadly.

Susannah's voice softens to speak to Sophie, our youngest contributor. Sophie is currently finding life very serious. She's living in the shade of her older sister Dottie, who now leaves her home planet daily to attend a whole other world, called school. 'Ok Soph, it's your turn, can you continue the story?'

'What was the movie Poppa?' says Dot.

'That's for Sophie to say if she wants, it's her story right now.'

Sophie keeps her head down but lifts her eyes to look around at us all, her lips rehearsing the story so far. After a long pause she begins.

'The Prin-cess,' Sophie stops, and gives a little sigh. She is enchanted merely in the presence of her name. 'Prin-cess said. "I would like. Ice cream."' Sophie looks around gravely at us all, and we all try to encourage her with smiles and big eyes. She continues hesitantly, '"A swing. And a. Cardigan."'

Susannah says, 'Oh well done Soph. She likes ice cream and she likes to swing, like you!'

'And she'd like a cardigan, with blue stars on it,' Sophie volunteers.

Susannah leans into the table, 'That sounds lovely. Does she need that because she is getting cold?'

Soph scans us all again, as if checking we are all taking this absolutely seriously. We are.

'The Prin-cess.' The enchanted pause follows again. 'The Prin-cess. Has huge. Tiddies.'

There are some airy nose noises, and a sudden outbreak of small adult coughs, as we all try to keep absolutely straight faces knowing we are being monitored by Soph. My teeth begin to hurt from being clenched so tightly.

This was the one story that couldn't get the usual neat summary and a sweet ending to send the children off to bed with. Because none of the adults were capable.

Susannah, initially with a kind of squeak in her voice and tears in her eyes, thanks Sophie, and us all for a beautiful story. Hank and I nod in solemn agreement.

'Time to brush teeth children. Say goodnight. I'll be up in a moment.'

'Goodnight Sophie, goodnight Dottie.'

'Goodnight Momma, goodnight Poppa, goodnight Grahamy.'

The three of us avoid all eye contact for as long as it takes Dottie and Sophie to be out of earshot, and then we simultaneously hiss with muffled laughter.

But despite our best efforts at self-control, Sophie's sensitive antennae have detected our instant love of the distinguished princess, and she will become a regular character in after-dinner stories. After all who doesn't love a royal with a problem?

VIC 2

On Sundays, Henry has his day off, and Vic and I move up a level; Vic becomes the head herdsman, and I become his assistant.

''Ere moit, step on me toes. Gaw on.'

'Are you sure?'

'They got internawl steewl toecaps.' says Vic, his pride of ownership making him even taller.

Having the right equipment for a job is everything. Always wellies for cow days. Vic is wearing his new big blue ones today, and I'm hoping they're not bossy-boots, like Perry wore whenever he was put in charge of anything: especially me. Wellies aside, penknives and adjustable spanners are pretty neat bits of equipment too, but the farm prize has to go to baler twine. Always to hand it can repair gates, be a tractor's throttle cable, hold a jacket together to keep out the cold, or hasten an arrival.

'Whatcha done so far?' says Vic, after he's finished milking and cleaning.

'Fed the heifers in the 20 acre, strawed and fed four yards, done a load of silage ready for afternoon milking, scraped the collecting yard, and I'm just going to empty the muck spreader.'

'Good *lad*.' I think I detect a hint of mockery in Vic's voice, as he does his 'Yawkshire' accent for me again.

When I return from making cowshit fly from the spreader onto the 50 acre, Vic seems distracted and serious, holding his bottom lip with his teeth. 'Let's check the loose boxes,' he says. We walk down through the olive concrete yard. Vic drawing the bolts on the upper stable doors, to look into each freshly strawed, skylit white-painted cube. He eyes the occupants in turn. 'Oi think, we moight give this one a hand. It's only her second.'

As Vic opens the lower door, the cow shifts to keep us in sight, and his voice switches to become quieter, and even more serious. 'It's alright gell. Let's have a look atcha.' A black nose, and two yellow hooves, poke out at the world through the cow's vulva. Vic gently swipes away a khaki ribbon of shit that has extruded onto the calf's nose, and turns to me, 'Can you get some bayler twoine?'

'Got some,' I say, pulling a hairy doughnut of it from my pocket.

Vic smiles, I think he might be pleased. But then I realise, he's still working on his impersonation of my northern accent, as he repeats '*got sum*.' Adding 'You're learnin' farst *old sun*.' Although he does revert to his own voice for the all-important instruction, 'Make loops loik a slip knot, and put em behoind the first knuckle joint.' I hand a loop to Vic and copy what he does.

'Wite until she pushes again, then puwl.' Vic's face is solemn, all his attention's on the cow. The cow, equally solemn, moos softly between straining. 'Roight. Here we go, puwl steady, in a straight loine.'

Like getting a cork from an old bottle of varnish, it seems like it will be impossible. The three of us strain and rest. Strain and rest. But then it happens, in just a second. The calf pours onto the strawy floor four feet away, like oil paint squeezed from a tube. A sudden new presence, in titanium white and ivory black, has joined us in the loose box. Glistening and beautiful, freshly painted onto this canvas of white and gold. A splash of liquid follows, a yellow bubble of it remains hanging in a grey membrane from the cow. Vic takes a piece of straw and standing astride the dazed calf, pokes it through the film that covers its nostrils. The shiny head moves. As the cow turns to greet it, Vic rubs a handful of straw on the calf's back and sides, and stands back.

'Now give her some spayce,' he says quietly, and I realise something. That he really cares.

The cow takes over from Vic, rasping its long tongue over the wet black and white body. Pleased with the calf's movement, Vic cleans his hands on some straw, and we retreat to the other side of the half-door. We watch the scene, as the calf is licked out of its bewilderment, and into life. And soon, encouraged by mum's nuzzling, it begins its first attempt to stand.

'We just need to wait and be sure the calf is feeding alroight,' says Vic, as if to excuse our presence to the cow, as much as to me. 'Can you go and get her a fresh bucket o' water, and fill a net bag with best hay?'

I return to find Vic still leaning on the half-door, gazing into the loose box and smiling. Something has changed. 'Look at that Groi-ham. Beats workin' in a factory dunnit?' He steps back to give me room to peer in, and I watch the calf standing to suckle, with its wet stringy tail swinging.

'See, you gotta be sure the calf gets the first miwk. It's full of co-lo-strum.'

'Co-lo-strum?'

'It's special miwk that gives it a really good start. Full of goodness.'

'Like a Sunday dinner?'

Vic smiles broadly, 'Toime for lunch?'

'You're the Boss today, Vic.'

'Whatcha got, mate? Jam sandwiches again?'

'And some cake.'

'Then it must be Sunday!'

We walk back through the collecting yard, and I ask Vic to tell me again the name of the special milk. He says 'co-lo-strum', twice over and in that moment I realise he just likes words. He isn't taking the mickey out of my accent at all, he's just enjoying it. Then in rising high spirits, he recites some more of his favourite words, chopping them into syllables so they sound as clear and separate as drinks on a silver salver. He is a BBC announcer, warming up his voice, before reporting from Bellaby Farm; 'Co-lo-strum, Hot Sau-sage Sand-wiches, Chill-i Will-i and the Red Hot Pep-pers.' He swings his big hands through the air as if he's waving a pennant, with each enunciated syllable on it. Then still smiling, he squeezes himself into his Hillman Imp for the drive home for his lunch, leaving me to climb into the barn for mine, and wonder to myself, if I ever saw a man looking quite so happy as I just did.

Like livestock, new thoughts can be born too. A different way of seeing things can emerge out of older ones. My new notion is: just because some of us don't speak the Queen's English, doesn't mean we don't enjoy language.

Later, at 6pm, we finish work. It is raining heavily and Vic insists on driving me home to Fenley, four miles out of his way.

'How come you don't take the tractor?' he asks.

'Henry said, Thurpley doesn't want me to anymore. But I will have my own transport next week.'

Wotcha gettin'?

'Motorbike.'

'Good. You gotta 'ave the roight kit for this job, you living ouwt at Fenley an awll.'

IN SERVICE

My jacket is over a chair close to the Rayburn in the kitchen, and Hank passes me a mug of tea, 'A wet day for you huh, Gray?'

'Yeah. That's December for you.'

'What did you do today?'

'Usual cow stuff, and then after lunch Thurpley drove over to tell me: *go stand on top of the hill near the wood and open the gate when anyone needs to come through.*'

'Why? Who was coming?'

'The local hunt. Thurpley's landlord is a bigwig in the hunt.'

'So you stood there, like a doorman?'

'Yep. So the gentry didn't have to dismount and get their fancy riding boots, red jackets or their jodhpurs dirty.'

'Well I guess they must have appreciated that.'

'Didn't seem like it. Some were talking, well you know 'hee-hawing' to each other like posh people do, as if I wasn't there. There was *one* woman who said thank you. But that was all.'

'Jeez.' Hank turns his mug around and we both watch the steam rise from my tweed charity shop jacket.

'How long before they all passed through?'

'About an hour.'

'You stood in the rain for an hour?'

I nodded towards the sodden jacket.

'What the fock?' He put down his mug quickly. It reminded me of my dad doing things quickly when he was angry. Then Hank lifted both hands and waved them around like he was juggling hot coals. 'You know, when you cross that road onto the farm, do you go into Victorian England? Like you are in service to Lord and Lady Thurpley? Don't you mind that? Do you bow and nod?'

'It's a job Hank. I don't bow to anyone. You should know that. I have some pride. Vic says, Thurpley does it to earn brownie points with his landlord.'

Headlights flash at the window as a taxi bumps along the pocked drive. 'Here's Susannah and the kids.' I say, but Hank's mind is elsewhere.

He puts his hand around the mug again, stares at me very seriously, 'Fock. You know Gray, one day there's gonna be a goddam revolution in this country. There'll be fighting in the streets.'

I'm puzzled. Then he adds in a different tone entirely, 'You must tell the story at dinner tonight.'

'Yeah the kids would love the horses and the colour.'

'No tell ALL of it. Did they catch any foxes?'

'None.'

Hank throws back his head and laughs. As he moves towards the hall he says with such enthusiasm, 'Great! That's so great!'

Sometimes I wonder if people hear different stuff to what I actually say. Can that happen?

CHRISTMAS TRAIN

'It's the kitchen! How did you do that?'

'It's just looking, and perspective. That's all.' said Susannah as I admired her drawing.

'Perspective is really hard.' I said.

'Simple rules.' she said, doing me some lines and shapes on the back of a Christmas card. 'Check it out tomorrow, train lines are a great example.'

That was last night after dinner, and here I am now on the train heading north, at last. Forget perspective though, I can't even see the rails yet in the early morning darkness, so I can't tell if the view changes as it recedes to some distant point, or whatever it was.

What I'd really like to know is; will I get close to any girls this Christmas? I've had a good bath, best Wranglers on, clean shirt and my new C&A jumper, so I've hopefully left the smells behind. On Bellaby Farm we all pong of stuff, and keep away from each other. The pay might be rubbish but we do have plenty of space. There's always a tractor width, or the swing of a muck fork between us. Perhaps we farm workers actually like some distance. In fact, it's a bit strange being so close to people at the station, and on the train.

Anyways, as Hank and Susannah say, I'm on my way, leaving Northants, and taking some well-deserved time off, after four months hard work. Time to relax and stare out of the window, as the sun comes up.

Clickety clack, clickety clack.

Telegraph poles, grey fuzzy trees.

Close cropped horse field. Like Johnny says, the closest cut of any grazer. The yellow dawn light picks out wet lanes, windier and muddier than the Bellaby.

Stubbly fields, awaiting the plough.

Apple peelings of ridge and furrow.

Toy Massey-Fergie, moving straw.

Probably wheat for bedding livestock. Remember my first load back to the farm? Placing them on the steep elevator, to Vic for stacking. Watching them rise into the barn with such pride, 'my hundred bales that *I* brought in,' I wanted to say. For weeks I could point out *my* bales, glowing rows of pineapple chunks. 'Well done old son,' says Vic in my accent.

Pristine milk tanker, miry track.

Sun emerges, faint and unsure.

Mangers and troughs, framed by poached land.

Cows in a yard steaming, remind me of Henry. 'Come on get in thur' it's milking time. If things don't change, they'll stay as they arre.' Calving, and wonder and smell of de-horning. 'Ave hot soapy water ready for t'vet, an' av some yersel' thurs shit down your arrm.'

Buildings - wood slatted, wind ventilated.

Painted Dutch barn, fingernail size.

Hedges, some gappy, laid, lofty, or flailed.

Boundaries of wire, neat wooden rails, squares of sheep netting.

Ploughing, some tidy, near straight as ours, by 'Johnny the Furrow', who sets up a rig as if with a rule.

Fields and farms are slipping by. Cereals poke through stony loams, ploughed land waits for frost and snow. Shiny wet meadows reflect grey clouds. I've come a long way for a failed sixth former. Heading back home, Yorkshire for Christmas! Feeling at peace, like walking the herd after teatime milking. I know this land as if it's my own.

'Birmingham next, change here for the North.'

Powerlines dip and climb between pylons, like doodles on the Fenley phone pad.

Sooted up windows, long dark ridges, black brick walls and arched manholes.

Tapering columns, steel spiked fencing, floodlights hover by jumbly scrap yards.

'Fragile roof - Use crawling boards.'

Subterranean Birmingham New Street, eerie green lighting, 'This train for Sheffield?' Thank goodness, last leg.

Platforms begin to slide away. Sudden dark tunnel, no lights on the train.

It's Friesian black. My thoughts just STOP.

The carriage's yellowy lights come on, and an orange coat appears close alongside me. It's as thick as my old greatcoat, but has large plastic buttons, like something my Aunty Kate might wear.

'Is this seat not taken?' says a young female voice. I lift my head to see that uncertain look that women give me. Her hair is not long, but has a natural wave more on one side than the other, the asymmetry heightens the pleasantness of her slightly flushed face.

'Er no. Sorry, yes. It's not taken.'

'Sorry, that wasn't a good question was it?' She laughs to herself. A musical chuckle.

'Er no' I say.

Her coat is off, and I hope I'm not blushing as I catch myself noticing her chest as she rolls the coat and stuffs it behind the seat with her ex-army bag. A round collar peeps from her green patterned sweater. With a whiff of old furniture fustiness and flowery shampoo, she sits down next to me. Aware of our proximity, I twist my legs inward, and lift my eyes up over the wooden window ledge to outside, as platforms, signals and concrete piers slide by.

'Birmingham is always so busy,' she says.

I eventually turn to look, having assumed she is talking to someone standing in the aisle, but she isn't. Her chestnut brown eyes are looking at me.

'Yes,' I say, supposing this to be polite conversation before she disappears into a book.

Through the window, we're back in the open, dead leaves float in a grey canal, and there's more grim brickwork and grey matt windows. A melodic question lifts a drain cover before the rivulet of my thoughts.

'Are you going home for Christmas?' She seems determined to chat.

I pause, but speak without thinking, 'Er. Yes I left my family this morning to go home.'

'Sorry? Where are your family?'

'They're in Northampton,' I say lifting my thumb.

'Then aren't you going the wrong way?' she says, pointing forward and then back in a vague sort of way.

'No, I'm going home, to Sheffield.'

'Oh. You have *two* families?' Her hand momentarily shows two fingers, as if she might be speaking to someone in a different language.

'No. Well, er, yes.'

'It sounds complicated.'

'How about you?'

'I'm going home to spend two weeks in Newcastle with my parents.'

'Why aye.'

'Sorry?'

'It's what they say in Newcastle. The Geordies.'

'Oh. Right, well I've never been there before, my parents just moved there from London. So it's not really my home. This is my first visit. I'm at college in Cardiff. Tell me about your *two* families, I'm intrigued. Were you adopted or something?'

'Adopted?' I query, but she isn't joking, her dark lashed eyes are as steady as a ship's compass. 'I live in 'as family', where I work. On a farm. But I come from Yorkshire, and I'm going back to see my parents, my real family, for Christmas.'

'So one is a real family?'

'Well, my new Northants family is real. They are very kind, they look after me and feed me pretty well. They have dogs, cats, loads of books and know so much. Although we argue sometimes, we have good fun together. The children like me to read to them, and we all talk together a lot.'

'That sounds really nice. What a great way to live.'

'Yes I suppose it is really. The parents often ask me about my home town, and I talk about school or the corner shop or hiking on the moors and they put down what they're doing and look at me as if it's the most interesting thing they ever heard. At first I thought they were taking the mickey but they weren't.'

'And your *other* real family?'

'Oh, they're very different. They don't talk much. Or sit down together at mealtimes, except for Sunday dinner. How about your family?'

'Well who knows their own family really? I mean you grow up with them and everything, so whatever happens it all just seems ordinary. My dad works for the government and is hardly home, Mum does lots of voluntary work. I think we make our own family. You seem to have found yours.'

Unsure what she means, I nod and look outside. She is so open and chatty. Why don't I meet girls like her? She's not winking, wincing or talking to her shoes. She is interesting and interested.

Trees. Trees in woods, in lines, occasionally ivied, alone or in hedgerows. Ones that stand tidy together in copses and ones that sprawl alone by streams.

'Where are we?'

'Burton on Trent.'

Our train stops and another train blocks the view. The conversation stops too and I wonder if this will be the end of it.

'Lo-ok,' she sings. 'I love that don't you? When your train is standing still, but seems to move forward because another train is pulling out in the opposite direction.'

'I see what you mean,' I say. Soon after our train moves off for real.

'What are you hoping for, in your life?' She says after she has picked some lint from her jeans, before adding, 'Sorry is that a bit serious?'

'No. Well it is, but it's ok.' I say, as she smiles broadly, and I feel a sudden blush from the awareness that I'm here, having this real conversation with a beautiful stranger. I decide to stick to the facts, 'I'll complete my year on the farm, then Agricultural College for three years, after that I'm less sure.'

'You sound like you've got things pretty sorted out.'

'For now.' It seems that we can talk about almost anything. 'I was just thinking about how my understanding of the countryside has changed. The strangest thing was that I seemed to be thinking to the train track rhythm. Is that weird?'

She laughs again, and ducks her head forward so that for a second I think she is scoffing. 'The *didulee-dum*? Yes! I know just what you mean. Sounds affect us don't they? I once spent a night on a ferry, and the engine was so loud, that I couldn't think anything other than *tub-tub-tub-tub* for a day afterwards. Although I was very tired. And a little drunk.'

Soon a familiar urban sprawl seems to tap on the window to get my attention. 'It's Sheffield,' I say, 'I have to get off here.'

'You sound so excited. It's been lovely to talk to you. Have a good Christmas, and enjoy the rest of your life.'

Christmas has started. I step off the train and breathe in the sweet, smoky air of Sheffield and the West Riding. Along the platform, is another young woman, in a long red coat. She waves. She is waving at me! Is she really waiting there just for me? After 4 months of being the stranger I'm home.

'Julie!'

Now it's over. It all went so fast that I haven't had a minute to think about it until now. Christmas is done. I'm back on the train to Northampton via Brum. I have to be at work tomorrow at six a.m. Back to moving the straw, the silage and the cow shit around.

But I have had a lovely time. I danced with Mary-the-Fabulous as Wizzard sang, 'I wish it could be Christmas every day.' I saw all my old mates in the pubs, and never got asked my age once. Only a few months to my 18th birthday now.

The train has just passed into a dark tunnel, and it's like something has altered in me, and I can't figure out what. Where was I? There I was leaving Fenley; looking for perspective from the train, that girl, then Julie waiting, the sixth form social with everyone telling me I'd changed. I remember my dad's beer-cheer wearing off before we'd even had the Christmas pudding, and all the time I was thinking to myself, how small all of this is; the house, my home town, and my life there.

Deep in the tunnel, my ears pop. The train is moving on, and Chesterfield has family houses all lit up, and I'm wondering if, one day I will live like that, in one of those proper happy family homes, where people talk to one another. And then I remember, that I *am* going back home, to the Mappledons at Fenley. What was that Slade song? 'Look to the future now, it's only just begun.'

JOHNNY 4

It's a very cold start to this February day. 'If you don't need him Victor, send the boy to help Johnny with the fencing.'

Oh how I hate that. Even when I'm standing next to Thurpley, he still doesn't address me directly. But Vic understands, he gives me a wink and tilts his head towards the sloping yard, I show him my thumb and leave to find the tractorman.

Down the slope, away from the steaming straw litter of cow buildings, the ice-dried air hits the back of my throat like needles. The grass and the hedges are sugared with February frost and the ditches are still iced, but it's time for a new task, putting up fences.

Johnny emerges from the workshop's darkness. He's been beyond the oil barrels, amid the museum of cobwebby curios that hang on the back wall; the woodwormed shafts of old pitchforks, the seed fiddle and dusty oat sacks. He is carrying a tool that looks broken, its metal end flip-flopping about.

'What's that tool called, Johnny?

He looks up the yard to Thurpley, who is back in the Land Rover, but talking now to Henry. 'I'll tell you later. Let's get loaded up.'

We stack a trailer with pointed larch posts, until it resembles a new box of pencils on wheels. We add reels of barbed wire, an old paint tin of staples and nails, wirecutters, axe, hammers, gloves and the billhook. We're all neatly provisioned as Thurpley drives away.

We lift the trailers tailgate together without needing to do '1-2-3,' and Johnny rescues the strange tool, which is being licked by a curious calf in the old stable.

'Now,' Johnny says, with the shaft under one arm, 'this yur's Ginny.'

'How does she work then?'

'She's a great piece of kit. Well you put the end of the barbed wire yur see, between her legs. Close her up, an she grips like a bloody mole.'

'So the shaft is a lever for straining the wire?'

'I pulls her round the post, knock a staple in behind the barb, an' there you go; a wire as straight and tight as a vicar in the pub.'

He drops Ginny behind the tailgate, and we walk around to the tractor cab.

'You sold that well Johnny, I'll take two.'

I stand on the link arm at the back of the tractor for the journey down past the sparkling fields, frosted nettles and the hovel. As we near our unenclosed field, Johnny explains the plan, 'I'll drive slowly round the 'eadlands, while you drops a post every 6 yards close to the edge. After that, we'll come back for the post knocker.'

'Ok. I remember this field. It's the one you sowed down with barley and ryegrass, I had to stand on the back of the drill and keep stirring the seed to keep it mixed.'

'S'right. He's trying undersowing. He'll put the cows in after combining see. The grass will be growing in the barley stubble. It's not a new idea, but 'e thinks it is.'

Posts distributed, we return to the farmyard, and hitch up a hired Heath Robinson arrangement. It's a heavy weight, lifted by a chain, up a greasy metal pole. We connect it to the tractor's linkage and hydraulics, and return to the open green field.

'We'll start in that corner by the far boundary. It'll give us chance to get the hang of it, where no one will notice, see.'

The post is positioned, and Johnny reverses the tractor up to it until the post is between two horizontal bars. 'Ready boyo?'

'Ready.'

I stand clear. The weight, like a lead-filled tom-tom drum, drops down the pole, the loose chain rattling in accompaniment as it hits the drumstick of the post, 'BUFF.' Johnny slides the hydraulic lever so that the weight rises again, he reverses the lever and it drops again, BUFF. It takes between 4 and 6 drops to knock in each post.

'Bloody lethal bit o' kit this, Johnny.'

'It is that boy. But it's better than swinging a maul. Can you line up the next post, an' guide me in?'

Johnny soon stops dismounting to check the line, and leaves the post positioning to me.

We continue and put in the first half dozen posts before baccer time; Embassy, Polo mint, and eyes scanning as we talk. Thurpley is a rare visitor while we're on the fencing job so sometimes in our chats we conjure him up. I say, 'I say, how are you getting orrn, Jaw-nee?'

'Veru wahl Mister Thurpley. Posts are goin in very nicely,' says Johnny, playing along.

'Ye-s. Lookin' like soldiers on parade. Reminds me of when I was a hofficer in the harmy.'

We can't keep it up and we giggle together like naughty children.

Talk continues intermittently between the BUFF, BUFF, BUFF of the post knocker. Johnny twisting around in the tractor seat as I arrange posts. There's something of our own French Revolution going on in our mocking of the toffocracy, who seem to run everything and tell us all what to do. Here's the ominous creaky rattle of the chain drawing the lead tom-tom up the pole, before it falls without mercy like a guillotine.

The work becomes easy for which I'm grateful, at first. Hours and days slip by, as we work and rest in the familiar pattern. In one break Johnny pulls the stop button and climbs out of the tractor cab saying, 'D'you know yet, what you're going to do boyo? After college an' everythin?' He strikes a match to light up.

I lean against the rear wheel, and take out a half tube of mints. 'College seems a long way off. I don't know.'

'You gotta know something.'

'I know I want to get an education, Johnny.'

'Are you sure? Our Mr Thurpley, now he's a man with a *Heducation*.'

'Did he go to the village school?'

'Naw. Not good enough for 'im boy. They sent 'im away to school. Like his kiddies now.'

'Oh private school. That's why we never see them. It must cost a fortune.'

'Only the best for his lordship.'

'Well. For me, first I've got to get through this year, and then think about whether I want to work with cows or arable, or sheep, or pigs, I suppose.'

'You don't want sheep boy, sheep is ard work. Always need somethin doing to em.'

One morning, there's a light scattering of snow in the field. Previously invisible parallel lines appear; up, down and diagonally over the winter wheat. In the ghostly light of the foggy March morning it's as if all the marks and wheelings from cultivations long ago are here. The dimpled snow of the headlands might be covering hoof marks from a ploughman's oxen. In wet patches, the wheat is lost in a prehistoric, prickled, stony surface of mud. The days may be slowly lengthening for another spring, but there's a mysterious trick that fog can play. Where you lose for a few minutes exactly where you are. And all of time, its days, seasons and our lives can pass; or simply stand still.

BUFF, BUFF, BUFF, BUFF. We're coming up towards a neat thorn hedge at the corner of our newly defined field. I sight in another post to keep the fence dead straight and call, 'What time is it Johnny?'

Johnny twists around in the tractor seat, 'You reminded me of the 'orse then.'

'Did the horse used to ask you the time?'

'He din need to, he knew when it was coming up to dinner time.'

'How do you know?'

'You'd reach the end of the field see like us yur, an e would stop, instead of turning round. You shake the rein see, an say, Walk on, an there e'd stand. As if to say *Are you sure? I makes it dinner time*. Move on you bugger I'd say, taking my watch out. It would only be half eleven. We're doing another down and back before then I'd tell im. An e'd turn to look at me, an then at the hedge, where my bag was hangin with his nosebag alongside it, an I'd have to tell him again before he started to move.'

'So he was trying it on?'

'He was, but you've got to admire that. Some orses is smarter than a lot o' people.'

He reverses to the post, stopping with it exactly in the middle of the post knocker's frame.

BUFF. BUFF. BUFF. BUFF.

It's been one of those muddy and cold mornings, when the grave like coldness of the soil grips your boots and won't let go. When only the warmth of the work and the cheery conversation keeps you from feeling the ghostly chill of death pawing at you, and imploring you to yield to winter's power.

A NEW ANGLE

If I'm working near enough to walk home, I'll have lunch at the cottage when we're fencing. It's good to have hot tea instead of the lukewarm tea in the flask.

Hank can be a bit distracting when he's around in the daytime. 'Hey how about taking the afternoon off today huh? There's a really good flick on TV, *The Maltese Falcon*, you'll like it.'

'No thanks, Hank. I can't not show up, when we're working on a job.' As Hank is always interested to hear about the farm work I've been doing, I switch topic and have a grumble.

'So, there's three tons of sugar beet pulp on a lorry in the farmyard to be unloaded, and Thurpley says to me, "Like this." He takes a bag from the flat bed of the lorry, and tries to *run* with it into the barn. But of course it's too heavy, and he has to stop and lean on the wall so that he doesn't drop it. Vic took the bag off him in the end.'

'Why did he do that?'

'It's another one of his attempts to make us work 'farster' as he calls it. He does these high-speed demo's and then jumps back in the Land Rover. He doesn't understand that you can't do manual work all day at top speed. Thurpley is such an arsehole.'

'That's OK.'

This is something Hank loves to say, *That's OK*. It might sound 'cool' to him but it's getting annoying.

'Hank, how can you say that it's ok that he is an arsehole?'

'Lemme tell ya. When you measure land for building and do a levels survey, you fix an arbitrary datum peg and compare all the reading to that peg. Later you can check maps and bench marks and readjust the readings to their true value.'

'Truly fascinating Hank, but…'

'So, you need some assholes in your life, to compare everyone else to. How else will you know who the good guys are? Would you like Johnny and Vic so much, if Thurpley behaved like he was your buddy?'

Sometimes, just like that, it all flips around when you talk to Hank. He just sees everything differently. You start off having a cup of tea and a bit of a whinge and bang, you're into a new philosophy, a whole new way of seeing things.

'Now orses is more delicate see. They don't eat like cows, tearing an swallowin. Orses is careful. You could take an old silver threepenny bit, as small as your fingernail, an put it in 'is nosebag. When e finished you took it off, an that tiny threepence would be in the bottom. 'E'd nibble round it see, feelin it, with his lips.'

We've been 'having a minute' from fencing and watching the bullocks graze in the next field. It's these bits of chat from Johnny that make the day, and maybe stop us both turning into machines ourselves.

Some days we fix barbed wire onto the posts, 'Top wire first boy, goolie height.' The monotony is broken by a bit of carpentry, as we strengthen the occasional post with angled props made from the broken or knotty wood. The wire is new, and it runs easily from its coil. Less easy is the handling of it, as we staple it onto the posts. Our hands are measled with scabs and fresh nicks from the barbs, despite our leather gloves. 'Bloody barbed wire,' utters Johnny, at each new scratch and puncture.

While we maintain an unspoken pride in our steady work rate, for Johnny, distractions are always welcome. As the tractor engine stops a robin alights on a low branch. Johnny stays perfectly still, 'You gotta beakful there boy, where you off with that? *Never you mind, e say, got kiddies to feed now see.* E's no time for talkin today.'

The coming of spring, with its promise of warmth, and work variety is a regular feature of our conversation.

Johnny says, 'the sap will soon be rising,' clearly meaning something else. 'I saw your friend Eveline Squeaney in the village yesterday. All dolled up she was. Haughty that one.'

'She's not really my friend Johnny, just someone I know from Young Farmers…'

I'll tell you what she needs…'

Despite Johnny's enthusiasm to offer me tips about love and lust, uneasiness makes me divert the conversation, although only slightly. 'Oh. I almost forgot, Mr Thurpley came by while you were watering the chestnut tree, he said to say, "Jawn-ee, when you've finished the 12 acre my wife has a job for you in the bedroom. She said only you could do it for her, if you wouldn't mind popping along. Don't take the boy with you." I told him you'd say, *Right ho.*'

At this Johnny creases in two like the post strainer, and when he straightens up, he is laughing as if he's releasing joy from deep inside. He does little whooping sounds for a moment afterwards. Composure regained, he has a broad smile, his blue eyes steady and the broken veins in his cheeks purple-red with exertion, 'I thought he was right h-yur for a minute then.'

It's my turn to laugh. He is as pleased with his own joke, as I am at his reaction to mine. A shared happy moment by the chestnuts along the Fenley road, where the wind stirs the lengthening Italian ryegrass around our boots. The sun has come out, and the warmer air feels full of something good. Thurpley might well dominate our lives, but secretly the two of us can dissent, make irreverent jokes about him, and thus find a little power ourselves.

The wind is roaring and swooping through the trees. The odd fallen leaf, still dry enough to move, blows acrobatically down our drive lit by the yellowy outside light of the cottage. From my window, in the darkness, the drive looks sprinkled with snow. It's not snow. A chap from the village has been to spread fertiliser on his fields nearby and he's accidentally spilt it, the granules have been crushed by our vehicles and the post van, I suppose it's a sign that spring is on its way.

Thanks for your letter with your news. Working in a post office now eh? Does that mean you get staff discount on stamps as a perk?

I'm surprised that Mary has gone to London. I don't know why I should be surprised. Perhaps now that I've moved away, in my head I think of everything at home staying exactly the same. I hope she is happy there anyway. Here's something else I miss about home, that I'm sure will still be there; the hills of Derbyshire, those lovely walks, the smell of my mildewy rucksack, the moors and peat and the feel of gritstone when you sit down to eat your sandwiches. I must stop now – don't want to get homesick.

I'm back working with the cows tomorrow, so an early start. Our one perk is that there's all the milk you can drink. We scoop it out of the tank with a plastic jug and it's delicious.

You asked me about new girlfriends here. Well I don't see many girls full stop really. I joke with Susannah that to me, she is like an older sister and girlfriend combined. The Young Farmers club is the only place to meet girls. There was one girl there, called Jane, who I asked out. We met one Saturday morning and went to Northampton together on the bus. She is very quiet and not easy to get talking. She has long hair and unusual eyes, they are very pretty. If you saw a painting of her face you'd think the artist had put her eyes too far apart. They slant downwards a little, in a beautiful but slightly sad sort of way. I was hoping she could tell me about Northampton and show me around, but she says she doesn't go there much.

It was a long morning. I'm not sure what she thought.

At one point she said, 'What land do your family have?' Then, 'Do they farm?'

I almost said, 'well my dad has an allotment,' but I thought better of it.

But it was on the bus back that I think it all went wrong. She said, 'Do you ride?' She didn't mean on the bus, or the motorbike. She meant horses. I know, because I had to ask. How else was I supposed to know? Suddenly, it was like I'd just failed an interview. Those sad sloping eyes looked at me, and for a moment, it was as if they might just slip from her face entirely. I could have talked about my occasional glimpses of the pit ponies in the field at the back of the coking plant, but I didn't think that would help. She looked out of the window for the rest of the time. I've not been to Young Farmers since.

Looks like you have had some success though. Your new boyfriend Nigel sounds a good laugh. I have asked for some leave at Easter, so I can make a week of it, and maybe see you too. I'm looking forward to a break. You might not recognise me though. I keep having my hair cut short. At the moment it's growing back and looks like a biro doodle of a Beatles haircut about 1964. It's practical at work though, and that is the main thing. People at home will think I've been away in the army. Remember Bernie Peats in the 3rd year whose dad used to cut his hair for him? Well it's a bit like that, but without the neck rash and nicked ears. Maybe it could be another reason why I didn't get off with Jane?

Will write more tomorrow. Must get to bed.

JOHNNY 6

It's another day, and another field, Johnny and I resume post knocking. The promise of spring is forgotten as heavy cloud threatens to rain us off at any time. This would mean returning to the farm and finding indoor work, abandoning fresh air and freedom for foul smells, dust or worse. Worse being Thurpley giving us different jobs, or a number of small jobs, that would make the damp day seem endlessly long. For now though, we're on our way to a new field.

'You vote, boyo?'

[Harold Wilson just became Prime Minister and the miners returned to work after their strike.]

'I'm not old enough yet, Johnny. Next year. Did you?'

'Always. You gotta vote after the war an everythin. I know the miners is portant and I'm on their whossname, you gotta be see, coming from the valleys.'

I'm standing on the link arm at the back of the tractor as we lurch and sway together over one of those tracks that has become very messy. Johnny spans the deepest rut by keeping one wheel on the firm strip between the long puddles, and the other on the field. The long heavy pole of the hired knocker is tall and pitching about menacingly, a sudden slip could damage it or us.

'But what I does boy, is, vote Conservative. I don' like em, but you gotta when you work in farmin. They look after the farmers see. And without them to give us work, we're buggered.'

There's more daylight in each day now, and the wind is losing its sting. Some days we can even take off our coats. But not today. Under this battleship grey sky it seems even more important to look ahead to the future.

'You'll soon be on the chain harrows while I does the rollin, then sprayin, next in May silaging starts, then a bit of shit cartin before harvest comes round again. You'll soon be out of here boy.'

My mind stays for a while, with the surprise of Johnny's voting choice, but then moves to consider the prospect of my year ending and all the uncertainty that will bring. *Maybe I'm not sure about this whole farming career.* Johnny continues talking, but a dark cloud all of my own has descended about my ears.

'We're getting a new machine for silage this yur. A John Deere, self-propelled, forage harvester. Yuge they say. American. E's in a syndicate see, three farms workin together. Costin thousan's.'

How can Johnny vote on behalf of Thurpley? After all he's said; the tied houses, the hovel, the long hours? Am I caught in some kind of rural trap?

We get to the field and crack on. *At least fencing is something clear cut, a field's purpose decided and its border delineated. Like the school careers teacher's neat diagrams where you progress from one box to the next. Or do you?*

I'm lining up another post; a little more to the right, maybe I need an adjustment too. *Is this how it must be? One day you're new on the farm, next thing you're Johnny. You're trapped there. You no longer vote freely, forty years have passed and cig breaks, lunch and sexual imaginings are the only respite. Is this what I want?* 'Ok Johnny.'

The lever is pulled, the pile driving tom-tom falls.

'Fuckin 'ell boyo,' Johnny shouts.

I never heard him shout before. In that same instant I see the horror film scene that I'm suddenly starring in. My hand is still holding the top of the post.

The weight is about to hit. I'm pissed off. *Life is not fair. I'm unsure about farming. My career in farming will certainly finish with a smashed hand. No more worries about 'cows or arable?' No voting dilemma. No more rebelling at the rural hierarchy. There will not even be a hovel for me to live out my days in. I'm a crushed hired hand, caught in this snare of hired sky-blue steelwork.* I notice the dried paint runs from the lumpy welds. *The machine, glossy and weatherproof will go on. More posts, more hands, more lives screwed. I'm just one more replaceable faulty cog in the countryside machine.*

The weight feels surprisingly light against my knuckles. It rises *up* the pole.

'Take your hand off the post,' shouts Johnny. The engine stops, and Johnny runs around holding the tractor seat sponge. 'You alright? Sit down.' He drops the seat onto the grass and I do as I am told. 'Fuckin' hell. I thought your hand was gone there, Graham boy.'

'I'm OK.'

'I saw your hand and pushed the lever back.'

'Thanks, Johnny.'

'Bloody hell I thought you was a gonner. Let's have a minute. Get your Polos out, it's baccer time boy.'

There's a sharp twisted robin call from just above us. Johnny doesn't respond.

'You 'ad me worried. I don't want to lose you boyo.'

'Sorry Johnny, I don't know what happened. I've put in loads of posts and never done that before.'

I sit in silence for a minute and then get to my feet and return the tractor seat foam. 'I'm fine Johnny, thanks for spotting my hand in time.'

'You nearly give me 'eart attack.'

'My mind wandered a bit. Maybe I should go back home more often. On the motorbike.'

Johnny looked at me through a 'V' of cigarette smoke. For a second I wondered if I was crazy, and what Johnny would say.

'Then it's thick newspapers you'll want. Push em down the front of your trouser legs see, for insulation. That's what I done when I was off to Wales on my bike. That cold can bugger your knees. An you want three pairs o' trousers on boy. I know some as would wear women's stockin's an all, just to get an extra layer for motorbikin in winter.'

You can't beat returning to practical matters in a time of potential crisis.

'An you don't want to work that engine too hard, see? 'Specially on a long run. When me an the missus goes on oliday in the van, I don't go above fifty. That's fast enough for me an fast enough for my van see. An I don't care if those buggers behind me on the motorway don't like it. I made up my mind, fifty, an tha's it.'

'Shall we carry on, Johnny?'

We resume work with the addition of a very loud, 'All Clear.' from me before the monster strikes, BUFF, BUFF, BUFF. We get in another dozen posts before the next baccer time.

'You know, I 'ad a best mate in Wales. I could talk to im jus like you.'

'What happened to him?'

'Oh he loved is motorbike. Like me. An e was a careful rider. But one day in summer, they found him dead by the side of the road. We couldn't understand it boy. He'd been down that road thousan's o' times. His bike was laid by a lamp post. It stayed there for three days, no one had the heart to move it. They had a whossname? You know when they don't know why someone…'

'A post-mortem?'

'That's it, a post-mortem. He was fit an 'ealthy they said, but you know what they found? A fly in his eye. He must've closed his eyes, an skidded into that lamp post. I bought some goggles after that.'

'I must get some, or a visor for my helmet.'

'We din ave helmets then.'

THE BIG APPLE

I've called home for breakfast on Sunday morning. Susannah has been listening to Radio 4's 'Letter from America' by Alastair Cook on her little cube radio while mending some clothes.

'New York. That's the place. It's all so, vibrant, Grahamy. You know what I mean? There's the Museum of Modern Art, Central Park, which you would love with all those crazy Americans jogging around, the trees are amazing and kids are skate boarding on the sidewalks. Oh yeah, and the Natural History Museum is nearby, and has all these dioramas. You would love the Statue of Liberty, you could take the Staten Island ferry. Aw Graham you would LOVE it. You have to go.' She puts down her sewing and stands as if to emphasize the instruction, stirs a huge casserole pan on the Rayburn, and returns to her seat.

Hank appears in the doorway. 'No Susannah! Don't tell him about New York. I don't want him to go there. He'll ruin it for all of us.' He walks in and touches my shoulder, 'Just kidding Gray. Hey, I'll fix you breakfast. Bacon and eggs?'

'That would be great Hank, but I can do it.'

'No siddown cowboy.' He takes the heavy skillet from the hook and puts it on the small electric hotplate, while reaching into the fridge.

Susannah now darning a hole in a child's jumper, pauses to stare dreamily. 'Gawd there's Maceys, Drive-ins and baseball on TV.'

'He must see a football game. You will wet your goddam pants Gray, when you see the marching band and the cheerleaders. There's iced beer, huge plates in the diners, every kinda steak, eggs done any way you like, hash browns, French fries, hickory smoked burgers, triple decker sandwiches.'

Susannah jumps in, 'Pastrami, olives, Belgian waffles, chocolate muffins mmm..., and, oh Gawd, *blueberry pancakes...'*

Hank breaks an egg one-handed on the edge of the skillet, splits the shell, and gently places the first egg by the sizzling bacon. 'Hey Gray, you really should go to New York. You can see a flick anytime, day or night. You just need to get some bread together.'

'Where did you learn to do that with an egg, Hank?'

'Here get one, I'll show ya. I was a short order cook in a diner. That's what you should do.'

'Work in a diner?'

'No, just work to get the bread. You don't have to be a slave to it. Then do something you really wanna do.'

'But...I think I just want to learn about farming, go to college and find a girlfriend.'

Hank neatly fills the plate, and puts it down on the table between the cutlery. *'That's two dots an' two dashes.* You gotta learn the language so; one egg's *sunny side up,* the other's *over easy.'*

'Thanks, Hank. That's great, what a treat.'

'Farming, college and a girlfriend huh? Goddam it, Gray. There's a whole fuckin' world out there. Sometimes you are cornier than Kansas.'

JOHNNY 7

Working outdoors and doing interesting things with people is ok, but maybe I should keep an open mind. Beside the sight of my hand in the post knocker's frame, I can't shake the image of that hovel. As if it is some kind of clue for me. Is this honourable labour, or rural slavery that I'm getting involved in here? A modern feudal system? I own nothing except my clothes, an alarm clock, an old motorbike and a few records. I work long hours to pay my board in lodgings that are provided on condition that I work for Thurpley. Someone who can't even bring himself to use my name. It's low pay, and long hours of moving heavy stuff from A to B. If my health falters, I will be jobless, and have nowhere to live. Like the poor sod in the damp hovel I'm a peasant, and the roof can come crashing down at any time.

Johnny and I both know that today the fencing job ends, and it may be our last work together, out in the open where we are free to talk. The drier weather and increasing sunshine will change everything.

'You are so different to how you seemed when I started in August, Johnny. I hardly saw you out of a cab.'

'First, I din say much to you. I thought you might be like Perry, but you're not. He had Thurpley's yur alright.'

'Will you be glad to get back to tractor driving, Johnny? Being out there, on your own, your own boss, like?'

'It's alright, but *you* don't want it, boy. Up the field an down, up the field an down, all day bloody long. You gotta make your mind up see. Be your own man.'

Maybe my near miss was like a baptism: we *welcome this child to the farm congregation, the unsafest workplace in British industry, with a free history trip back in time*. My allegiance wasn't clear to me, but it certainly lay closer to Johnny and the glimmer of enlightenment he had brought me about my possible future, than to Thurpley.

Our last fence is the long side of the 50 acre. 'We'll have a nice long baccer time when we put the last staples in there, boy.' Johnny had said some days ago and now it's almost done. Johnny and I look down the long straight fence. There didn't seem to be much poetry in wire fences compared to the serpentine old hedge boundaries.

'You've a bloody good eye, boy. Thas a picture.'

'The fence?'

'Sright. It's a masterpiece. A masterpiece in posts an barbed wire. Straight as a die.'

We've worked our way back, adding the bottom wire, until we're back at the old oak gate post where we originally secured the top wire. Johnny passes me the last staple. 'Here you go boy, put one extra staple in the old post, for luck. It's your fence this one.'

I hammer it in after parping 'Last Post' through my open fist. We both salute and laugh.

'Oh Johnny, I just realised, we can't get out. We've fenced ourselves in. We're stuck here in the 50 acre on Bellaby farm for good. There's no escape.'

Johnny indulges my silliness. 'You gotta make your mind up now, boy. What you gonna do? Stay yur on the farm?'

'I might climb out over the top wire.'

'Then for God's sake mind your goolies!'

'What will you do, Johnny? Will Mrs Thurpley come to your rescue?'

'Naw. I'd rather see my missus, tell you the truth. No one bakes like she do. I'll serve my time an then leave by the gate.'

He exhales smoke into the air. 'Come an ave some tea at my youse next time you walks through the woods to Benby.'

DEPARTURE DELIBERATIONS

I'm home for a distracted lunch. I keep putting my sandwich down while I think about the cancellation of my Easter leave at short notice. I sit in my room and decide to write Thurpley a list of my grievances. I return to the kitchen to pick up an apple from the fruit bowl, and something makes me pause. The room smells of the week's meals, the book cover for Maurice Sendak's *In the Night Kitchen* is sellotaped to the wall next to the pot of wooden utensils with their oily patinas, all perfectly normal. Perhaps it's the strong cold blue light from the April sky that makes this place somehow seem different today? So unlike the warm table lamp yellow that has lit all our evenings in here throughout the winter.

Only Hank is home, and the stairs creak as he comes down for some tea. I lower my head while holding the unbitten apple.

'What is it, Gray?' His voice is soft as if he has just woken. He takes a large white mug from the drainer and pours from the chipped teapot.

'I made the tea twenty minutes ago, you might want to...'

'It's fine. What's eating you?'

'Oh, it's the bloody job.'

Hank opens the art gallery fridge door, and automatically thumbs Dottie's sea lion picture back as it springs its curled corner. A ritual we all do as we take out the milk. 'Uh huh.'

'I know it's a great chance to see the farming year, and all that, but I've had enough of Thurpley. I can't stand him.'

Hank lifts the dimpled foil top from the milk, whitens his tea and replaces the bottle. 'Ok.'

'When I do learn something new, I do it over and over until my mind rots. I'm not actually learning very much.'

I realise I'm waving the apple around as I speak, which suddenly seems silly, so I put it down on the table and continue. 'How come Perry knew so much about the farm and everything?' I assume Perry's newsreader voice, *The spring wheat will be next to combine won't it Mr Thurpley?'*

Hank smiles and gestures for me to sit down at the table with him. 'Oh he went to see Thurpley one evening every week, to discuss the farm and ask questions.'

'Bloody hell. He'd really got his feet under the table hadn't he? Thurpley barely knows I exist!' I feel the force of my voice leaving my body. It's different to usual.

'Graham, is this like the, "take the boy with you" thing?'

'Basically yeah. But this time I've written Thurpley a letter. Can you check it's clear?'

'Sure.'

I take the envelope from my back pocket, carefully open it, and pass the letter to Hank.

He reads it with a serious face, reaching out to give his mug a half turn on the grainy table, as if checking it's still there, and then picks it up as he puts the letter down.

He exhales noisily over the warm tea. There's silence. He puffs up his cheeks and blows again quietly, 'This is really important to you isn't it?'

'Yeah.' He is looking me in the eyes, and narrowing his own, as if the light is too bright. 'Hank, how do I know what the right thing to do is?'

'Jeez, that's a big question, Graham.' The tea is put down and he leans across the table with his hands together. 'I think with this one, what matters is, what feels right for you.'

I stare blankly at him. Maybe he is going to bamboozle me with some clever stuff, and so I look away. My eyes are taken by the incongruity of a small oblong among the glass storage containers, it is a small green bean bag laid plumply on the cork top of a pasta jar on a low shelf, it has Sophie's favourite yellow sparkly ball carefully placed on it in a little hollow. It looks as if it might roll off to the floor.

'It's clear you feel strongly about this. You're angry. He's really got under your skin.' Hank looks at me with a kind of concern that I haven't seen before. 'You seem intent on confronting him about how he treats you. And I admire that.' He pauses, leaning away from the table and looks into the air for a moment.

I'm pleased to have Hank's admiration, but I don't think I have the solution yet. He returns his arms to the table, sliding the jam jar of wilted bluebells and celandines to one side with the back of his hand, as if it might get damaged. It leaves an arc of pollen and dust.

'You *could* tell Thurpley to fuck off, and then leave. And maybe, you'd feel good right away.'

I shrug, seeing something clearly at last. 'But then I won't get a reference, and I won't be able to go to college.'

'So what's the alternative huh?'

This is so hard. I stare at the terracotta floor tiles. 'I could stick it out.'

'And the muck carding, that you're sick of doing?'

Another good point. I am so sick of shit. 'Well it can't go on forever. It's silaging in May, which means overtime and working on other farms too.'

'What's the worst thing about "sticking it out"?'

I'm feeling flushed and hearing that voice again, that is rising from my own chest, but sounding as if it's someone else's.

'Thurpley. He hates me. He never speaks to me, it's like I don't fucking exist. Yet I do all this work for him.'

'So do you have to work so hard for him?'

'Yes because I can't let the others down. I like everyone else.'

'Johnny and Henry and Vic, they'd miss you if you left early?'

'Yeah, they would. I know.'

He leans back and slowly rotates his tea mug a full circle on the table. 'The kids would miss you.' He looks away, out of the window and up the drive, and turns back to me. 'Susannah would be in pieces.'

'Really?'

'Yeah.' He looks away again and then back at me his eyes seem redder and tired but he wears a resigned half-smile, 'Course, I'd be pleased.'

'You would?'

I would run up a motherfuckin' flag. It would be great if you just fucked off back to the North. I'd get more pies, there'd be no more stinky socks in the laundry basket, I COULD READ MY OWN GODDAM KIDS A FUCKING BEDTIME STORY INSTEAD OF, *but Poppa we want Grahamy to read.'*

I turn around in my chair, clunk open the fire door of the Rayburn and throw in the letter.

Hank smiles. And then he says something in his own voice that sounds almost genuine. It's not in a movie voice, or mock-shouty, or any of his other voices. 'After all you are our SON and we love you.'

I'm not sure what else to say. I look out of the window up the lane and pocket my apple.

'Thanks, Hank.' I glance around this dear kitchen, before I stand and we shake hands. Hank slaps my back as I go for my coat and motorbike helmet to return to work. 'It was the pies that did it.'

'Attem cowboy.' Hank calls down the hall as I slide into my wellies in the porch.

VIC 3

With days lengthening, impatient for the spring, I walked up the drive last night to listen to the wind shooshing in the trees. The sky was all stirred up and full of change. But this morning it's calmer and the land is dry enough for me to ride my motorbike slowly over the farm track, snapping through the fallen dead branches. I pass yellow smiling celandine, goosegrass stretching up from the hedge bottoms and vetch leaves pushing their leaf ladders against the bottom wires of fences. The cereal fields are at last beginning to look more green than brown, although around the ruined hovel the nettles are waking and thistles bristle with new needles.

I'm at the farm at 6am to start a new cow day, and Vic has already got the milkers into the collecting yard. The generator starts up as I open the dairy door and cross into the parlour to call, 'Mornin Vic, how's your belly off for spots?' This is one of Vic's newest phrases and I can't believe he isn't picking it up.

'Mornin, Groyam mite.' he says.

Perhaps he's a bit fed up of the weather. 'I'll start strawing and feeding.' I say.

Later, after breakfast I return from feeding the heifers on the far field and reverse the trailer up to the silage clamp ready for the next refill. I jump down to see Vic looking a bit strange with his default smile absent. He says, 'Now then, now then.' which always cheers us both up, but then he returns to that odd lip holding face, as if he's supervising a difficult calving.

'Can you do something for me mite? There's summin' oi can't do.' This is an unusual request. One of the unwritten rules at Bellaby farm is, never ask anyone to do something that you're unwilling to do yourself. Thurpley excepted of course. 'Come wiv me, old Sun.'

I follow Vic down to the lower collecting yard which he has partially scraped free of its layer of cowshit. A drain cover has been lifted, and next to it is a stack of sugar beet pulp bags. 'Sorry mite, it's blocked. An oi can't git moi 'and down it.' He lifts his shovel paw, as if he needs to show me. 'Can you 'ave a go?'

'OK.'

'You'll need to take your shirt off.'

I remove jumper, shirt and t-shirt. 'This might be as near as I get to becoming a vet.' Vets always seem to be undressing in farmyards.

I lie down and get on with it, scooping handfuls of cold and increasingly fibrous cowshit out of the four inch drain, until I feel something hard. 'I've got somethin' Vic.'

I pull out a corroded blackened bolt.

'It's from the crush. Good lad. Come with me. I've got your clothes.'

Then just like the vet, I'm led to the dairy, where Vic pours warm soapy water down my arm, and then leaves me to wash in a fresh bucket of warm water. With the vet's scented soap and a large soft nail brush, I scrub the smell away. Paper towels replacing the fresh-from-home cotton towel the vet has.

At lunch, I think how Vic is always kind to me. He led me to the pub in the village after harvest and introduced me to the landlady. After that I felt like a local as I could order, 'A pint of Best please, Nora.' He also took me with him to the Speedway track at Coventry one evening. I almost enjoy him imitating my Yorkshire accent now, his attempts always sounding so terrible.

In the afternoon with another task done, I drive back into the farmyard my RAF greatcoat heavy from the steady rain. There's a tall brown cone floating about the side of the 165 tractor. It has blue wellies underneath. It's Vic wearing a paper sugar beet pulp bag, the cut open edge is folded back like a long turn-up to stiffen it into a giant hood, to keep the rain off. 'Can I help, Vic?'

'Get me the pliers, wiw ya? It won't start. Oi think it's water in the fuel.' He turns a nut and a clear liquid dribbles down the side of the crankcase and into the mud. As the flow turns pink with diesel he closes the nut and says quietly, 'Jus turn 'er over.'

I step up onto the tractor, check it's in neutral and turn the key. The starter motor whines, the crankshaft thumps around and then the engine starts. Vic raises his hand immediately and I pull the stop button. 'Got yer you barstard,' he says, and smiles. A farm day can be made with a small triumph like this.

'A question for you. How d'you *learn* all this stuff, Vic?'

'What stuff?' He waves me to follow him towards the workshop.

'Bleeding fuel lines, milking, calving, helping lorry drivers re-sheet their load, doing the knots an' everything.'

'You just pick it up mite. Like you're doin.'

'Am I?'

'How d'you bleed a diesel?'

'Tip out the fuel filter, undo the nuts in the fuel line until the water runs out…'

'There you go. You only saw me do it once dintcha an' you got it. You're gonna be alroight.'

It's true, that is how you learn here, by watching and helping. Some things you only need to see once, like taking a tractor seat sponge off on a wet day and keeping it somewhere dry. Occasionally there's instruction too, like, 'stop the engine before you connect a PTO shaft,' or, 'always put stay bars on when you fit the 3-point hitch.' But there's some learning that is much harder, with no instruction or example to copy.

'Ere, let's get in outta the rain for a bit, I got somefin to tell ya.'

The rain drips off the pantiles, of the workshop's unguttered roof, forming a thready curtain between us and the rest of the farm.

'Y'see mite, I got to leave Bellaby farm.'

'Leave? Why?'

'Oi got another job over Leamington way. Head cowman. Not so many cows as 'ere mind. I gotta letter at lunch toime.'

'Congratulations' I say, unconvincingly, from the way Vic is looking at me. I stare at the neat red bricks in the rounded pillar that hold up this old farm building. 'So you're leavin' us hoi polloi?'

Vic smiles. He likes hoi polloi and repeats it a couple of times. But he reads something in my face.

'Look Groyam, me and Marion's got a bab now see. An' you gotta think twoice about the roight job wiv a family. I bin Thurpley's 'boiy' a long time. A long whoile afore Perry an' then you come along.'

He is talking to me dead serious. Like the calving or the clogged drain. As if I am a grown up.

'I gotta move to get a crack at a herdsman's job. Oi'll always jus be, "Village boiy Vic," to 'im. There's no future 'ere for me. This place by Leamington's not so many cows as 'ere but it's a start. The new boss's letting us 'ave an 'ouse. Marion loikes it.'

Something is changing and I don't want it to. It feels painful although nothing is physically hurting.

'Anyway you have a barth next Froiday mite, put ya gladrags on and join me an' Johnny down the Partridge for a point o' Nora's best. I'll boiy you one, and we'll chuck some arrers.'

'I know you've got to take it, but I wish you weren't going, Vic.'

'I know mite. We've 'ad some good fun din we? Speedway.'

'Yeah. Watching the shale fly.' I name a Coventry rider. 'Gerhard Whatsisname from East Germany.'

Vic smiles broadly before repeating the name twice slowly, 'Gerhard Uhlenbrock', then holding his nose to do his tannoy voice adds, 'From Sweden Jan Simensen and Soren Karlsson. Nigel Boocock.'

'Where's he from?' I ask knowing full well.

'England,' he says and laughs. I laugh to see him rolling vowels around like a kitten with a ball. 'Remember what you said 'bout speedway?' he says, not giving me chance to reply, *A fan-tas-tic night Vic,* you said.' I laugh again at his 'northern' accent.

We go quiet and listen to the rain as it plops into the mud that holds pink diesel in little puddles by the 165, calves rustle through straw next door as drops fall from the roof in a line.

Suddenly Vic pronounces seriously, 'I'm gonna have to ask yer to do somefin else for me as well.'

'What? Another drain?'

'No. Look arfter cow 129 for me, with 'er big oiyes and 'lashes.'

This is the Ayrshire that I once told him reminded me of an old girlfriend. He has never let me forget it.

Then in his best mangled imitation of me he says, 'You must tell her every day, *Yew are bewtiful,*' and he laughs until he makes a noise like the hiccupping of hot parlour rinsings in the dairy's gulley. 'I'll always remember that' he says.

Strange really, that a man who seems to love his cows finds it so funny that someone might see beauty in a cow's eyes.

'Thurpley will miss you.'

'He won't.'

'Do you think I'll get promoted up the ranks and he'll stop calling me *the boy*?'

'Fraid not mite. Oi 'ad five years of it.'

'I think the rain might be stopping,' I say stepping beyond the drips where I can see the lane up to the woods.

As I look, a recent memory replays of Vic at the top of that lane after a field calving. He lifted a new calf over his head and carried it across his shoulders, as if it was a soft toy. We walked back chatting while 'mum' followed behind bellowing softly until she realised her baby was perfectly safe.

'It's gonna be a struggle putting up with Thurpley without you, Vic.'

'You'll soon be out of here mite, fouwr mumfs.' He holds up four fingers, then inclines his head to indicate getting back to work. As we walk up the slope in the running mud he's brighter, 'Here, I heard Thurpley's having you chain harrowing with the old grey Fergy next week, when it droies up. You'll loike that. Proper spring job that is. Unless you wanna stay on the shit cart?'

I roll my eyes.

'Cus I know how you love your farmyard manure!' He repeats, 'Love Your Farmyard Manure,' changing it each time as if it is a new advertising slogan, or an imperative being delivered by an old stage actor in a Government Public Information film. I think Vic is going to be alright.

AFTER VIC

Vic was right. Better days came. Despite the cold mornings, some afternoons had spells of eye hurting, blue-shadowed brightness, and the sun lit up the braver trees that had cracked open their hopeful buds for a new growing season.

A week after he left, I was chain harrowing in between helping Henry with the cows. I had to harrow all the permanent pasture that would be used for grazing in the coming summer. A good two weeks of having work of my own to do. Pleasant spring days when at last the sun grew brighter, even warm enough for me to take my coat off and wedge it under the Ferguson's simple seat. Chain harrows drag out the old dead grass and spread out the cow pats. I took pride in my straight lines. The green stripes made each field looked like a mown lawn, and lasted for weeks.

In the less permanent pasture sown with Italian Ryegrass, known as grass leys, Johnny was out rolling. Slowly pressing down the stones, so they wouldn't be picked up by the machinery, and flattening the surface soil crumbs to conserve moisture. These were to be the silage fields around which farm life would revolve for many weeks ahead.

So it became clear why Thurpley had cancelled my leave. He needed me to do Vic's work until cover could be arranged. Of course it would have been great to be told that, or that I was indispensable to the farm, at least for a little while. But Thurpley wasn't that sort of a boss.

Eventually relief agency milkers came and went. All poor substitutes for Vic. Some of them kicked the cows, and not one of them practised Received Pronunciation phrases when they were happy.

A SCHOOL STORY

It's another one of those after-dinner table-lamp lit conversations around the remains of dinner, in the yellow-orange light. It could just as easily have been candlelight, or firelight in another age, when people entertained themselves.

'Ok Grahamy, your turn. Can you tell us about when you realised that you were gonna leave school?'

'It was on a stormy afternoon of wind and rain…'

'Like today!'

'Yes Soph, a day just like today, but almost a year ago. I was rolling downhill on my bicycle, going home from school, when there was a big noise, like a door SLAMMING in the wind. I pulled hard on both brakes together as quickly as I could.'

'Did you stop suddenly?'

'No Dot, I didn't. Because the brakes didn't work. Until they'd squeezed the water off the rims. Then as the brakes started to bite they juddered and squealed and I was thinking, *maybe there's been a car accident behind me.*'

'Like Mr Squeaney and his pickle truck!'

'Yes something like that Soph. As soon as I stopped, I looked back through the rain, there was no car crash. But, in the middle of the road, was my green Field Biology ring binder. Now Field Biology to me, was like Dot doing bubble painting at school. It was my favourite thing.'

'Like my doll with the orange hair. And my sparkly ball and my…'

'Shhh' gestures Susannah.

'Yes Soph, it was my best bubble-painting, red-haired, sparkly-ball subject. I'd been working on it for three weeks, and it was my last hope of being allowed to stay on at school. If my work was good, I could stay. Oh, I really wanted to stay at school. But there it was, my work, lying there open on the shiny, wet tarmac. The rings had opened with a loud SNAP.'

'Like a crocodile!' Dot claps her hands together.

'Yes, imagine a crocodile that SNAPS when it opens, *as well* as when it closes, its jaws.'

'Yes but then, the other naminals could run away…'

'That's right Soph.'

Hank puts his hand on Sophie's head. 'I think that is a great story for another time, Sophie.'

'So the binder was laid open, and the wind was BLOWING the pages out and spreading them all over the place. They were twirling in the air, like seagulls following Johnny's tractor. Some were twisted around telephone lines above me, some were landing across the road and sticking to a fence.

It all seemed to happen at high speed but also very slowly. Like I was watching a slowed down film. I grabbed some pages…'

'Did you cross the road?'

'Yes, and before you ask Dot, I did stop to look right, then left, and right again before I crossed. But by the time I got to them in the pouring rain, the ink was already just a pale blue wash on the written pages, the drawings had tyre prints over them.

That sound, was the sound of a big door slamming alright. The door to my chance of going to University or becoming a teacher like most of the other sixth formers wanted to be.'

'Fuck! That is some tough shit.'

'That's right Hank, but let me finish. And that, is when I got a job on a farm, and came to live at the cottage in the woods, with Dottie and her sister Sophie, and their Momma and Poppa. So things didn't turn out so bad after all.'

SILAGING

Our farm's syndicate is a summer beast. Three farms work together to share machinery and labour related to silage. Johnny was right about the 'new bit of kit,' it's a star attraction. Other silage cutters are towed by tractors, but this forage harvester is more like a combine with a cab that is sealed up like a diving bell. It has large tinted limousine windows, and people stop at the side of the road to watch it working, or maybe to see if a Hollywood actor might step out of the cab. Johnny is the sole appointed driver, and sits there in his American John Deere baseball cap. The first baseball cap I've ever seen.

From early May, there is an almost constant background roar of engines, and mowers, and always the whine of the forage harvester's cylinder. A bright yellow auger, with fins that appear to rotate in opposite directions like some crazy 1960's psychedelic cartoon, draws the cut grass into the cylinder. The grass is then chopped into tiny digestible bits, and sprayed with acid, before being spat out through a long swan-necked chute into the silage trailer.

Our high sided trailers are drawn, rattling and banging, alongside the shiny prima donna in its green and yellow livery. The aim is to perform a noisy mechanical pas de deux of tractor and trailer movements, so that the harvester is never alone, a trailer permanently alongside to collect the grass. A gracefully efficient performance that will leave the field, so bare, yellow and tyre tracked, that it will look as if it might never recover.

The silage is hauled back to each farm's silage pad, an expanse of concrete surrounded on three sides by walls of railway sleepers. Here, each trailer tips its load, before returning to the field for more. The long days, mostly 7am to 7pm including weekends, pass slowly with lots of short trips, but slightly quicker when the fields are further away from the pad.

One day we are told we're working until 9pm, but not to worry about food, as Mrs Thurpley would bring us all our tea in the field. She turns up and drives her car onto the field while about seven of us gather round. It's been long hot day, and some of these blokes are much bigger, thirstier and hungrier than I am. She passes out paper plates from the boot, with one small triangle of cucumber sandwich and a miniature piece of cake on each. Paper cups are half filled with lukewarm tea. She beams at us, delighting in her Lady Bountiful role. We all thank her politely, and mentally note that we need to bring more food, in case this should happen again. No one comments about it. This is the way things are. No wonder Mr Thurpley doesn't do any work on the farm, he must be starving.

On the silage pad, a Volvo loader resembling one of those yellow longhorn beetles you see on domes of hogweed flowers, scurries back and forth, heaping and then rolling the grass cuttings, pressing them down to exclude air. When the pile is deemed sufficient, the covering ceremony takes place. Half a dozen of us bustle about like ants on the green mound to roll black plastic over it, and then weight it down with old tyres.

The excitement of this new work soon wanes, but it is good to meet other farmworkers, see different farms and fields, and drive other tractors. I meet Rab from Glasgow, another farm student like me, who plays me a tape of a band called Queen, when we drive off to buy chips one day. I see Johnny sometimes in the 30 minute lunch break, if he isn't too busy with visitors eager to inspect the celebrated machine.

'How aroo, Graham boy? I 'eard you ad accident.'

'I did, Johnny. I was driving the International - with the big round indicators - and turning right off the road into the track.'

'What happened?'

I felt a bump, and then this van passed me and slowly tipped up onto two wheels. It carried on down the road for 40 yards like that, before it fell onto its side and slithered to a stop.'

'Bloody hell, boy.'

'It all went quiet, and I ran over. The driver was crawling out of the window of the passenger side. He said he was alright, and he was sorry, it was all his fault.'

'That's alright then eh?'

'Well it wasn't all I was hoping to hear, Johnny.'

'What you mean?'

'It was a pork pie van, and I was hoping he'd say, "Well we can't sell these pies now you might as well have some." but he didn't.'

Johnny took his cig out to laugh. 'Bloody good job you're alright boy. The police come did they?'

'Yeah, but Dan Glaston was following up behind me, he saw it all. Said the silly bugger tried to overtake me even though I'd indicated. I gave a statement and then Dan dealt with it all, told me to forget it.'

'E's a good boss is Dan. A proper gentleman 'e is.'

'I know. D'you know Johnny, he always speaks to me *and* uses my name.'

'Thas a good boss for oo.'

'Say Johnny, is it true we finish on this farm today, just in time for the weekend?'

'Thas right boy, but we're back at Bellaby tomorrow.'

'Second cut, already?'

'S'right. They reckon there'll be three 3 cuts this year if we get the rain.'

DEARJULIE JULY 1974

At last, time to resume writing to you. I never seem to finish a letter in one sitting.

It's one thing being a taxi driver for grass clippings for 6 weeks - 'Where to Sir?' - 'Silage clamp please' –

but when silaging at last comes to an end, you'd expect the next pick up to be better wouldn't you? But it's a case of - 'Say hello to your new regular client - stinky manure!' If you're thinking, I'd finished that job, well so did I. But the farmer is sharing his staff, i.e. me, with other farms too, so I have their cow muck to cart as well. But I will see the year out.

I look at the tractormeter on my tractor for inspiration. It counts the rpm and the hours that the engine runs, (unlike a milometer on a car). A tractor engine can be working when the tractor is standing still; running a saw bench, a pump or turning a shaft. And I think, I am like that now, counting the hours regardless of how humdrum the work is.

So much of the work has been enjoyable over the year, so it's a shame to end on a duffer. Cow days now seem richly varied in comparison. I'd hoped to see the straw carting start, as that is where I came in. But I have annual leave outstanding, so it looks like I will have to finish a bit early and miss the bale-bashing party.

I'm sure you will want to know how the cereals are. Well the wheat crops are all a bluey-green and you can easily tell them now from the lime-green barley crops. The barley is the most handsome, it is stirred by the lightest breeze and sways like the sea. Patches of seed filled ears curve downwards so they look like shoals of small fish leaping together. It's a lovely sight especially when the swallows flitter over them.

Hey this could be my last letter from here. I really am coming back home. But of course everything seems to have changed. I don't feel like the same person that started here nearly a year ago. I think my life will never be the same again. I know home has changed too – I left the West Riding – but I'll be coming back to South Yorkshire.

I was thinking about my letters to you. You know how in Maths they always said, 'show your workings'? Well I suppose that's like me doing these letters, I'm working out what I think; about where I am and what I'm doing. Before I start to write I've no idea what will come out. I'm not saying my letters are algebra equations or anything. Perhaps they're more like the mole cadavers hung on the fence by the mole catcher, to show where he's been. Although I hope they're not quite that gruesome!

Here's a funny little thing I noticed, on the roadside verges; strawy stems of tall grasses swish around as tractors and trailers pass. It's as if they are waving excitedly to cheer each trailer of grass on its way. They'll soon be doing that for me, as I go the station for my train home.

It's been a whole year of change. The family who seemed so crazy to start with feel like my own new family now. Just walking into the main farmyard seemed so alien on my first days. To think I could hardly understand anyone that first week too. It makes you hopeful doesn't it to think how we can change ourselves to fit into new situations?

Anyway, I must get to bed, so I'll pop this into an envelope for the postman to pick up tomorrow morning. I'll ring you when I get back in a week's time.

Yours sincerely,
Graham xx
Your farming correspondent

LAST FARM DAY   AUGUST 1974

I am breathing in the smell of summer cowshit concentrated by the August sun. I've taken a sick cow some extra food, and as I walk back down the hill towards the caramel stone farm buildings, I look out across the collage of green and yellow fields. I'm thinking how I'm happy here in the beautiful countryside, apart from the one rogue thought that has circled me for weeks like a persistent dung fly; that a permanent rural life isn't for me.

As I return to the farm where, in front of a cloud of spinning spheres of little black flies hanging around over dark puddles of silage effluent, Thurpley and Henry stand chatting by the silage clamp.

It was always a sign of Henry's status on the farm that the two of them seem to have friendly little assemblies throughout the day. They break into laughter as I approach. Thurpley puts his cap back on, 'I was just saying to Henry, that when I looked up the hill earlier, and saw you striding up there with a bale of straw on your back, I said to myself, *That boy has come a long way!*'

I am embarrassed for myself, and for Thurpley too that this is the best he can do for a compliment on my last day at work. Of course given the occasion I say something polite and thank him for the farm experience, and say I was lucky that he chose me as the pre-college student. 'Did you have many applicants, Mr Thurpley?'

'Yes. Invited half a dozen likely lads for interview. All much the same. But don't you know, you were the only one who came without a parent! Anyway look, I may not see you before you leave so I'll say goodbye.' We shake hands.

Vic came by Fenley last week on his day off with Marion to show us the baby and wish me well.

Johnny arrives at the farm driving the combine, fresh back from its annual service. It's engine noise echoing around the yard. The stop button is pulled and Johnny descends its steps. 'Tomorrow's the big day boy.'

'Yep. Henry says, you're cutting the first of the winter barley.'

Johnny laughs, 'No you daft bugger, you're going home.'

There's something about the combination of the last three words and Johnny's rising voice that makes my eyes sting and my lower face begin to shake. I bite my lip and somehow the energy is converted into a laugh and Johnny joins in. We laugh for longer than any joke warrants.

'Get that heducation you want, boy.'

'I think I had it working with you, Johnny.'

'No you can do better than that.'

We walk up towards his van.

'Ok I will Johnny. Hey, its five past five. Mrs T will be wondering where you've got to.'

'I know, an' it'll be the last tea at normal time, now we got Bessie back yur.'

He throws a thumb towards the combine harvester and turns to drop heavily into the crinkled leather seat. He shakes my hand warmly and I stand back knowing that, silage and harvest excepted, *nothing* stops this man from going home on time. 'An' one other thing, I don't want you hever to pass by yur without calling in to see me an my missus. There's always cake for you boy, an all the tea you can drink.'

'I know Johnny, I'll come back and see you. As soon as I get a faster motorbike.'

'Righto.'

I watch the old green Morris van go down the winding concrete road and then return to my cow jobs.

In the shortest hour I ever worked, I straw some loose boxes, refuel and park up the tractors tidily in the yard while Henry finishes the milking. Henry and I shake hands and he wishes me well before I walk the cows back to the 20 acre.

There is always something so peaceful and timeless about walking the cows to their field at the end of the day. The orange dust they kick up is occasionally damped by the cows defecating as they walk along, flies buzz around us excitedly and there's the sound of horny feet hitting the stony earth in a steady unhurried rhythm. I say my goodbye to the cows at the gateway as they move eagerly into the new grass. I close the gate, on them, and my farming year.

LEAVING FENLEY

It's a sunny start to the day, with a cool breath of early autumn passing through its morning light. But this is how those hot dry August days can start, and before you know it, the thunderflies are out of the corn, flying around, and sticking to your sweat.

Hank is unpredictable to the last. When Hank pauses in a sentence, it's best not to say anything. I only ever once suggested a word when Hank paused. He switched on his angry-face, glared at me, and said quietly through his teeth, 'don't *ever* fucking do that again, OK?' Then his face broke into an apparently friendly smile, as if nothing had happened.

'Got any wise words for me as I leave, Hank?' You can say things like that to Hank.

I wait. This time he doesn't hesitate for very long. 'Sure, here's what you gotta remember, *never give a sucker an even break.*'

My last minutes at the cottage, and still the new experiences keep coming. The nearest I came to hugs in the farm year was holding calves for Henry to put in ear tags. I'd seen Fenley visitors get the hug treatment, but never imagined my turn would come too. We're all outside in the sunshine, I'm taking a last look at the veg garden. My suitcase is waiting on the chalked clay tiles.

Here comes Susannah, with her dancer's poise, 'Oh Grahamy.' She is heading towards me shaking her raised arms, as if she is either anguished or drying her hands. No one else but Susannah will ever scoop catshit and disinfect the floor while imparting seriously life changing information to me. My role as a bewildered onlooker, in scenes from Susannah's Italian opera/ballet, is over.

'Oh Grahamy, I am gonna miss you SO much.' She hugs me tightly, but then suddenly lets go in order to take hold of my arms and gently shake me, 'You must write me, Ok? Promise?'

'I will.' Another hug.

Hank shakes the car keys, 'Ok cowboy. We gotta go.' He points to Dottie and Sophie who are stood crying by the gate.

'I'm afraid you don't get away so easily,' says Susannah, doing a sad frowning nod towards the children.

Dottie and Sophie are wearing their dungarees and look like two lost little workmen. Dot has her bottom lip curled out under her wet cheeks, while Soph holds both her hands to her mouth like the most mournful harmonica player in the world, a pair of rivulets connecting her sad eyes to her hands. I kneel to hug them, both together. 'Would you like to share the record player I left in my room?'

'Yes!'

'I will have to come back to see you, as I don't have anyone else to read stories to in Yorkshire. So it's just a bye for now.'

'Bye, Grahamy.'

Hank and I walk to the car and I turn to wave at the sad sight of the girls and their tears.

Hank glances at them and then narrows his eyes at me over the roof of the car, 'You ba-ersterd,' he says in mock anger, and he smiles as we drive away.

We get to the last curve in the stone track and I stop waving and turn to face front. Hank is smirking at me. 'You know that I told them they'd get candy when I got back from the station, if they turned on some good tears for you?'

I don't rush to respond. There's a sound I'm waiting for. We reach the tarmac road, and I hear the familiar old tunes of the two cattle grid pianos for the last time, the sound that signals I am off Bellaby farm land for good. Then I turn to Hank to reply, 'You bastard.'

He throws back his head to laugh, and slaps the steering wheel.

On the way to the station; there is no road rage incident, there are no obscene gestures to other road users, no terrible swearing. Or maybe there is, and I just don't notice, because it all just seems perfectly normal for my family.

TRAIN HOME

From the train I look out at the ripening August countryside. Sycamores have baby bunches of keys hanging, nettles are full height and fully armed, while mildewed cow parsley and browned hogweed stems lean in from the margins of hay cleared fields, as if to enquire, 'What just happened here?'

There's a late summer feeling of things half done. Cereals stand drying in the sunshine, awaiting the combine, enclosed by green haws and nightshade hung hedges.

I know I will miss the Mappledons of Fenley, and one day I will understand what they have done for me. For now, all I know is that there's been some kind of a change inside of me.

Change is everywhere: the Yorkshireman Harold Wilson is prime minister, and in the States Richard Nixon has resigned the presidency. It seems as if the whole world is altered for ever. Although, as I look out of the train carriage window I see a countryside that, despite its ceaseless transformation, seems reassuring. I have a slowly dawning feeling, that in my head, I am somewhere new.

My mind frolics with memories of smells and sights of my past year; pink diesel in mud, apple pie with cinnamon, cows and the Christmas spirits-cupboard aroma of ripe silage. Voices come and go between my ears like colours in a kaleidoscope; '*What!* You never had garlic?', 'Thas a picture, a masterpiece, boy.' 'Goddam sonovabitch.' 'Oi know mite we ad some fun din we?' 'That boy has come a long way…without a parent.' 'Do you ride?' 'Prin-cess' 'Hoi Polloi.' 'Hell-o-o-o.' 'I thought 'e was right hyer for a minute.' 'Jolly good.' 'Get that heducation you want boy.'

But outside, in the present, the dew has lifted and sent the combines to work. Lorries are hauling straw bales. Outside farm cottages washing hangs to dry, between green shirts of horse paddocks with thistle clump buttons, and fawn sheets of cereals, while power lines rise and fall against the blue sky, as the train heads north.

The feeling rising in me for the first time, is that of being fully present here in my comfortable 18 year old body. A body that moves easily, and carries in its bones the sense of fulfilment from a job well done. I have seen the farming year through its cycle.

All these different lines of thought criss-cross like a mad railway junction inside my head, before straightening to a taper and then converging like a perspective drawing. I close my eyes and for a moment, everything makes sublime sense, and then it's gone into the dot of a vanishing point. Gone to wherever the memories that make us, are condensed and stored away.

GARDEN

FIRST ENCOUNTER AUGUST 1974

Dear old early morning home town: red bricks and purple slates, factory smoke and tarmac. It's good to be back. I'm opening up the Honda 90's throttle on the new by-pass, then coasting down the hill towards my turn off for the new job. Left at the bus depot by the huge concrete cooling towers, and then a dramatic change. All is flat and cool. Small trees line the road and between them water shimmers in the August morning light. Life is getting better.

In the coming weeks I'll see it differently. I will see that if ever mankind owed nature a break it was here. Dantley Flash Nature Reserve is a token recompense for a hundred years of damage done. Mother Nature might have looked down on Brownton power station and its humming transformers next to the screechy coal train line, clocked the wheels of Dantley pit's headgear and its grey spoil heaps, glanced at the polluted river, and sobbed until she formed pools of tears either side of Low Meadow Road.

But for now, my new commute is to be savoured. Down into second gear for the climb up to limestone country. At the junction I wait in front of a welcoming white outcrop while a combine harvester passes, and then I'm up around the wooded bends to Linklater College of Education.

I recognise the head gardener from the interview. He does an odd narcoleptic sort of nod, and flashes a quick wave at me across the stable yard from one of the doorways. 'Morning,' I say.

'Mornun,' he replies abruptly, stepping back into a room that is lined with yellow boards which are pocked and striated like old bananas.

'What should I call you?' I ask. I have yet to learn that here words are like weed seeds, not to be scattered freely.

'Sit there.' He points to a dirty arm chair with a blue back and a torn pink seat cushion. 'They,' his eyes move around the room as if there are other people there, 'call me,' he hesitates until his eyes come to rest on the pile of grey coke next to the boiler in the corner, 'Bert.'

'Should I be doing something? The rule on the farm was if you're on your own, find something to do, sweep up or clean something, don't waste a minute. On the farm…'

There's a sudden harshness in his voice as if I'm threatening trouble, 'You sits there 'til I say.' He turns and looks out of the open doorway. After a couple of long minutes his large head drops and lifts in another clumsy nod.

A serious Yorkshire voice says, 'Mornin.'

'Mornun, Ray.'

A man enters with a face brown and creased like the underside of a tractor's foam seat. He wears bib and brace overalls, and a flat cap with a button on the top. His pace slows as he nears his chair under the room's one window, as if he's reluctant to sit down. He throws a Tupperware sandwich box onto a small pile of old newspapers in the window bottom, and turns to sit looking straight at me. Without taking his eyes off me he addresses Bert, 'Bright.'

'They give rain,' responds Bert, mysteriously.

'Aw ar. An oos this?' says Ray.

'E's Graham.'

'Ow do.'

Soon after the big head rocks again, and again as Colin, Kennedy, and Tim enter the banana room to begin another working week, and each one is reluctantly introduced to me in the same economical way.

The next thirty minutes pass by like an eternity punctuated by short questions and answers.

'Race t'pigeons Saturday?'

'Ar.'

'Win owt?'

Ray shakes his head.

Silence returns. Bert stares out of the open door.

'On't beer Foxie?'

'Ar. Fifteen pints Satday.'

Silence.

'Workin, Tim? OY TIM. A said, were you working this weekend?'

'Tombine.'

Ray twists around to Colin, who spares him the trouble of asking, answering, 'Painting.'

At 8.30am we are all sent to hoe a shrub border. But we have barely started before someone says 'Its break time.' And we all troop back to the cabin, as it's called, to drink tea.

In the cabin people ask me where I've been working, and I soon learn that, 'down south,' is all they want to know about Bellaby farm.

I reach the end of my first day and go home with a strange sensation, I am not at all physically tired. It's good to be back in Yorkshire.

PUB LIFE

Join us here, for a night in the Fettlers Arms, and I'll tell you something. One great thing about home is being known and recognising everyone. As people come through the pub's door, I can name most of them, or know where they live or work. I've seen them over the years coming and going, I can remember what school uniform they wore, or the names of their children. The people round this table in the corner of the lounge are all old friends, ones I've known since I was five; we played football on the back streets or went to Sunday school together. These are proper old muckers who will never see you go without a drink.

I know I've had a couple of pints, but everything is good. Pub life is great, even the smell feels welcoming; beer, perfume, cigarette smoke and after-shave. Old Charlie comes to join us, he's not seen me for ages; where have I been? On a farm, down south. He wants to buy me a drink. No thanks I've just got a fresh pint.

Earlier I asked each of them about their work. Every one of them groaned, and said something like, 'I don't want to talk about it.' As if, like the beer going off, stepping on a broken glass or someone lining up Paper Lace, Abba *and* Peters and Lee on the juke box, it would spoil their night out.

After last orders we're going round to Chris's house. He's just got Clapton's 461 *Ocean Boulevard* LP, and he's been talking about it half the night.

'Come round, we'll make some chips, and play it.' he says.

His mother has just bought a fancy cutter to do crinkle-cut chips.

As we all leave the pub he says, 'Hey, I'm not sure now if you're all coming round for Eric Clapton, or the chips.'

What a laugh. I'll tell you what is great, as we walk down our street to his house, people are calling across the road to one another, 'Have you had a good night Stan?' and 'Goodnight love.' Sometimes you hardly know them but they're so friendly.

Charlie says to me, 'I bet you don't get this down south.'

I say, 'It's great to be back home.'

And he says, 'I never spoke to Stan in my life before, and he's just asked me if I'll marry his daughter.'

After chips and 45 minutes of air guitar, but just before we break up and walk home along the quiet streets, I ask if anyone would like to join me for a walk in Derbyshire tomorrow or next weekend.

They all say no, and Charlie quips, 'I always walk on Saturday: from the Red Lion Inn down to the Black Horse via the Fettlers.' Everyone laughs.

THE GARDENERS

Linklater College of Education is a teacher training college based at the 18th century Linklater Manor. Hundreds of students are working to get their Certificate in Education which takes three years of study and teaching practice. To get a place here you need five 'O' level passes and to have done two years in the sixth form. To get a job here as a garden labourer, it's probably best not to mention 'O' levels at all.

I meet Kennedy walking towards the stable block at the start of a new working day. Out in the open he looks much less menacing; short and stout like a city post box with his wild orange-red hair and ruddy complexion, less angry than he appears from across the cabin.

'Morning Kennedy,' I say politely.

'Don't call me that. I fuckin 'ate that. Only me mother an Bert call me that. Call me Foxie, like everyone else.'

'Ok I will.'

We cross the yard to the bruised banana room, 'Mornun Kennedy,' says Bert as we enter.

When we are all present, Bert the head gardener reads his *Daily Express*. Perhaps he's trying to stimulate discussion during our compulsory half-hour confinement, by occasionally making announcements from behind it, as if he is the only person in my new village who can read.

Troubles in faraway lands are summarised as, 'Rum do in Cyprus/Merica/Argentina.' They elicit no response from anyone, until he turns a page and says, 'School zam results is out Thursday.'

Old Ray with his rubbery face one huge frown, comes to life, and gives a mocking, 'Huh.' He lifts his head suddenly, so that the back of his flat cap pushes his lunch box against the glass window with a dull tap. 'Fuckin 'O' levels. Shit levels more like. What good are they when yer car won't start eh? When watter's pouring though yer ceilings? When you've thirty yards of stud wall to purrup? I told my lad, ni mind omework an bloody 'O' levels, gerr art theer an get playing football, it'll do thee more good. He's playing for Leeds United nah. Fuckin 'O' levels, puh.'

The cabin's off-coloured silence meets his testy comments, as it meets everything said here, like a smothering coke-dusted blanket. I return to my own thoughts in order to comply with the contemplation ritual. I don't know how long I will be here for. Maybe three years like the students. I have no plan, just a vague notion of learning about horticulture by doing it. I'm just glad to be back north and listening, with the exception of Bert, to some broad Yorkshire being spoken.

'Reight,' says Bert signalling that it's time to go to work, 'Colun and Graham, tidy up flahr beds by Manor house.'

We all walk out into the welcoming bright sunshine and cross the stable yard to the store that looks like the horses only recently left. It has stalls with iron bars, flakes of whitewash on the boarding and wall mounted mangers.

Colin straightens his brown trilby hat and selects a wheelbarrow, 'We'll take the Daimler for a run today. You tip her up, and we'll make sure she's silent.' He squirts an oil can either side of the axle and spins the wheel. 'Lovely. German engineering see.'

Colin seems the most thoughtful of the garden labourers, and possibly slightly crazy in a way that I think I like. 'You can be driver,' he says, nodding at the wheelbarrow as he puts two Dutch hoes over his shoulder.

'Flahr beds?' I query.

'Flower beds. What did you do on the farm then?' he asks as we walk.

'I had a go at most things, lots of tractor driving.'

Colin stops and leans the hoes on one shoulder, takes out a silver lighter from his pocket, and tenderly lights the pipe that he stripped down and serviced during cabin time. 'Did you live on the farm?'

'Yes on the farm estate, but not with the farmer. I lived in with an American family.'

He draws breath through his pipe three times before the bowl's contents glow and smoke, and then he exhales with great satisfaction, after my short curriculum vitae has been laid before him. We resume our walk, and after what I take to be a reflective silence he says, 'I'll tell you what I hate about Americans, they can't do owt without changing their hats. Different bloody headgear for everything.'

I'm soon learning how to use edging shears by keeping the lower blade still and out of the soil. How to dead head flowers, hand weed and throw back the soil edges neatly with the hoe.

But I also learn something that was unthinkable on the farm; Colin watches me work and says, 'Steady on lad. This is a nice little job that could last us until lunchtime.'

Soon it's break time, and we retrace our steps back to the cabin. 'I wouldn't be surprised if Bert has you grass mowing with Tim after break.' Colin says, 'He's a grand lad is Tim, about your age, but as deaf as a post. Born deaf, lives on a farm, didn't learn to speak for years. He can't make some sounds. You'll get the hang of it. Look after him won't you?'

Later, sure enough, I'm with Tim and two 24 inch Atco mowers in the yard. He shows me the routine daily checks. 'Pill up wid petrol.' Den, 'check diptick.'

Where - is - the - oil - kept? I ask.

'In deer,' Tim replies, pointing to the oil can he brought out with the petrol. Next, 'Air pilter.'

'Do - we - clean - the - sponge - with - petrol - first? Like - on - the - farm?'

'Ar.'

O - K. What - next?'

'Adust bades.' Tim demonstrates the long socket tool that adjusts the bottom blade of the cylinder mower. 'We need tum paper.'

'News - paper? I'll - get - some - from - the - cabin.' I march across the yard and return with the front page of an old Daily Mirror. 'Got - it.'

‘Tum ‘ere.’ Says Tim, gesturing with his finger. Something about his innocent expression and slight eye roll reminds me of Stan Laurel. He stands and exaggeratedly puts down the socket tool on top of the mower’s petrol tank, and turns to face me.

‘Dook,’ He points to both his ears, ‘am depp not dapt da knows.’

‘Sorry, Tim.’

He holds out his hand.

I add ‘So - rry - Tim.’

And he laughs as we shake hands.

ROCK

There's an outcrop of limestone that runs through the rolling grounds of the college. It might be a geological fault line, a discrepancy in the landscape, but it's quite an attractive feature in places. Sometimes it's a yard high with summer bedding at its base and cheeky *Aubretia* in its crevices, the plants looking especially transient clinging to rock millions of years old. In places it's a ten feet cracked wall that looks blue-grey on dull mornings, but bright cream in afternoon sunlight. In other spots it's a steep bank, thinly covered with soil.

But a fault is a fault. Something not quite right. With limestone comes fossils. Stone replicas of animals that lived in a time long past. Like the cabin in the morning, where no one speaks for ages and when they do, it's to talk about their pre-war schooldays. Sitting in that place is the hardest thing for me. It's like visiting my grandparents several times a day. Loads of inactivity, while waiting for knowledge to be passed on, but just like my grandparents nothing so far except lots of tea.

Perhaps there's no rushing this process of fitting in at a new workplace. Henry on the farm said, when we go to work we are selling our time. But the farm was about learning to do useful stuff, and exercising new skills, this place is mostly about surviving with these cantankerous characters. I have a sentence to serve, doing whatever I'm told to do forty hours a week, even if that means sitting on my backside. At least the pay is better at £23 a week.

Possibly rock has the answer. Not the workaday limestone of Linklater, but the gritstone edges and limestone dales of the Peak District that I can enjoy at weekends. Then there's rock music of course. I'll walk in Derbyshire more, and go to more rock concerts at Sheffield City Hall. I'll bring my New *Musical Express* to read in the cabin. *That's* how I will get through this.

FOXIE AND BERT

Foxie is a strong, stocky, red-haired animal. He's about 25 and very physical. Drinking, fighting and fornication are his main interests outside of work. Although he doesn't call it fornication. He talks a lot about previous jobs, 'on the buildins,' driving JCBs, and drots, which are small mechanical diggers. Show him a hint of polite interest and he'll tell you all about different kinds of buckets, hydraulics and slewing levers in more detail than you'll ever need. It seems that women flock to a man with these kind of talents.

Foxie is the only one allowed to drive the single tractor here, a round-nosed, old-fashioned petrol engine Massey Ferguson 135. I'll never drive it. Bert is very clear on that.

Bert overhears Tim asking me what kind I drove on the farm, and then as I leave the custardy suite, Bert pulls open the door to the tractor shed and says to me, 'See that tractor? Well you aint gotta touch it. Only Foxie see?' I nod, and he says, 'You got that?'

'Yes, Bert.' I say.

Bert is being as polite as he gets. For him talking without swearing is polite, but eye contact is another thing. He does have eyes of course, but he never uses them for looking at anyone he talks to. You know how those old cameras, the ones before SLRs, always 'look' in the wrong place? The viewfinder image looks alright, but when the photos come back, the subject has moved to one side, or even slipped out the frame altogether.

Well, I think Bert's vision is like that, he's always looking somewhere else. He occasionally talks to your boots, but mostly he is at least 45 degrees out. He never sees me properly at all.

Foxie's eyes on the other hand can pierce you like ray gun beams. His eyes aren't especially small, but they appear to be, it's to do with his face - there is just so much of it. He has a deep forehead over those piggy peepers, and a wide head that makes his quota of hair look thin as it struggles to cover the breadth of that great cannonball.

But I should be careful, because Foxie may be Bert's favourite. Sometimes in the morning Bert is chatting away to him as I near the cabin's door.

'E say, "These is your grounds now Mr Merrin. You must do as you wish."'

Foxie looks on expressionless knowing only that Bert likes to tell him things when he arrives first thing in the morning, before 'the men' arrive.

'Tell you summin else, you knew where you stood with the ole Principal, I'll give 'im that.'

'Aw yeah,' says Foxie, uncomprehending.

Bert always stops when I appear.

Foxie resumes one of his long and apparently contemplative stares at the litter, today a blue penguin biscuit wrapper in the base of the coke pile, which has escaped the furnace for now.

Bert opens his newspaper. Sometime later when everyone is present, and I am submerged in the pages of the NME with my head in a hairy world of wordiness and rock and roll hyperbole, I become aware of him muttering more loudly. It's something angry about immigration. I tune into the diatribe in time to hear him say; 'Al tell you summin else about fourinners an all. You kin ardly tell what they says. They can't even speak the Queen's fuckn English they don't.'

Let's hope the rain keeps away and we get out of here to work soon.

WEEKEND WALK

One of the joys of life is Friday at 5pm, when it's time to forget about work for over 60 hours.

I can choose whatever I want to do with *my* time. Tonight, I rode my motorbike to a quiet layby in Derbyshire, locked it up and walked up the nearest hill. The nights are drawing in now, so there's no time to hang about. Here, I am totally free. Wearing my favourite boots and warm walking clothes. I have the top of Win hill to myself, and it's so beautiful. The sun is going down behind Rushup Edge, and the fields in the valley are glowing green in the orange light. There is nobody about. It's the perfect antidote to work, and to home, where five of us live in a two bedroomed house. I can't believe I am so lucky.

About three hours later, I'm lying in my sleeping bag, within a bigger plastic bag, to protect me from the rain. I am lying on a slope in the top of a conifer wood with my feet against a spruce tree. The rain is pattering gently. The air around me is completely still, even though I can hear the wind stirring the treetops above quite violently. This is freedom. I can't sleep very well with the noise, but I'm safe and snug. It makes me appreciate buildings and beds. It's worth coming for that alone.

When the dawn light comes, I'm glad to get out of my damp sleeping bag. I put on all my spare clothes, before pouring the condensed water out of the plastic bivi bag. I take out my stove, make tea, and pour hot water onto a muesli and dried milk powder mixture and crouch to eat it from the billy can's lid. I'm cold, and so sleepy that my eyes won't open properly until I heat more water for a good wash. I'll change my walking plan so that I end today at the Edale youth hostel after a walk across the peaty moor of Kinder Scout. I can't tell you how luxurious that hot shower and bunk bed are going to feel!

FIXTURES AND FITTINGS

We're installed in the mustard room, again. A few weeks in, and I feel like an ill-fitting piece of furniture. Half an hour at each end of the day, plus tea breaks and lunchtime, we're sat here. Even longer if the weather is wet.

Foxie and old Ray are getting on each other's nerves. Ray always has to chip in. This is a typical one, with Foxie talking of a night in the pub.

'E said, "am Manny Birkin, mediumweight..." Yer can stop theer, a said. Cos I don't care oo you are. Nobody speaks to my girlfriend like that. Nobody. I caught im dead centre, knocked t'breath art on im. Yer berra pick im up, I said, to is mates.'

Ray pipes up, 'Aw ar. I 'ad to do that wi...'

'Hey up, hey up. Eer we go.' Foxie scoffs.

'It's true. I ad three on em int Fox an Pullet. I said, you best put them stools dahn, unless yer *want* to go to casualty.'

'Deh. Gee over wi t'barm,' says Foxie, meaning give over, and stop this nonsense.

'It's true. Yer can ask Dave Spansell, e were theer.'

Ray has to beat every story, whatever it is. Most of his tales can't be true, unless he *is* the real Superman. With his alias, *not* the reporter Clark Kent, but an ex-plasterer, with a bad back, pushing fifty and working as a garden labourer. Although this Superman has probably blown his cover with all the boasting.

I'm learning to tune in and out of these cabin conversations, and to read or occupy my mind with my own thoughts. At least the furniture in here only *looks* like it's been thrown around in a pub brawl. These easy chairs, once proudly padded and bright, sat in staffrooms, or student rooms, and facilitated discussion and debate of a much higher order. Now faded, they sag with broken springs, bearing stains, and spills with sides split like seed pods, exposing their fluff. A chair can only take so much; so many tears, so many scratches, so many falling backsides, before it is rejected and offered down the hierarchy, eventually to the handymen, the cleaners and the gardeners.

'New boots, Colin?' says Ray.

Foxie hacks, and spits into the coke pile.

'Old un's polished,' says Colin.

Tim yawns.

Here they are, my new workmates: Bert the shifty puppet master, Foxie the muscle, strong as an ox and as rough as a hangover at sea; Ray, full of swagger and tall tales; silent Tim, and slightly detached Colin, who thinks he is so cool with his pipe. As if he needs only to hold it to become Sherlock Holmes, or Richard Hannay in *The 39 Steps*. But his cool is of another age, an age of cardigans, and Glenn Miller. And me? I'm the misfit, although after Foxie's recent wrestling hold on me, when I couldn't breathe and was close to passing out, I could easily have become Graham the brain-damaged one. I'd have fitted right in here. What the hell are we *all doing* here?

Like the chairs, we just kind of ended up here. Even a chair can only take so many rejections. When everyone says, 'No, too scruffy,' or, 'I'm *not* sitting on that,' or, 'beyond repair,' this is where they come, the end of the line. Their last station before the bonfire heap. Stood on the horseshoe chipped tiles and pushed against the boarded walls; their cushions doubled or trebled to compensate for missing springs. Here in this lowbrow backwater, of base banter and curses, where standards are close to the ground, they are all approved by the gently falling coke dust and the grateful rumps of gardeners. But pity those chairs, they must really miss the conversation.

MOW, SWEEP, LISTEN TO RAY

Tim and I take three days to mow around all the buildings and flower beds, and apart from the constant mower noise, it's a pleasant walk really. Not the tennis court banks though, they're steep and pocked with holes from rabbit scratchings. For these we bring out a different cylinder mower. It has two curved handles like horns, and two side wheels instead of rollers. Its instability causes the mower to kick and twist as you walk behind it, making it harder to hang onto, even before you get onto the uneven slopes where your boots slip into holes hidden by the longer grass. The engine is so old that oil leaks past its worn piston rings and burns, making chewy black exhaust smoke which pop-pops noisily through its tiny silencer. It's called the Antelope, but Loud Oil-burning Bucking Bronco would be a better name for it. But any job at all is better than the slow brain death of Cabinosis.

Foxie loves mowing with the tractor's gang mowers and making the clippings fly in green arcs. You can tell because he sings. He sometimes stops to chat while Tim and I are mowing all the edges and the rings around the trees.

Out of sight of the main buildings, Tim has a joke with Foxie, 'Now den, is dis your pirst day divin a tactor? Is tumfin wrong wiv d' teerin wheel?'

'Why?' says Foxie, smiling.

'Cos you've missed tum.'

This mild criticism is enough to make Foxie dismount, and while still laughing, he suddenly puts Tim in a steel scrapyard grab of a headlock. He holds it until both their faces go red, and Tim shouts, 'Mind me hearing aids,' before making choking noises.

Students and lecturers pulse along the paths between classrooms, dining hall and library as I mow. I envy them learning things. I wonder what they think of us? Does a student ever look up from lecture notes to see us, and envy us doing outdoor work that requires no thought at all? The other man's grass always being greener. No one, with even half a mind, would probably last very long out with the gardeners.

The lawns and mature trees make the college look a very nice place. Sometime people stand in little groups to chat, but move away as I approach with a noisy mower. Mostly it seems as if no one notices us at all. The lecturers seem to live in a sports-jacket-and-tie, book-carrying, cheese-and-wine world very different to ours. Although there is one exception, a younger lecturer with a beard and long hair, who always says 'good morning' to the gardeners. His name is Ben, and he started here only a year before me.

One day I am wearing my 'Keep off the Grass' tee-shirt, and Ben stops me to ask, 'Is that an anti-drugs message?'

We laugh about it and talk a little while. He repeats some of my words and tells me he is interested in

English accents and dialect words. It's the first time anyone has spoken to me from the academic staff.

Friday is sweeping up day. In two's, we work along all the college roads to pick up soil, leaves and litter. It's a more social job without machinery, and everyone talks differently when we are away from the jaundice ward. Tim and I meet up with Colin and Ray at a junction. Without Foxie there to stop him, Ray gets into full flow when he hears Tim talking to me about a farm bull.

'Awww ar,' or, 'Al tell thi what...' is his regular opener.

Thrifty old Yorkshiremen, who don't say much, get a lot of wear out of these little phrases. Long before the expression, *been there, done that, got the tee shirt*, there was, 'Aw ar.' The straight translation is, 'Oh yes,' but the meaning varies from a polite display of interest, as in, 'please tell me more,' to the bitter, 'so that's what *you* reckon is it? Well I don't believe a word.' It can also be an affirmation, 'we're agreed on that.' But Ray's long drawn out 'awww ar,' is an interrupter, that signals he is about to take over the conversation. This may be because has a correction, or more likely considers he has a superior tale to tell. Ray has perfected the use of 'Aw ar', and then worn it to tatters, because it's a rare day when *he* doesn't say much. His, 'al tell thi what...' is a demand for full attention.

Having interrupted Tim, Ray lifts his cap's peak like a knight opening a visor, 'Al tell thi what...' He pauses to collect his thoughts, pulls the peak back down again, and begins.

'This prize bull escaped from a pen at t'Partford Agricultural show. Ther were folks running abart, women screamin, mayhem it were. There were blokes laid theer wi brokken bones, blood all ovver their show coats. Mayhem.' He slowly pivots his head from side to side as if assessing the scene.

'"Ray, Ray," they shouted.

A walked ovver. And a stood theer in t'openin to t'public area. A lerrim come reyt up to me. Aif a ton o' best beef.' Rays eyes move between each of us ensuring we are paying full attention. 'Snotty and snortin he were. Then, a just went like that,' he extends two fingers, 'straight through is nose-ring. An then twisted.' He flips his wrist and points down. 'He went straight dahn.'

[The real version might have been more elaborate, but memory is a merciful editor.]

In the silence that follows the bull story, he says, 'aw ar.' And then, after a long pause, makes two breathy 'ar' sounds, as if to say, 'I can hardly believe it myself.'

Whether *we* believe him or not, Ray works tirelessly to convince us all of his heroic past. Sometimes Ray uses Colin, his contemporary, as his stooge. Scooping up some roadkill on his shovel prompted another tale.

'Al tell thi what Col, tha'll remember when Randolph Wrekin got hit bi that coil [coal] lorry?'

Colin has learned *not* to respond to these attempts at corroboration. If he says, 'No I don't remember him or that incident,' Ray will go into excruciatingly long diversions, involving other places, events or family trees. For example:

'Tha *does* know 'im. His lad married that lass wi't big 'eead, she came from Handel Street dahn Bleawell. Her mother died in childbirth. Her father married agean, t'Elsie Tucker.'

We all learn not to question Ray or show too much interest, because the story will continue anyway.

'So, Randy allus wore a big flat cap, nivver took it off. Like a dustbin lid it wor, tha must remember that? Anyroad, when they pulled his body art from under t'lorry, he were a terrible sight.' Ray scoops some soil, and flicks it over the flattened blackbird corpse in the wheelbarrow. 'A tell thee, terrible.' Ray pauses and shakes his head, as if he can't go on. 'He wor a mess, a reyt mess. His body all mangled up, and his face, well it looked like two pound o' raw mince. Terrible it were. His own missus wouldn't've recognised im.'

Ray pauses again for one of his breathy affirmations. 'Ar.' He switches from hugging his parked broom with one arm, to hanging from the top of its shaft with both hands, looking Colin straight in the eyes. 'But tha knows. An tha'll not believe this Col. That bloody titfer, wor still on is ead. And a tell thee, it looked as smart as t' day e bought it. Ar.'

The delivery is grave without a hint of humour. His tone dares us to not take these stories as seriously as he does. If you challenge him, or laugh, he will go into overdrive to verify it, producing names of witnesses or even more background details. Like Bellvine (*Calystegia sepium*) roots, in the shrub borders, Ray's tales can go on and on.

The best response to the end of a Ray story, is Colin's, a polite pause before changing the subject. 'Shall we sweep these steps then Ray? Or do you want to save that job until after lunch?' Questions are always good because Ray cannot resist giving answers. In his view, there isn't much he doesn't know.

JULIE 1

Tonight I'm staying in as the Front Room is free. This room, that in the past I've been evicted from for the offence of 'taking it over with homework', is now open to me as a board and lodgings paying guest. It's the one like a pub's taproom; cream anaglypta walls, fringed wall lights, whisky miniatures and a standard lamp with hunting scenes on. I am trying to eliminate the pub ambience by lying knees up on the small settee chewing a Biro, filling the coffee table with LP's and having James Taylor singing, 'You've Got a Friend' from the radiogram. 'You just call out my name and you know wherever I am I'll come running…'

On my A4 pad, I've got as far as, 'Dear Hank and Susannah, It's an autumn night and the darkness is closing in.' I'm thinking about what I can possibly say to them about my new job, now the shine has worn off, and I seem to be losing my sense of detachment about being back home.

There's a knock on the door. It's Julie with her new boyfriend that she wrote to me about while I was on the farm. Nigel has driven her over from Doncaster in his Mini because Julie wants us to meet.

Introductions over, I hang up their coats in the hall as Julie chirps, 'Hey, didn't you say you've got all your farm pictures back from the chemist now? Can I see them? Don't tell me, let's see if I can get their names right. You see Nigel, I know so much about everyone cos Graham wrote me letters.'

I pass her the Kodak card wallets of photos and she says, 'How's the new job? Is it as you thought, an old head gardener like Percy Thrower from the telly?'

'Hmm. Not quite. Tell me how you two met.'

We spend the evening chatting amicably enough and it becomes a regular event. Sometimes the three of us go out to the pub. But it's never too long before Julie says, 'Have you found a girlfriend yet?'

'No. How is Mary?'

Mary is Julie's best friend from school, who I last saw at the sixth form Christmas disco last year. It was over a year since my final date with Mary on the hot August night before I left for the farm, and my new life, forever so I thought. It concluded in a longing passionate embrace under the railway viaduct where, full of optimism for the wonderful future that surely lay before me, I insisted that we must break up.

'She's moved away, down south with her job in a bank.'

My shortlist of possible girlfriends just got shorter. It's also clear that Julie is no longer a contender, smitten as she is by her new man who has it all; a car, a dark moustache and a talent for impersonations that means TV and film stars can manifest at any dull moment. Mary, my old flame, is lost to the south, and any other candidates Julie or I name have lost touch, become engaged or gone to college. Life in the old town has changed. My love life is in casualty. Something has to be done.

Julie puts her head on one side and says, 'What about…'

And that's how it all started. A succession of dates with girls we knew from school. With some I got as far as second or third dates, sometimes joining Julie and Nigel for a night out together.

'What about… that girl you were going to bring to that party, but she had a cold? The one in the year below us. Her skirts were always a bit longer. You used to really like her.'

'Oh yes,' I say, 'that's Fiona Pearson. She often has a bad chest. Well not a bad chest. She has a beautiful chest. Oh God, you know what I mean, she would get infections - always had a cold.'

'Did you ask her out?'

'Yes.'

'What happened?'

'She had a cold then too. I'll try again in a couple of weeks, she only lives around the corner.'

'This is what I call a Donny race morning,' says Colin, as we all walk out of the yard with Springbok leaf rakes over our shoulders and into the crisp clear cool air.

The St Leger meeting runs in September every year at Doncaster racecourse, and Colin reminisces about the old days when he ran his own business and could go. I like the way Colin tells me more serious stuff sometimes. It's a change from all the daftness.

But Foxie is closing in behind us. Foxie in a playful mood is like a deep-chested spaniel with an unquenchable appetite for pushing, nudging and provoking. He catches the heel of Colin's boot with his wheelbarrow, deliberately.

Colin removes his pipe, 'Al not tell y'again about that. You better not make me drop this when I've just filled it wi fresh bacca.'

Foxie laughs. We are going to rake fallen leaves out of the flower beds, even though the blue lobelias were browned by frost a week ago, it's not explained why we are doing this. Bert never explains anything.

It's not long before we are back in the custard box again for morning break.

'Hey Col. A saw Freddy Barber dahn t'allotment,' says Ray.

There's a pause when I wonder if Colin will say he knows him just to spare us the tangential stories. But Colin seems to tease us by stretching that pause out to breaking point, before saying, 'Aw Freddy, how is he?'

He widens his eyes slightly and drops his chin as if to say, *here we go again.*

Phew, there's no family tree today from Ray. 'He's awreyt. His allotment's near mine. He makes some great compost does Freddy.'

'Oh yeah?'

'I asked him ow e does it. "Layers." he says. Green weeds, deead leaves, tea leaves from ome, an then strawy hen muck when he mucks aht ivvery Setday mornin. Breaks dahn in no time. It looks like crumbs o chocolate cake in six months.'

'Sounds like good stuff, Ray.'

'Aw ar. A teld im. Tha could win shows wi that stuff Freddy. An e said, "Ar lass would be happy wi just some decent parsnips, she loves em, roast, souped or mashed wi taties, but ar can't grow em."'

Between taking bites from a sandwich, Ray continues, 'Al tell thi what to do a said. Tek thi iron bar, and mek some deep oyles in a row, in March. Fill them oyles up wi thi sieved compost, and then sow t'seed on top.' Satisfied with his own advice, Ray affirms to himself, 'Ar, ar.' Before adding, 'An e did an all.'

'An…er.' Colin plays with the question, he knows he is expected to ask. 'What…happened?'

'E ad parsnips like bloody Saturn rockets e did. Show winners, all on em.'

'Oh aye,' says Colin non-plussed. 'Was his wife ovver t'moon wi em Ray?' Colin's face so straight he has to be joking.

But Ray isn't listening. 'There's somethin abart that compost stuff, when you gerrit reyt.' For a moment Ray's deep brow furrows develop secondary furrows that appear to collapse his entire face, like a corrugated box under a lorry wheel. 'It's a bloody marvel that stuff. It's onny dee-ad things e's purrin it, an yerrit *feeds* plants like that. Freddy nivver uses any fertiliser, just is owd compost. S'like witchcraft that is.'

Bert, our sole professional gardener has returned from his break in the flat above, and joins us for the end of Ray's talk, he makes no comment. He might know about plants, but I imagine Bert doesn't do wonder.

After break we are doing something new. Not mowing for a change, because the grass's growth had slowed now. Foxie takes the trailer down to the flower beds, where Bert supervises us for a few minutes before walking away. We fork out the Geraniums and drop them into opened out plastic fertiliser bags. For one red variety we pile the plants onto a big hessian sheet and it takes three of us to haul them up onto the trailer.

Foxie is still being Tiggerish, and he trips Colin deliberately again by the flower bed. Colin surprises us all by dropping his fork, and passing his pipe carefully to Ray, before putting up his fists to Foxie.

'Come on then,' he says, forearms held high, as he moves surprisingly lightly in his steel toe-capped pit boots. Foxie puts up a single fist and smiles. Colin's face is solemn, 'Come on, if you want to fight.'

Foxie, twice the bulk and half the age of Colin, laughs, but looks uncertain before saying, 'Deh' and waving his hand dismissively and trying to laugh it off some more. He has spoiled the pleasant atmosphere, and inside that heavy skull, even he knows it. He doesn't bother Colin anymore.

They all disappear and Tim and I are left behind to dig the beds over. 'Ploughin,' as Tim calls it. We can indulge our secret. We both love working hard. Without the others to stop us, we hack cubes of soil and flick them over carefully to leave weeds and debris buried.

Without pausing Tim says, 'Ey, teady on,' in imitation of Colin.

I respond with a Ray impersonation. 'Aw ar. I once dug 30 acres on me own by hand, wi just a trowel, aw ar.'

Later, I straighten up to ease my back, and Tim stands too, he reads my face and says, 'Are d' birds tingin?'

'Yes,' I say, 'a mistle thrush I think.'

'He's telling them all it dinner time,' says Tim, pointing to the clean brown earth and the worms we've just exposed.

On our way back for lunch Tim asks if I have a girlfriend.

'I'm working on it,' I say.

'How do you det one?' he asks.

Realising that Tim is actually behind me in dating expertise, I say, 'Find a girl you like, and ask if she would like to go out with you, for a drink maybe.'

'Den what?'

'Well you have to play it by ear, see how it goes. Ask her if she would like to see you again, and decide if you'd like to see her. Try and do something together you both like.'

'Like Poxie?'

We laugh. 'No. In fact whatever you do Tim, DON'T try to copy Foxie.'

A little while later, when it has rained for two days solid, and no one, not even Bert, can tolerate sitting in that crazy yellow room anymore we find ourselves work. We sweep and tidy the cabin and the tool store, scrub the tea mugs with Vim, file the hoes sharp, oil all the hand tools, sharpen shears, polish the kettle and the teapot, wash the windows, thin out the newspapers, restack the compost and fertilisers, clean the toilet, check all the mowers, scrub the sink and shine its single cold tap. And when we've done every other task we can possibly think of, only then, does Bert allow us into the hallowed space, of the greenhouse.

The uprooted Geraniums have to be trimmed and prepared as cuttings. Foxie and Ray show us what to do while Bert looks on. We prepare old seed boxes by lining them with newspapers and then filling them with compost.

I say, 'What's in the compost, Bert?'

'Never you fuckin mind,' he says.

Bert wanders off after a while and we stand trimming cuttings, pushing them into compost and writing on wooden labels; 'Pink', 'White', 'Red' or 'Mixed.' There is a calm for the entire time we are under glass. It's so quiet I look up to check, yes, there are *five* of us working in this Geranium-scented peace, lining out cuttings into trays, and laying them out on the dry pebbly benches. Even Ray is hushed.

It will be some time before I will learn that these plants are Zonal Pelargoniums and not actually Geraniums, that the days of growing them in this way are over in more progressive places, and that here at Linklater, despite a stable full of sharp, clean tools, I am not working at the cutting edge of modern 1970's horticultural practice.

A DAY FISHING

I bump into Ade in the pub. He left school at 16 for an apprenticeship with the National Coal Board. Along with Dean, we'd shared a great holiday together when we were all 16.

'Did you hear about Dean?' he says dropping his eyes down to the head of his pint, his tone suddenly sombre.

'Yeah, Julie sent me a clipping from the *South Yorkshire Times*, last year.'

'Very sad. Perhaps it's true, *the best die young*. He was only eighteen.'

'What made him do it?'

'Don't know, maybe she was pregnant? It all happened so fast. That's a blessing I suppose.'

'Yeah.'

A respectful silence follows as we think of the disappearance of our friend into the institution of marriage. An institution we feel outsiders to. But then Ade brightens slightly, 'We've got to make the best of the time we've got. Do you fancy a fishing match? We're trying to fill a bus for next Saturday.'

'I've not been fishing for ages. Go on then.'

'See you outside the Miners' Welfare Club at half six next Saturday morning.'

Any spaces on the coach between the bodies and the fishing boxes are filled with crates of beer. The miners are keen for a good day away from work, and their wives, in the relatively wide open spaces of the banks of the river Witham in Lincolnshire. The jokes are funny, and alternative lyrics are sung loudly over the pop hits on the coach's radio. Free's 'Alright Now' has 'There she stood, in the nud', John Denver's tender 'Annie's Song' becomes an ode to lust, 'Let me lay down beside you and slip it inside you,' is probably enough of a sample of it. The rattle and chink, from empty beer bottles rolling under the seats, rises in volume as we pass down the A1.

Ade's memory for jokes, like his Les Dawson demeanour, might well have developed to cope with life down a coalmine, and days spent match fishing. We arrive and draw tickets for numbered pegs on the bank along the long straight waterway. Ade's peg is a long way from mine. All banter and jokes stop as the fishing commences.

Oh it's a long cold day for a bank side vigil. The sky is a thick grey eiderdown, slipping off the bed in a cold north-east wind. I cast out, and settle down to contemplate the candle flame orange tip of my slenderest float in the company of a plastic box of maggots. There is some consolation as I sit on my wooden box, that all these experienced fishermen around me with the latest glass fibre rods, padded plastic seats and special catapults for placing ground bait, don't seem to be catching anything either.

Every float in my home-made tackle box represents long solitary meditations. The time spent making each one from scraps of wood and cork, plus the hours I spend in doleful waterside soul searching, staring at the tip. I know that I will even see the familiar Day-Glo tip as sleep beckons in bed tonight, sometimes with ripples around it, that first sign of a bite. This always happens after a day's fishing. The bite that I long for rarely comes, except in dreams.

The day passes very slowly. So dull and cold that the even the mutely restless maggots are slowing down. I lift my tackle box lid to gaze at the float colours as it's the only respite from grey-green, rain-prickled water, and morose grey men surrounded by fishing shop merchandise.

As the rain becomes heavier, green umbrellas come out, and I pull up my hood, tighten my scarf and put the lid partially over the maggots. You maggots at least have each other for company, whereas the fishermen are isolated on their boxes. Although to be fair, you lot couldn't organise a bus trip. Granted though, you are not slumped in a drunken torpor after coming here straight off night shift either. Maybe life's about getting yourself into the right kind of group or, learning to fit into the company that you're in, even if it's not ideal. All that camaraderie on the coach and look at us now, participating in a solemn, river-staring competition as if we're in some strange institution. Where is the truth about life? Somewhere between the solemnity and the camaraderie? It's hard trying to work all this out by yourself. It's alright for you larvae, writhing in your little community, rejoicing in your youth.

'Are you talking to your bait?' says Ade.

'Don't call them that they don't like it.'

Ade is normally keen on fishing, so he has surprised me by appearing at my side mid-afternoon. He loses interest quickly in my minimal kit, and starts reporting back on others. 'Ey, he's got luminous floats for night fishin in is box.'

'Aw no, we're not 'ere all night as well are we?' My enthusiasm for fishing is dropping with the rain. My feet have long since turned to frozen kippers inside my wellingtons. 'I didn't bring enough snap.'

Ade continues surveying his competitors critically, 'Eugh! Look at him across there, he's just taken a piece o' cake from an old bait box.'

A distant sonorous whistle blows to indicate it is, at last, the end of our shift. The match winner has only about two ounces of fish. I think I have caught a cold.

I seem to be surrounded by conventions and wretched traditions. Nothing, not even marriage, could be worse than another day of 'leisure' like this. Since boarding the bus, and later joining in the fishing ritual of men bowing their heads in the presence of the river, I have been feeling like an outsider. There must be better ways to experience freedom, or live a life, than this?

The day is not wasted though, because I've made a decision. I will never go coarse fishing again.

AN AUTUMN CHINK OF LIGHT

The leaf fall continues to occupy us. Yellowing lawns are cleared one by one, but like supermarket shelves, they refill during the night. We use large wooden hay rakes to create first rows, and then piles of leaves that smell of stewed tea. They are removed by a team effort, using Springbok rakes like wiry hands, to lift them up and put them into Foxie's trailer as he tramples them to get more in. 'Just like that,' we say in imitation of Tommy Cooper, as we drop the leaves and then shake the rake heads clean. But just like that, more leaves blow in.

One morning Colin and I are released from the team inanities, and sent to clear the leaves from the back of the Manor House, picking them out of the gulleys to keep the grates clear.

'It's cold today,' I say, as we guide our barrows down the crunchy frosted path. It's the kind of cold that can still find your ear lobes under two layers of woolly hat and pinch them like pliers. 'But at least that wind has died down.'

'It's cold,' says Colin continuing,
'It's cold, it's fucking cold.
It's as cold as a frog in an ice bound pool,
It's as cold as the end of an Eskimo's tool,
It's as cold as the hairs on a polar bear's bum,
As cold as the kiss from a whore when she's 'come'.
It's as cold as charity, and that's fucking chilly,
But not as cold as our poor Willie,
Poor bastard

He's dead.'

'That's great, Colin. What is that?'

He pauses to remove a glove, and pokes his pipe bowl gently with a finger. 'I think they called it, 'The Rear Gunner's Lament.' I wanted to go in the RAF.'

'Why didn't you?'

'They had a system of allocating your National Service at that time in the war, you didn't get a choice. I was sent to work in the pits, they called us Bevin Boys.'

'That's as far away from the sky as you can get. But at least you weren't a rear gunner. Can you say the Rear Gunner's Lament again? I'd like to learn that.'

As we brush and rake we run through it a few times and imagine the terror of flying in a bomber full of high explosives and being shot at. Hand picking dead leaves out of the drains doesn't seem so bad after that. Nor does the cold.

Colin pauses light his pipe, 'My father was a miner. I always like to think I'm a product of the 1926 strike.'

'You didn't stay in the pits then?'

'No, but I'm glad I did it. It makes you appreciate the hard work that goes on; hewers working at the coal face, and then rippers coming in to lift the height of the roadways before the next shift comes on. I've seen men doing the sort of graft my father did, and you've got to admire it. The camaraderie is great, but every time that cage goes down to the pit bottom you're thinking about if you're going come back up again, alive.'

'So did you leave?'

'No we couldn't. This was our national service, two years, like it or lump it. Some of the lads stayed afterwards. But it wasn't for me. I couldn't wait for the paddy mail to take us back to the pit bottom for the cage back up at the end of a shift.

At first we thought it was just meant to be until the men came back from the war, although they made us do our full two years anyway.

Then I got a job with a painter and decorator. Learnt the trade, the old way. I was lucky, I had a really good boss. Taught me everything he knew.'

'Like Bert with me?' We smile weakly at each other.

'He asked me to take over the business when he retired. So I worked for myself for years. My wife helped me with the book keeping. Did all sorts, even travelled abroad doing holiday homes. I really enjoyed signwriting. Such a skill in placing letters so they look right. I did a few pub signs and that led to me starting oil painting.'

'How come you've ended up here then?'

Colin's look changes suddenly. We've stopped for a break with our task almost finished, but we're near the blind corner of the building. 'Don't turn around. Bert is coming towards us.'

Bert only comes out once a day to check on us. Normally he can't sneak up on you, he stands out too much for that. He would be very tall if he was straightened out, but his arms swing like a man doing a poor gorilla impersonation in a cap, and he walks with a stooped and effortful lurching gait as if slightly drunk.

This look is accentuated by his jacket flapping more on one side than the other. One pocket is weighted with the stones he collects to throw at pigeons and cats.

Don't turn around,' Colin repeats. 'Follow my lead, turn slowly, and point.'

Colin moves animatedly to point at a sycamore, and then after lightly stamping his feet around to signal he's turning, he suggests I point to another big tree. Which I try do as if Bert isn't there and getting closer.

'Leaves *and* branches,' Colin says strangely and deliberately, before stopping as if he has only just noticed Bert. 'We were just saying Bert, there's more leaves to come, and a bit o' dead wood in them trees that'll be down this winter.'

We'd said nothing of the kind.

'Yurs,' says Bert, 's'nature's way.' And he turns to walk on up the hill back to the stable yard.

We return to the task. Colin, lifting leaves with two floorboard offcuts he found by the bins, says, 'Always look busy for the bosses. We used to say, *never cross the pit yard empty-handed*. Pick up a tool or a piece of paper, always looks like you're on your way to a job.'

'So what brought you to Linklater, Colin?'

'Ey up lad, it's nearly lunchtime. Let's get these leaves done. I'll tell you later.'

On the way back to the stables I say, 'You know I don't mind getting sent to work with you. Why can't I have a decent talk like this with the others?'

'Life is hard lad. Go easy on em. Like us, they're all coping the best way they can. Keep talking a bit o' daft occasionally, and you'll be alright.'

CABIN VISITOR

Foxie is in the stable yard, already at work, when Colin and I arrive to start our day. He is washing salt out of the tractor-mounted fertiliser spreader with a bucket of warm water. Foxie is the only one of us to get paid overtime for coming in early on frosty or snowy mornings to grit. Bert is speaking loudly over the tractor's engine noise and he hasn't seen us. Despite his volume there is an unusual softness in his voice.

'They was all goin off to war, so I git under gardener, wi me leg see? He say, "You can't fight if you can't run, Merrin." Genkleman he was. "Best *Delphiniums* I ever seen," e say to me. Thank you Sir, says I. Her ladyship was orlright an all. "You is a proper gardener to me, Merrin," she say.'

'Mornin Colin, morning Graham,' calls Foxie. Bert suddenly stops his tale and scuttles into the cabin ahead of us, opens the boiler door and stirs the cinders around with a long iron bar, before laboriously heaving in several shovels of coke and clanging the door closed.

After the noisy activity he drops himself surprisingly silently onto his chair, like spit falling onto grass. There he sits enthroned in front of the old sideboard, his habitual seat of power near the door. He is also symbolically blocking access to the sideboard's store of hand tools; trowels, shears, knives, dibbers, secateurs, gloves and string. *He* decides when we will work. He also guards the way to the kettle, tea mugs and our half empty pop bottles. This is a man who knows how to control his staff.

Ray, Tim and Foxie join us, and the sitting ritual complete with its stilted conversation can begin. Except that this morning, there is an interruption.

'Good morning,' says a new bright voice outside our door, 'you must be Mr Merrin.'

'What if I am?' replies Bert, standing to adjust the door so that the rest of us are hidden.

'I understand you might be able to help. I'm Dave Berwick, the new captain of the second eleven college football team.'

'Oh yea.'

'We have an away fixture with Dewthorpe on Saturday, but they've cancelled because of a drainage problem.'

The student pauses, optimistic that Bert will see the solution and propose it.

'Well that ain't my fuckn problem.'

'Er no, but I wondered, is it possible that we could play the match here on our pitch instead? I checked and the first team are away.'

'It ain't as simple as that. You hev gotta to go through head of PE, to book the playing field.'

'Oh.'

'An if you think we can jus drop everthin to mark out a football pitch and git nets up an all that, you are fuckn wrong.'

I'll ask Mr Pendleby then?

'You can do what you like but I'm tellin you there'll be no fuckn football ere Saturday.'

'OK. Thanks for…explaining that to me.'

Bert sits down and flicks his arm in what could be a half-hearted wave, or a dismissive swatting gesture.

The cabin remains silent for a long moment.

'That's told him,' says Ray.

'Fuckn students,' says Bert, reaching to pull the door to its half open position again. He shakes open his *Daily Express*, 'they don't think about nobody else they don't. They think you got nothun else to do.'

INTERPLANETARY POST

Amid the banality and frustrations of daily life I often think, *did I do the right thing coming back to South Yorkshire*? Not that I had much choice. The farm, which I increasingly think I just imagined, was so stimulating and challenging compared to this job. Now and again though a really good thing happens, and I realise it was all true.

I get home after work to find, underneath the letter rack stuffed with bills and 'important' paperwork, an envelope with my name on it. Susannah's energetic looping script is immediately recognisable. I take the letter somewhere quiet to read and imagine Susannah in the evening, her hand pale orange under the table lamp's light, writing while a placid cat looks on.

In some way I don't understand, I grow when I read these letters. There are thoughtful reflections on life in Oxford, where they moved to soon after I left, and comparisons with quiet Fenley; Dot and Sophie's progress in school and their parts in upcoming school plays; Hank is always doing something amazing like directing a play in London, designing a building, or writing a book. There will be interruptions by dogs or children, and advice for me; 'your life will work out,' 'you *must* go to college,' and always, the undertone of caring hopefulness. A regular feature is half a page demanding that I come to visit, 'because the children miss you', or because relatives are coming over from the

States that 'you *must* meet,' and even, 'Hank says he misses you.'

Like a prisoner in jail I read the letter over and over. Finding always that it is hard to connect their reality and mine, as if we're on planets with different atmospheres and gravity, lit by different stars. They are in beautiful Oxford, and I'm in a mucky corner of Yorkshire living life as a garden labourer among some unhappy people. My sense of separateness from the sadness thinning a little more each day.

I book train tickets at the travel agents to visit them just before Christmas. Writing back, I confirm I'm coming, and try to be as entertaining and as thoughtful as I can. Sometimes I fear that I grumble. But it doesn't matter, Susannah will still respond with warmth and encouragement, 'Your letter was so funny Graham!' And whatever she says, it will be unfailingly positive. The underlying message, occasionally made explicit, is that I am loved and will always have a place as an honorary member of her family.

TREE PLANTING FEBRUARY 1975

Tim has his cap reversed, as he always does for digging, the neb projecting over the collar of his jacket which is lifted up against the cold. We have almost finished turning over the Dahlia border on the edge of the principal's garden. I hear Foxie laughing and peer into the freezing fog. I nudge Tim and flap a hand, 'Slow down Tim, they're coming.' Initially like ghosts, the motley band approaches with wheelbarrows and tools. Bert is leading them with a fistful of small canes.

Bert limps about the lawn puffing his cheeks and pushing canes into the turf in three approximate lines, and then says to Ray, Foxie and Colin, 'You know what to do.' before walking away.

As soon as he's gone, all their tools are put down and they walk over to us to admire our work, I think.

'Tha wants to watch that, Tim,' says Ray.

'Whatta matter?'

'The way you're doing that digging. You could get into serious trouble.'

'Eh?' Tim, like the rest of us, has no idea what he means.

'Horace Tuplin used to wear his cap like that. And you know what happened to im?'

'What tat den?'

'He liked to do a ton on his motorbike, down that straight road where you come down from Sickle bank. Aw ar. One day they found im covered in blood in t'hedge bi that bend, is arms an is legs bent anyroad.

Ronnie Coalhouse found im, he were int' St John's. He stopped a car an got Emily Sprakes to go ring f't ambulance.

Ray turns to Colin, 'Tha'll remember Emily, Col?'

'Aye,' says Colin, unconvincingly.

'Anyway, Ronnie stayed wi Horace till t'ambulancemen came, an then 'elped bring im dahn out o't hedge. Horace looked shockin', is eead covered in blood. But they managed to find a pulse.'

Tim picks up a twig and began to scrape clay from the edge of his spade.

'It weren't to be though, Tim,' says Ray, detecting a lapse in Tim's attention. 'It were n't to be.' Ray shook his head and Tim copied the action. 'E were dead bi t' time they got im to t'infirmary.'

Tim took off his cap in mock respect.

Ray ignored him and continued, 'Bert said they put im an is bent legs on t'stretcher, they rigged up a drip, e'd got two o' them tourniquets on is legs and he semt to be doin OK. Ar Ar.'

'So what happened then, Ray?' says Colin.

'That bloody medic int ambulance, looked at his cap, then went and turned his 'ead rahnd.'

There's a long pause in which Foxie looks genuinely surprised before scoffing dismissively, 'Deh.'

'Ar.' Whispers Ray respectfully. 'It's true. So, you should allus keep thi hat on t' reyt way round, Tim.'

It doesn't matter that Foxie jeers and says, 'Nay, gee o'er wi t'barm,' because Ray, only protests all the more.

'It's true, it's true,' he says, adding, 'tha can ask Ronnie thissen. He saw im do it. Come to t'Fox an Pullet on Friday neet, e's allus in then.'

'Anyway, Ray,' says Colin patiently, 'are we gonna get these trees planted or what?'

Tim and I finish the digging. We're then sent to wheelbarrow down the young trees that were delivered this morning.

'Handle em carefully,' says Colin, 'they must have cost a King's ransom that lot.'

This is something new and special. There are lots of trees at the college but none are very young. The new trees, some potted, others root wrapped, stand together just where they were lifted down from the nurseryman's lorry on the edge of the stable yard. They look alien, vulnerable, and very cute, like first year kids at school, with name labels on. Although, no one knows what the labels mean.

We transport them the last leg of their journey to the Principal's lawn. Soon after, I'm planting one with Colin that looks to me like a Christmas tree with a bent tip. I'm talking about finding my way in life, or walking, or women, or some topic dear to my heart, but as I pick up the string to tie up the bent shoot, Colin interrupts.

'Ahm goin to tell you something now, lad. You did say to tell you if I could help you to learn?'

'Go on,' I say, ready for enlightenment by wise old Colin.

'You'll remember this for the rest of your life. Always tie your string to the post first, then around the stem, going left over right, right over left.'

'The post and the string being?'

'The cane and the three ply fillis. To hold the shoot up.'

'Oh yeah.'

'What did you think I meant?'

Over two days we plant twenty-odd trees just as Bert instructs us. But throughout Colin and Ray mutter together. I ask what's up, and Colin explains, 'It's a rushed job. You've heard of, 'Plant a Tree in 73?'

'Of course, the campaign to replace the trees lost through Dutch Elm disease.'

He holds his pipe by the bowl and uses the stem to draw an imaginary line around the mini forest before us. 'Well this here is 'Plant a Tree and Watch it Dee.'

'What's wrong then?' I ask.

'Should be bigger holes, with muck in, bigger stakes, rabbit netting. Bonny young trees like these, going into this clay. Not enough space either, it's not right. We're spoiling the ship for a ha'porth o tar. But Bert won't hear of it.'

'Ey, Col,' shouts Ray, trying to decipher a tree's label, 'a think this one might be a money tree. Like oliday Webb had.'

'You'll be lucky. Stick to your football pools,' says Colin.

Later when I'm digging a hole for a conifer Ray is nursing, I ask, 'Is that his real name Ray, Holiday Webb?'

Ray begins unwrapping the hessian strips bandaging the tree's rootball, 'Naw. A f'get nah what it wor. Everybody calls im oliday.'

'Why?'

'Cos e's nivver worked a day in his life.'

'How come?'

'His Dad wor an accountant, deed young an left 'im money. When that ran art e married Viv Darnall. Her Dad ran t'cash an' carry an a chain o' paper shops.'

'Oh I see.'

'It wor oliday as said to me, "Claim compo for thi back, Ray." E knew ivvery fiddle gooin e did.'

Ray's clear admiration for this man is eclipsed momentarily by the pale blue conifer he is holding. Its perfectly round rootball is full of white and ginger young fibrous roots. 'By, that's a lovely tree is that.'

TRUTH IN STONE

We're back St Custard's with the Ray and Foxie tag team wrestling their opponents, the Truth and Reality. Both gardeners are giving their rivals quite a pummelling, but as usual they are more in competition with each other.

It's no surprise that they are talking about sex. After all Foxie sees sex everywhere. This a man who last week looked at some callusing on a tree trunk and saw a naked female pudendum. Although he didn't call it that.

Meanwhile in my head, I'm out walking on Dorset cliffs with John Hillaby, because I'm engrossed in his book, *Walking through Britain*. But despite this, and the background hum of familiar voices in the sleepy atmosphere, I detect the noise level rising and tune in to the conversation.

Foxie is claiming that despite having had sex several times on Saturday night he still had an erection that was, '*Like THAT*,' he takes hold of the end of the cabin broom's handle to illustrate.

Ray is in the ring. 'Nay tha *can't* have.' Ray's eyes do a sideways movement when he is thinking of what to say next, as if he is reading from an invisible crib sheet. His eyes are doing that now. Seeing this, Colin passes him a small pencil stub from his pocket, anticipating his need for a different visual aid.

Foxie laughs, and moves on to discuss the viscosity of his semen in considerable detail.

Ray tries to conclude with, 'Nay, I'll bet thi owt, bi four o'clock in t'mornin it were like tatie watter.'

Unusually, it's Bert who rings the bell to call the bout to an end. He pulls out his pocket watch and laboriously rises from his chair while simultaneously straining to say, 'Reight.'

We are all spared further details of Foxie's genitalia or fecundity.

Colin and I are sent to 'git flahr beds tidy by Old Manor.' We walk out and see dirty swabs of clouds lying in the steel curved dish of sky. By the time we are at the beds we can smell the rain coming. The Polyanthus flower buds are just breaking and showing tiny samples of their colours. We hand pull a few weeds, pick up the litter that looks brighter than the spring bedding plants, and make the edges look tidy. We fear we are in for one of those long grim days in the jaundice ward.

'Let's just take a look at the rose beds by the buildings.'

'Are they untidy too, Colin?'

'Not really, but we'll give 'em a coat of look at just the same. I can't get my pipe lit in this wind. Just follow me and try to look intelligent.'

Over the entrance to the Manor are two weathered stone animals, and underneath them is an inscription.

'What's that actually mean, Colin, *Nisi Dominus*?'

'Nay, lad. I only said *look* intelligent. Let's pick up these bits o' litter and bugger off before it chucks it down.'

As we thought, it's the wet day routine, but luckily there is sufficient work to do that extra cabin sitting isn't required. Lots of summer bedding seedlings need pricking out, and some Dahlia tubers have to be boxed up in compost for cuttings production. This work really saves the day because I'm hitting a bit of a low spot with all this dull routine. We get talking about seed sowing and I build myself up to ask Bert about the skill of seed sowing next time he appears. 'Will you show me seed sowing sometime, Bert?'

Heads stay down, but the sound of tapping dibbers momentarily stops.

Bert, doesn't hesitate for a second, 'I does all that, never you fuckn mind that.'

Later at home, after tea, I walk over to the town library and look up that entrance inscription. Probably added later by some clergyman, apparently, it's from Psalm 127, sometimes translated as 'Everything is in vain without God.'

The truth I am fighting within myself, is that I feel dull and uninspired. I have lost my way. 'Everything is in vain,' seems to perfectly sum up my life at the moment.

JULIE 2

Love is strange. There's only so much I want to know about working as a manager in the local pits. Each to their own but; calculating air volumes, installing fans, slide rules and gas tests? As conversation? Nigel loves his work, but maybe it's good that most people don't talk about work, too much.

We're in the front room at home and Julie seems quite absorbed in Nigel's talk. She was always quite good at maths though. But it's not too long before she finds a pause to ask the inevitable question, 'Anyway, what about your love life, Graham? What happened with Elsie Greenwood?'

'We managed three dates; drinks, a walk and the pictures.'

'Are you still seeing her?'

'Well, she's another one of those amazing looking girls that doesn't need to ask questions, or work stuff out, as if she has all the knowledge she wants already.'

'So are you still seeing her?'

'No I think we'll let it peter out.'

'What about Fiona Pearson? Could you go round and ask her to come for a drink with us?'

'It's Wednesday. She might be washing her hair.'

'Why not go round now and ask her?'

'OK.'

So I do.

If the council houses on Polly Avenue have been especially allocated to the bashful, it's only surprising that more of my teenage girlfriends don't live there. Just around the corner from home, Polly Avenue is full of privet hedges, different in character at every house, from delicate medical screens to gappy clouds and engineered oblongs. Some have curved tops as broad and as solid as railway carriages, others are looming over paths and threatening to deny access, occasionally they're wild and flowering, rearing like frothing horses. All of them shielding the lives of their house's occupants.

Fiona Pearson has natural Bambi eye lashes and a shyness which keeps her face looking down, at pavement and roads mostly. I wish this was because she is entranced by my presence and feels to be floating on air, so much so that she needs to check the ground has not vanished. But in reality it is more likely that paving slabs, and tarmac, hold more fascination than me, or my conversation. Standing by her doorstep I try, yet again, to persuade her to venture beyond the privet's protection.

The futility of my journey is clear, damp hair and rollers under a headscarf say it all. If only her eyes would lift to the porch's pebbledash I'd be encouraged, because it begins two feet up the wall. On our sporadic dates, low brickwork and pub wallpaper beneath dado rails, receive great scrutiny. If we were ever to look up at trees or rooftops together, it would be tantamount to an engagement and warrant celebratory rings.

Eye contact with her is very precious. There is something I know and understand deeply about her way of being, but I can't explain it. When she smiles, and when she looks at me, I feel very special indeed. She has the darkest brown eyes, and a face that speaks to me of love and possibility. Her perfectly formed mouth however, says mostly as little as possible; 'Yes', 'Maybe' or more frequently, 'No.' I think I would give up the world for her with only a hint of encouragement. But it never comes. Making her laugh now and again is the only way I can find to free her, and myself, from the disease of reticence we've had since childhood. How can anyone be so beautiful, and not know it themselves?

I return to Julie and Nigel who are sitting on the sofa holding hands. Mam has been to see them and made them coffee. They're the picture of togetherness.

'Well? Is she washing her hair?'

'Yep. Maybe I'll see her next Friday.'

'What happened with Elsie Greenwood?'

'Can we talk about something else?'

'No.'

'She told me we weren't right together. Well not directly.'

'Ooh mysterious. Tell me or I'll scrag you up.'

'Scary! Ok. We went to see *That'll be the Day* at the pictures in Barnsley. When we walked back to the bus station afterwards I asked her what she thought of it, and she said, 'It was alright,' in that way that meant it wasn't really. Then she said, 'What did you think?'

'And what did you say?'

'I said it wasn't a great film, but I liked the music and David Essex and Ringo Starr. The atmosphere was realistic if a bit glum. The end was a bit strange, downbeat I suppose.'

'What did she say?'

'Nothing for a while. We walked down by Bacon's book shop and I was looking up at the starlings roosting on the church ledges, when she said, 'That's your trouble.'

'Sorry? I said.'

'That's your trouble. You think too much you.'

Julie quickly puts down her coffee and drums her feet on the floor as she laughs.

They go off about 9pm. They could've had enough of John Lennon's *Imagine* LP, or perhaps my search for love is too agonising to witness?

Julie turns back as they're leaving to say, 'Don't be going off walking in September without telling me will you? Nigel and I are getting married.'

FIRESIDE CHAT

We're in the woods tidying up some wind damage. But a new storm is about to strike. Escalating tales of bravado from Foxie and Ray are nothing new but this one, about feats of strength, is about to hit a new level. It's a hurricane and there could be structural damage. It blows up out of nowhere.

Ray is perching on the handle of his fork by the bonfire. Suddenly he stands outraged, and scoffs, 'Pah. Yer just *can't* av lifted a trailer tow bar on yer own. You daft bastard.'

Foxie throws down his rake and steps close to Ray. Enunciating slowly to indicate a line has been crossed, 'Don't call me that. You can call me anythink you like. But not that.'

'Am only seyin'...'

'And I am telling yer.' Foxie is talking through his teeth now. 'Don't. You. Ever. Call me. That. Again. I could snap you like a fuckin' twig.' He bends and picks up a warty bit of dead sycamore to demonstrate. 'Like thet.'

The dead branch cracks loudly. A dead silence follows. Ray's eyes do their usual side to side movement, that this time make him look as if he is checking for escape routes rather than thinking what to say next. A distant rook caws, and an orange-grey burning branch wheezes and falls into the soft embers.

We'd never seen Foxie like this before. His blocky head is red with rage. The sight is scary. He's a bull mastiff that's been kicked hard, and let off the lead.

Nobody breaths or moves for what seems like an hour. Then Colin takes his pipe from his mouth and ducks his trilbied head as he steps to Foxie's side. Then waving the pipe as if in hesitant apology, he touches Foxie's sleeve and says softly, 'Sorry, but I didn't quite catch that. Snap like what?'

Foxie's chest begins to shake and he bends forward to pick up another twig, this time doing his high pitched squeaky-toy laugh before repeating, 'Like THET.' We all join in laughing, with the relief. Like the wood smoke in the wind, the tension suddenly goes away. For now, the fight is off.

BIKE BREAKDOWN

The walk across to the bike shed on the car park at 5pm is the necessary preliminary to liberation. The transition to freedom begins with this routine; I adjust my scarf, put on my helmet, zip up my coat and buckle its belt so it won't flap as I speed down the hill to home.

But today the bike won't start. It's now 5.05pm and getting dark quickly after a long wet day. I've got the tools out and I check for a spark at the plug. *Nice fat blue one, so the electrics are ok.*

'Got trouble?' calls Ray, across the car park. *Oh no, that's a voice I've heard quite enough of for one day.*

'It's alright' I say, wishing it was. He'll soon be gone. I hear his door open and close again. The other have left. *It could be water in the carburettor, maybe I can drain it out without taking it apart.*

His engine starts up first time, and I hear him pull away over the stones of our rough car park. 'What is it?' he shouts, from the window of his Morris minor van.

Oh shit. Here we go, whatever I say he will know all about it. He will have repaired Spitfire engines in the war, while standing on the wing at ten thousand feet, or some such bollocks.

'Just a carburettor problem. I've had it before.'

He lets the van roll backwards down the slope as he speaks. *He might be a self-proclaimed all out genius, but his clutch control is shit.* I've just found the Phillips screwdriver in the half light, and I can soon have the bottom of the carb off. He stops, gets out of the van and my heart sinks. *At worst he'll take over, at best he'll distract me with some grandiose tale.*

'You best gerrit int van. We'll just catch Oggie Bennett oppen. E'll sort it for you.'

'Thanks Ray, but…'

'E's gorra bike shop in Bleawell. Ther's nowt e can't fix.'

'But…'

'I know, lad. Let's jus purrit int van. Come on. We're wastin' our own time nah.'

We haul it up into the van. It lies there on a diagonal. Ray doesn't fuss about the smell of petrol, or the tyre marks we just made on the van floor. The journey down the hill is made in neutral, 'rubber gear' as Ray calls it, to save petrol but otherwise we get there safely.

Oggie is quiet and bespectacled, not at all like I expect a friend of Ray's to be. He has the carb off quicksticks, and blows through the jets with an airline. He puts it back together, and adds the leg shields as I pass him the bolts. He refuses to take any payment. I'm riding back home in no time at all, mulling over how some people can take you completely by surprise. Maybe, just sometimes, Ray is actually right.

SPEAKING OUT

I know two Bills. One without sight and the other without speech, or so you'd think. Blind Bill delivers newspapers for the newsagent in Linklater. He wears a long old coat, buttoned right to the top of its sticking up collar, a wool balaclava and wellies. He dresses like this for three quarters of the year. You can't be too careful when you work outside, especially as weather forecasts are unreliable and clouds sneak over mostly without audible warning.

The other Bill is a friend I've known since Sunday school. He joins us in the pub once a week, when his work shifts allow. He is less distinguishable by his clothes, although he is quite tall.

Both Bill's lost something in their youth; Blind Bill his sight, when he ran into a hedge; Sunday Bill, his voice, as many of us to do, in order to fit in. Both of them like to walk.

Blind Bill can occasionally give cause for alarm by appearing in the middle of a lawn, or being found standing still in a broad expanse of tarmac like the one by the busy college entrance. He has his own means of navigation; a map in his head and a Wellingtoned foot that's dragged discreetly in contact with the kerb. We'd intercept him and hear his gentle voice on approach, 'It's that dropped kerb by the garages that throws me.' A voice soft and kind, as if he knows only the best of human nature.

'Take my arm, Bill,' one of the gardeners will say, and lead him back to a kerb. Blind Bill is probably an unsettling sight to those who see him wheeling his bicycle along, especially if they assume he is about to ride it. But he only ever walks with it, a second canvas paper bag hangs from the crossbar, and his coat is folded over the handlebars in summer. I suppose a blind man with a bicycle, like a mute man with a megaphone, can give the wrong impression.

'What's that smell I always get just here?' he asks, and for a while you have to think about it.

'Oh, it's the bed of wallflowers, Bill,' you hear yourself say, never realising before they even had a scent.

Sunday Bill can help make you see things differently too. He is the only person in the pub to take up my offer of a walk. We leave the town and explore the local countryside initially, but soon Derbyshire beckons. This Bill specialises in companionable silences, so it takes a while before we find we can share our secret. The shameful fact that has to be kept from our families and friends and played down with work colleagues. It feels so bad, we never speak of it within the town.

One day, walking by some woods, Sunday Bill just comes out with it, as brazen as you like, as if he has no shame at all. 'Are you, reading anything at the moment?'

It feels like someone just kicked the stereo, while it was playing the track of squeaky birdsong and wind noise on one of those BBC sound effect recordings. I presume he doesn't mean the *Daily Mirror*, or the one-inch OS map of the Peak District I'm holding.

'Er yes,' I say nervously, 'A book by John Hillaby, a walker and journalist. He walked the length of Britain for his last book, and now I've just started reading his *Journey Through Europe*.

I wonder if I say too much sometimes. Perhaps 'a book,' was all that was needed. But the silence doesn't last. Bill's voice comes back with, 'Is it like the Wainwright guides to the Lake District?'

I stop walking. I'm in conversational shock. We don't normally say this much. Not much that isn't, 'What time's the bus back?' or, 'time for a pee/coat/lunch stop?'

'You've read Wainwright?' I say.

Bill's eyebrows drop, and he looks studious for what seems a whole minute. 'Cantankerous old bugger isn't he?'

'You have read him!'

That Sunday Bill speaks more freely when away from home is good news, but realising that he reads and loves to discuss books and ideas is a revelation. We seem to live in a place where to appear 'clever' is sinful, and to be interested in anything much invites ridicule. So it is liberating to put on a rucksack and walk and talk of interesting things. Not just the books or ideas, we can throw off the restrictions of our limited daily vocabulary as well. Despite the wonders of the South Yorkshire dialect that we both love, there are ideas impossible to convey in it.

Another day he asks, 'Have you read the *Naked Ape* by Desmond Morris?'

'Yes. I say, 'Is that why you're growing a beard, Bill?'

'No, just having a break from shaving.'

'Are you skipping other daily ablutions then?'

'No. I just thought, why should I shave? Why would I want to remove my secondary sexual characteristics?'

'Maybe that's the function of sideburns?'

There's an unspoken agreement between us that if we know a word we can use it. The self-consciousness isn't easy to overcome at first, and we can't be pretentious, neither of us will allow that, but we can explore how life really is for us and how it might be in the future if we communicate and share our reading & thoughts.

Like Blind Bill having a new letterbox to deliver to, getting there can be a bit of an adventure, but once you've done it a few times it gets easier. The mental map gets modified, and the worst that can happen is that you find yourself in a quiet open space waiting for help to come along. That's how this new discovery is with Sunday Bill too. Learning to talk seriously, amid the quietness, for the first time.

LEAF MOULD

Like the gardeners' talents, the bountiful oak and beech leaf-fall is also squandered. Back in autumn, we wheelbarrowed and trailered fallen leaves away for disposal to various hidden corners; the woods, the back of the sewage works or the ditch of the old ha-ha among the trees. It's here at the neglected ha-ha that we pause, one early April afternoon, to allow a shower of rain to pass over. Ray kicks away at some leaves and pushes his cap to the back of his head.

'Here, Col. Come and look at this.'

'Have you struck gold, Ray?'

'Gowld? It's better than that, Col. It's bloody best baccer.'

Ray puts his hand into the leaf mould and shows it to us, 'St Bruno's fuckin' Flake. A wish I 'ad a few barrows o' that on me allotment.'

He kicks again, and takes another handful from lower down, this time smelling it before rubbing parkin coloured crumbs through his fingers, 'By heck ,that's lovely stuff.'

Unusually, Colin is quick to agree with Ray, 'Ought to be in the flower beds or that nursery garden. Just right for breaking that clay up.'

'Al tell yer weer else it should've bin an all,' says Ray, wagging his stained finger accusingly. 'Under them young trees we planted.' His head begins to shake slightly as if in disbelief.

Tim copies the shake.

But Ray's case for the prosecution isn't quite finished, 'But you can't tell that bastard anythin.' He concludes by spitting into the curly undecomposed leaves alongside.

It goes quiet.

Since Foxie's outburst in the woods the 'B' word is not a word that anyone has used. A magpie squawks in the distance and Tim taps my shoulder to ask, 'What tappenin?'

I explain briefly, and Tim brushes his boot against the exposed peaty leaf mould.

Colin considers. He taps his pipe bowl out against the rough ridges of an oak trunk, and says, 'Well he's the boss, Ray. Whether we like it or not, and whether he knows owt or not.'

Ray spits again, this time at the young nettles emerging alongside the pile, and turns his head away. 'Bert. He knows fuck all.'

Respect for our head gardener is eroding with each new horticultural atrocity identified. The dirty wooden greenhouse trays, plant pots that are never washed, the young trees planted without proper soil preparation, but worst of all this, not using the finest oak and beech leaf mould that any gardener would swap his best boots for.

'Yer might as well just fill yer pipe up wi' it, Col.'

'Perhaps he doesn't know it's here?' I suggest.

'He knows. Foxie's told him. I've told him.'

The rain stops, but nobody moves.

Colin says, 'When I was a Bevin Boy at the pit, they said, "Bosses don't *go*, Lad. They fuck off."

From that day we adopted the phrase for our head gardener, whenever we felt sick of him and Foxie wasn't around. So someone saying, 'Has Bert gone?' would be corrected with, as Tim learnt to say, 'No, he's pucked off.'

WIND AND WILDFLOWERS

I catch half of Bert's monologue as I'm returning from the toilet across the stable yard.

'...all o them fuckn 'ologies. Jonesy is the fuckn worst one. He say, "Can we 'av a little wildflower area, Mr Merrin?"

I say, you mean fuckn weeds.

"Oh no," e say, "choice native species."

No, says I. No you can't. I ain't avin weeds left to grow all over the fuckn place. I say no, an that's final.'

He reaches his foot out to tap Tim, who is sitting with his eyes closed. 'Tim, I SAY TIM, an Graham.'

Tim wakes with a start and hasn't a clue what is going on, but knows I will explain later. 'When you mows back o' Science, be sure an cut as close up them fuckn buildins as you can. I don't want no weeds gettin goin.'

Tim and I nod, Bert opens his newspaper, and a relative peace descends.

Foxie, for whom no urge can pass unheeded, *can* sit still in the cabin, but sometimes he's like a fruit machine in a pub; one that flashes, winks and plays a jingle. He'll shuffle and yawn loudly or roll his eyes about like Robert Newton in *Treasure Island*. Occasionally he practises his threatening stare, and if he catches your eye he'll say meanly, 'What are you looking at?' Or he'll try to provoke Ray by mimicking his, 'Aw, ar', repeatedly.

After the pause following Bert's outburst, Ray and Colin begin talking coal. As Ray sees himself as an expert, on everything, his lack of experience in mining is no problem. But Colin has natural authority on this and is gently putting Ray right.

'Damburgh pit was sunk long before that Ray, about 1910. They hit the Barnsley seam about half a mile down. Very good quality coal in that seam.'

Ray does a very rare form of, 'Aw ar.' One that subtly conveys in its softer delivery, an acknowledgement of a superior presence. What a special day.

Colin pauses to relish this rarity too, and then continues, 'But they had a problem with firedamp, as they called it, until they had a special ventilation system put in for methane drainage.'

When he isn't being the fruit machine Foxie can sit and stare at the floor, or some fixed point, as if in deep and thoughtful contemplation. Occasionally he belches, and follows it with a giggle of joy at his creation. If this fails to attract some attention, there is another talent he deploys from time to time, something that no one can ignore.

Foxie is sitting high on the orange and purple double cushions of his chair, lifting his short legs up and down.

Ray says, 'Just a minute Col. What's tha doin, Foxie?'

'Am sortin me socks art.' Foxie says, and smiles to himself, and then does his crazy-man squeaky laugh.

'Hang on' says Ray, 'That's not t' smell o' socks. Ow's that canary doin, Col?'

Colin lifts an imaginary cage and look into it, 'Well, e's stopped singing.'

'But is e still keepin' time?'

'E' s vamping. No, I think 'e's humming.'

'Somethin's hummin,' coughs Ray, 'Bloody hell Foxie.'

Colin is still holding up the bird cage, 'No. E's gone. A think it's firedamp. Can you open that door a bit more, Bert.' Then under his breath he adds, 'And call Mines Rescue.'

As we all spill outside to escape the stench, Ray says, 'Fuckin ell Foxie, *nobody* should reek like that. It's not natural. Thers summat up wi thi guts.'

Foxie laughs, revelling in the attention, and shouts to us all outside in the yard, 'Ee that Teckleys were good last night.'

I notice Bert's face. He is laughing, but also looks strangely delighted.

HOEING WITH RAY

Ray is a bit quiet today. Maybe it's because the others are all on leave. It's a cold, but dry and fairly bright April morning in the Easter holidays. We walk out from the tool store with Dutch hoes over our shoulders. The bolder trees are defying the cold air, and starting to leaf up. Some new leaves hang like corrugated silk flags while others are waxy tissue papers ready for the spring ritual of the delicate unfolding.

'Just me n' thee today then, Graham.'

'Yep.'

'Yer keepin that earring then?'

'Yep.'

My ear piercing has caused quite a stir. I had it done a week ago and I'm wearing a small gold ring. Colin and Ray have been quite shocked; these old blokes just don't understand, and I have nothing else to say about it.

Arriving at the shrub border by the empty student block it's surprising that despite the brutality of Bert's anti-shrub campaign, where plants are regularly sheared of all their new growth and hacked into unnatural domes, there are actually signs of new life. Some yellow *Forsythia* flowers have survived the butchery, and the flowering currants hold out pleated green palms of leaves like tiny hands raised in surrender. Even our head gardener can't stop the spring.

Soon the fruity scent of bruised currant is in the air, as Ray and I chop at the coarse clods of soil with our hoes, between the sad green light-bulb shapes of the shrubs.

Ray's arms stop their slow jabbing as he looks up at a flock of birds passing over.

'Pigeons?' I ask.

'Ar.'

'Hey, they have rings!' I say, but Ray isn't listening. He's still not himself somehow, and without the others to gee him up, it doesn't look like there is much work in him today.

He carries on looking up, leaning his chin on his fist atop the end of his stationary hoe shaft. For a moment Ray reminds me of the common man in an old religious painting, looking up to heaven in wonder after seeing the rolled stone, risen saviour or the water to wine thing. The peak of his flat cap emphasizing the direction of his gaze and making a band of shadow across his eyes.

There's a pause, another 'Ar.' This time a soft breathy one, as if he is exhaling to steam up a mirror. He stands perfectly still, with that habitual downturned expression. Then Ray does something that he doesn't do very often. He speaks quietly.

'Ar. There's nowt like that. When racing pigeons pass ovver together, in that rush o' air. Wheelin this way an that. It's like am up theer, wi em. Lookin for ome. It allus gets me when a see em. Dunt tell the others.'

After this revelation there's another, longer pause. Then the normal boastful volume resumes, with that irritating proprietorial tone.

'Ar. A told Benny Worksop to release some youngsters for a training flight from t'other side o' Grimsby this mornin. Fifty mile.'

'Who's he then, Ray?'

'Oh, he does all t' Barnsley District bird transport. He's alreyt. A bit slow in t' head wi too much boxin, but he looks after t' birds well.'

'So you think those birds are on their way to Bleawell then, Ray?'

'Oh ar. Thull be droppin dahn to ar lofts in abart four minutes. They'll av a bit o' corn an a tread,' he does one of his cackles, 'an then they'll settle dahn. Al rest em before t'weekend's race.'

'Hey. Talkin o' corn Ray, have you seen what time it is?'

'Fuckin ell lad, stick thi hoe in. It's break time.'

Now the usual Ray is back.

Foxie is the chosen one, selected and elevated from amongst the rest of us to receive Bert's wisdom. Today it's his management tips.

I'm zipping up my motorbike coat to go spend my lunch hour in town, when I overhear Bert amplified by the bare walls of the tractor garage, 'You hev gotta keep authority see, gotta be ready to punch em if you as to.'

Let me get out of this madhouse.

In town, I bank some of my wages, and queue in the bakers for a meat pie where I nod to the friendly lecturer, Ben.

When I go outside, he's waiting for me, 'I'm having a pint would you like to join me?' he asks.

The Fox and Pheasant is quiet. 'The juke box is broken and waiting for new records' the landlord says. I think he tells us this because of our youth.

'It's good to get out of college.' says Ben, taking a bite from his Cornish pasty.

'Yes, agreed.'

Ben takes a thoughtful sip from his pint, 'The gardeners are quite a lively bunch aren't they? I was talking to Colin and Ray yesterday, they were working outside the warden's flat. I bet your boss is a stickler.'

'You could say that. But it's a job. Let's just say I'm glad to get away at 5 o'clock each day.'

'He's a bit fierce isn't he?'

I laugh. 'Have you had much to do with him?'

'Well I play for the staff cricket team, so we have to speak occasionally. And there's been the new trees…'

'Oh, hang on Ben, I thought you taught English?'

'No that's *Ronald* Jones. He's been here since year dot but he's a good guy, played cricket for Leicestershire in his youth, and campaigned to get the students a TV room.'

'Oh *you're* Jonesy from Biology.

'You speak as if I have some kind of a reputation?'

'Oh sorry. Bert has mentioned you that's all.'

'An honourable mention in despatches I trust?'

I laugh and screw up the meat pie bag tightly, and poke it into the large ash tray that is still full of cig butts and ash from last night. 'Tell me about the new trees.'

'Oh that's been quite a project. Initiated by Ronald Jones originally, he was keen to find a way to commemorate the 25th anniversary of the college. I took it over later, once it was decided that 25 new trees around the campus would be appropriate. Trees being such a feature of the place.'

'Colin said they must have cost a lot.'

'Yes. That's why the principal agreed the college would plant the trees but not fund their purchase. We asked for contributions from staff and students. I made a list of species that were not represented in the grounds. And people donated money, tree by tree.'

'I'm surprised people were so interested in trees?'

'Oh yes, people and trees go back a long way. Trees are important to us. After the ice age ten thousand years ago Britain became covered in trees. Our ancestors would have crossed the land bridge from Europe into a forest. We lived with them, learned about them, ate from them, built houses, tools, weapons and ships with them. Our oak ships defeated the Spanish armada, explored continents, won the battle of Trafalgar. Yet now, most of the school children we take around the grounds know only one tree, the horse chestnut. It's a great loss of knowledge. Do you know your trees?'

'I suppose I learnt some on walks as a kid, and more on the farm I worked on. Can I ask you about the name labels on those trees? Why are they so long?'

'Well, what time is it?'

'Oh, yes, it's time to head back.'

'Very briefly, they're Latin names in two parts. Genus and species. For example, all oaks are the genus *Quercus*, they all have acorns, but otherwise vary widely. There are hundreds of different species, the one on the planting list is *Quercus rubra*.'

'So it's like the school register, surnames first?'

'Yes exactly. We should continue this conversation.'

'Yes, I'd like to. Do you know the Fettlers Arms? I'm in there every Thursday from seven.'

'What's the beer?'

'John Smith's.'

'Excellent. See you next Thursday.'

I ride back just in time to join the last five minutes of the lunchtime meditation session in St Custard's, my head buzzing with new knowledge.

BETWEEN FOXIE'S EARS

The cabin has been repainted over the weekend. It takes a few minutes to adjust. It's now a fresh pale blue. But apart from the cleanness and smell of fresh paint, nothing has really changed except that Foxie's orange hair looks more vivid than usual. Today he seems fairly calm, and not doing his fruit machine impersonation, at the moment. He is cleaning his ears with a matchstick.

Colin smiles, 'Are you picking a lock, Foxie?'

'What?' Says Foxie, unsure what he means.

Ray lifts his heavy eyelids, 'He'll be disappointed.'

'Why? What do you mean?' says Foxie, in a lighter version of his threatening-someone-in-the-pub tone.

'There's nowt to pinch in theer.' Ray smiles widely.

'Ey watch it,' says Foxie, before noting Colin's laughter, and joining in. He flicks the match into the coke pile.

It's a relief to me that he's in an accommodating mood, as I'm sent to work with him, loading barrows of topsoil onto the trailer to fill a new rockery, on this squinty bright spring morning.

Foxie, busy with work, is a different person. He is normally like one of those reactive metals kept in oil. A dangerous mix of a slow wit and a menacing volatility. But the threat of violence is switched off if there are plants to be tended, or demanding hard graft to be done.

He has really taken me by surprise today though. We are in the wood. He is leaning against the tailgate of the trailer which is half loaded with topsoil that we've just dug out from a slipped bank. Behind him is a blackthorn tree with a few white flowers hanging on, amidst the vicious spiny branches. He is pretending to have a shower, and is massaging his broad head and shaking it as he sings. *'I'm gonna wash that man right out of my hair, I'm gonna wash that man right out of my hair, and send him on his way.'*

I look around to check no one is about.

'Tell you anuvver good un, *Calamity Jane,* that's a good un, *Oh the deadwood stage…whip crack away, whip crack away, whip crack away. Oklahoma!* that's full o' good un's an all, *I'm just a girl who cain't say no, I'm in a terrible fix, I always say come on let's go, when I should say nix.*'

All I said was, 'What do you like do when you're not at work?'

Once he'd mentioned drinking, 'Teckleys ale', and having sex, although he didn't call it that, he jumped straight to this, 'A love musicals me.'

Touchingly open as he is I don't like to mention that all his examples are for female voices.

'So *why* do you like musicals, Foxie?'

'A just like a good show an some good songs. Mi muvver used to tek mi when a was lickle. Now a tek her.'

I ask something I've wondered for a long time. 'You know how you always prune the rose pergola, and do the glasshouse stuff, and the tractor work, did Bert teach you how to do all those things?'

'No. I learnt tractor drivin where I used to riggle taties on the farm. Then on the buildins I drove JCB and drots, which is similar to tractors but with more levers an that. Then a worked on a nursery before I came ere, they taught me cuttins and prunin.'

'So Bert didn't show you anything, either?'

'No. Tell you another one I like, *There once was a maaahn who loved a womaaaain.*'

'You've a strong voice. Ever thought of singing in a musical yourself?'

'No, but av thought of askin if I can help with the musical society.'

'Hey that sounds a good idea.' I say thinking, listen to me, *I just turned in to Hank at Fenley doing his counselling role.*

Just for a moment, Foxie looks unusually deep and thoughtful. And then says, 'Right come on. Let's get some more barrowin done.'

Kennedy Foxton is strong. I know from when he seized me that time, it was like being held in a machine. Something to be avoided. But if you want to imagine being like Foxie, this is what you must do; push a barrowful of damp earth for 50 yards.

As you do it, feel the weight tearing at your fingers and wrists, feel your chest tighten and your arms being stretched all the way down from your shoulder joint. Feel, as you struggle to resist gravity; the muscles contract, the heart pump, and bones creak, doing the work they were meant to do. And feel good. Feel the sense of achievement as the barrow hits the smooth planks at speed and the momentum takes you up onto the trailer. You arrive at the destination and make the last great effort, to tip that heavy load over the wheel.

Imagine doing this all day, every day, and becoming as fearless and as solid as an ancient oak tree. That's Foxie. Just the guy you'd want stood beside you on an ancient battlefield, pike and sword in hand.

'Tell you one me muvver likes, *West Side Story, I feel pretty, oh so pretty, I feel pretty and witty and bright...'*

Soon with the trailer well loaded, I sit on an upturned wheelbarrow on the soil pile, and Foxie drives us over to the rockery site, where the others are waiting. Foxie cannot hide it when he's happy. He's singing, *'Nothing could be finer than to be in Carolina in the mor-hor-hor-ning.'*

He's oblivious of the innuendo, and in far too good a mood to pay attention even when Ray points it out to him. What a surprising morning. Maybe Foxie *doesn't* thinks about sex all the time. And could his volatility actually be checked by a light syrup, instead of oil?

LIBRARY FORTRESS

I'm reading *As I Walked Out One Midsummer Morning* by Laurie Lee in the cabin, although in my head I'm in the parched land of Andalucia bathing in sunshine and poetry. But I can't concentrate as Bert is getting heated about something. My eyes stay in the book, but I listen to him growling.

'Fuckn librarian. "But he's a visiting professor," she say.

I says, I don't care if he is the fuckn King of Siam hisself, no one parks on my fuckn graarss.

"Charmin" she say.

Oh I got choicer than that I say. An I don't fuckn report to you I say, you hev better talk to Principal if you as a complaint or you don't like my language.'

Sometimes I imagine I'm dreaming all this. It can't be real. It's so dull and repetitious that I sometimes feel slightly superior and then, I'm disgusted with myself. Who do I think I am? I've only got three 'O' levels so I'm no genius, but even I can see that something needs to change. Bert is taking out his watch. Stand by for instructions.

'Reight. Library is avin a big delivery o furniture. Cos it's 'eavy and they give rain, we bin asked to help the handymen,' says Bert, sounding as if he is reading from a declaration.

'That's not…' begins Ray, our self-appointed shop steward.

Bert cuts him off sharply, as if the interruption was expected, 'Don't worry they ain't makin a habit of it, I told em fuckn straight.'

The declaration continues, 'When you sees the removal lorry, leave your job, an walk up there. You gotta unload the furniture, and put it jus inside library doors, only. You can't carry nothun in the library. Garden staff ain't allowed in there.'

The job is done in half an hour, It's as close as I get to being inside the college library, and then it's break time *again*.

Oh I don't know. I suppose this work isn't bad, just undemanding. The pay's better than farming, the hours shorter and predictable. I can't afford a flat, but living with my parents is cheap. I've friends to drink with, and can walk in Derbyshire any weekend. I'd like to be learning more, and I mean to find out about going to college.

If only job exchanges were possible. Although I'd need to find someone who thinks that sulphurous flatulence is hilarious, that base conversations are great, and for whom learning is abhorrent. They would love it here.

Meanwhile I'm stuck here, I'm 18 years old, and this job can't be forever. Someone in the pub has got tickets to see the Rolling Stones in London this summer, Ben Jones says he'll drive us. I can hardly believe it! London, the Stones; they're *still* touring *ten years* after their big hits.

'Back to the library,' explains Colin, after a briefing from Bert, 'looks like we are manning the barricades.' We take our wheelbarrows up to the side of the library.

As part of Bert's 'graarss' protection measures we are installing obstacles that are sure to scratch through the underseal if not damage the brake pipes of any cars attempting to park on the grass by the library. The limestone blocks will function like reverse ha-has, standing prominent and ugly, at the grass edges.

Colin and I are struggling to move a rock, I flag Foxie down as he passes in the tractor.

'Can you help us, Foxie. We're trying to slide this big one down a plank into that hole, I think it needs the three of us.'

Foxie jumps down from the cab, pull up his trousers, paws his crotch, and inflates his barrel chest so that his neck seems to disappear. 'Stand back.'

He bends low and picks the rock up in an embrace, turns and drops it into just the right place. He straightens, and steps back into the cab, waving away our thanks and admiration of his strength. We shout after him making a fuss as if he is a big red dog that just retrieved a stick.

Colin turns to me, smiles cheekily, and slowly nods approval. 'Well done lad. You're learning now.'

As we work I tell Colin about Laurie Lee, who is only a bit older than him, of his adventures in Spain and his artist's eye.

'There comes a time, when we've all got to walk out of the village,' says Colin, 'but first we have to find a better place to go.'

LARKING WITH TIM

Tim and I are mowing, and as usual we meet up half way, by the leafy Japanese cherries between the library and a hostel block.

As I arrive, he looks up guiltily. Tim has accidentally broken a low branch and he trims it off neatly with his pen-knife, folding the sappy twig to fit his pocket, so it can be thrown away discretely. He spits on his finger and picks up a crumb of soil to rub into the wound. It's a dirty practice we both saw Bert do once. It makes the fresh wound more difficult to see in the short term. It may be the only thing Bert's taught us so far.

'It's hot,' I say, miming sweeping sweat from my forehead.

'Am puckered,' says Tim exhaling dramatically.

The grass growth has slowed now the summer is well underway. It's always like this Tim says, grows like mad in spring then eases off. So we ease off a little too. It takes less time than it used to complete the mowing circuit. But we make it last, as it's good work for us that we like.

Although Tim is about my age, he always seems much older just as the Young Farmers always seemed to be at Fenley. He likes to joke and lark around a bit when we're together. I think he misses the times we worked in the woods in winter, where we could talk without anyone seeing us idling. We always got the job of logging trees that fell across the paths using a big two-handled saw. One of those jobs where we can work as hard as we like just for the joy of it, in between the chatting and larking of course. One of his favourite games is to talk to me as if I am new and deaf, and he is giving me instruction on anything to hand. My part is to simply play stupid. A role which comes quite naturally to me. Today it's about the mower.

'Watch my lips. Now, dis 'ere is d 'park plug, see?'

I look naively around and say, 'Dut a minute,' and fiddle with an imaginary hearing aid, as he sometimes does, before saying, 'Tarry on.'

'Don't touch d' park plug when d'engine is unnin.'

'Why not?' I ask with my best Stan Laurel face.

Tim mimes an electric shock by lifting his hair up and staggering backwards. 'Like Poxie' he adds.

He has done this sketch before, with the others nearby, the laughter drew Foxie over. The requested repeat performance ending with another 'playful' duffing up by Foxie. Tim's need to play, and have a bit of fun, being greater than anything, even his fear of Foxie.

BEECH TALK

It's one of those dry windless days. Still enough to hear lorries changing gear on distant bends, a fuzz of music from student rooms, and the soil crumbs crunching under our feet, as Colin and I move around the dahlia border tying up plants.

Left over right, right over left, trim the ends for a neat job.

As we work, the sky is darkening from seagull grey to pigeon wing, but before it gets to jackdaw breast, we're on the move just as the first light spots of rain fall.

As Colin puts it, 'We need to stand back and have a look at this border: from under that beech tree over there. Just walk nice and steady, so as not to draw attention.'

A mature beech tree can take a lot of raindrop hits before water starts to drip down to the soil, making it a good place to shelter from a shower of rain. We're standing on bare ground because the shade is so dense, not much can grow under here. An old beech may have a few wiry grasses and bluebells under its great leafy sunshade, but that's about it. And these small plants can only survive by making all their growth before the tree's canopy leafs up in spring, and mops up all the light. I say bare ground but, between the sloping buttresses of tree roots, there are several years' worth of accumulated beechmast insulating us from the cold clay.

So here we are, Colin and I, in the pre-rain quiet waiting for this July rain shower to pass. Here comes one of his regular sayings, I almost say it for him, Colin looks heavenwards 'Right. Chuck it down, David.'

He fingers tobacco from a creased, Old Holborn, plastic pouch into his pipe bowl and snaps his lighter. He sucks the flame down into the shreds and tamps down the glow with his hardened brown thumb. 'You see people have preconceptions. Look at this bark. It's not brown at all.' We look up at the bulging column of tree trunk covered in elephant skin. 'What colour is that, Graham?'

'It's grey except where the green algae grows on it. And there's a duck-egg blue-green to the lichen patches.'

'That's right. I'd paint that like the grey of new steel, and notice how smooth it is. Not all bark is rough.'

'Look at these branches, Colin.'

'I know. Ask most people to draw a tree and they have branches going up into the air. These older branches are falling downwards about 20 feet. You just have to look.'

This may not sound like an Oxbridge tutorial or anything very erudite to you, but it is like oxygen to me in this stifling time. An intelligent conversation. A whole new way to experience the visual world. After a few minutes of observations and colour theory the rain begins to pattle in the leaves above us. 'Take a look at beech bark when it's properly wet and it's totally different. Like copper. Of course then you need to think about reflections.'

'Reflections?'

'Watch that wall carefully as that delivery van passes it. See that? What colour was it?'

'Well the wall is a dirty cream colour but I think I saw a flash of pink. Or did I imagine that?'

'No that was a reflection from the red van. The colour of an object changes according to the colours around it.'

The rain is heavy now. The grass beyond the canopy is soaked and puddles are forming, but under the beech we're snug and engrossed in our conversation.

Sometimes I get drawing lessons from Colin, 'You don't need pencil and paper to draw. If you get a minute just stand and look. Look carefully.' Sometimes there are discussions of great artists, Stubbs, Hals, Carravaggio. 'Did you read that book I lent you? What did you think?'

'Well it was hard reading, with its big words and complicated ideas, but I liked Carravaggio. It surprised me about the problems he had, all because he painted the disciples as looking like common workmen. Although he was a bit of a rough lad himself, wasn't he?'

'He was. But some of the book isn't right. Always remember with art books, that *nobody* really knows what the artist thought or was trying to do. Sometimes these authors and critics get on my nerves.'

Twenty minutes alone with Colin under a tree and the day changes. The ties binding us to the mundane work, and Bert's crushing routine, are loosened. In our minds at least, we can escape. The air begins to smell sweeter.

OLIVIA 1

'It's so hot. Should we have our lunch here?' We sit on a sun-warmed rock in broken shade, and lower our feet into the cold water. It's so peaceful and quiet, with only the quiet chuckling of the young river Wye as background music. Derbyshire is always lovely whatever the weather, but being here on a blazing early August weekend with a female companion is something new.

'What was that white flash?' Olivia says.

'Oh you'll like this, keep your eye on that same area of water.' A bird soon emerges and Olivia is amazed. 'It's a dipper. They search out grubs and larvae that live under stones.'

Olivia sees me as her guide to all things rural. On the walk from Castleton I've been asked about cows, geology and tree identification. She's from Berkshire near London. She works in an office, and as people do who work in offices, she tells me nothing about it. 'I'd really like to hear more about that,' I say, but she just asks me another question or talks dreamily of a vague future since her divorce. I'm not complaining though, she is easy to talk with, and it's so nice to have company on a weekend walk.

She's quite a different kind of girl to the ones I know at home. I realised this when we were talking together on the minibus that was taking our group, and a trailer of kayaks, back to the youth hostel from South Wales.

I always wanted to go canoeing again after trying it at school, so I booked myself a YHA adventure holiday and drove down to Hereford on my motorbike last month.

When this articulate woman in her mid-twenties wearing a cheesecloth shirt and bangles took my hand, and slid it between the denim curves of her thighs, I knew this was going to be a very different relationships to the ones I've had with the local girls. Olivia was clearly not tied to a hair washing schedule, or considering taking holy vows. How I ever walked away from the minibus into the Youth Hostel I'll never know. But thankfully my Levi jeans were strong and the copper rivets and the brass zip held.

We've been writing to each other for a while before she arranged to drive up and see me at home. I think her life in the south is very different. Like with Susannah's sister, who came up here in June to 'see Yorkshire,' I have to do a bit of translating sometimes. South Yorkshire, like China, being somewhere not yet opened up for tourism.

We walk out into the heat again, although not for long, as Olivia is keen for us to stop for pints of shandy and ice creams. Treats I normally don't allow myself. We eventually arrive in one of the little dry valleys, as the sun is dropping and the grass has that bright green look of greengrocer's matting, in the declining orangey light. It's time to set up camp and get the Vesta curry cooking.

I love my little tent and all the gear. It seems like my true home, wherever I put it. Olivia is very interested and asks me about all the equipment and how I manage to carry it all. She says she loves the stove's windshield made from an old umbrella, and the tiny tin opener. I explain how it all packs away one thing inside another, it's just a matter of being organised. Nomadic people must do this all the time. She thinks she'd like to meet some real nomads, or maybe work on a farm abroad for a while.

The next morning she is pleasantly surprised at the menu; muesli, bacon, eggs and beans. She doesn't even complain at the prospect of washing from an improvised plastic bowl with only half a pint of water each. 'Where's the toilet?' she asks.

I pass her the flattened half toilet roll, 'Choose a tree or a rock, and take this knife to cut a triangle of turf out.' We strike camp, and she likes that we leave not a trace that we were ever here at all.

She talks all the way back to Castleton where we left her car. 'You know that I'm searching for something Graham, some kind of direction for my life?'

'I know,' I say nodding sympathetically. As if this is a conversation I have with all my girlfriends.

COURTING TIPS

Tim is not someone who needs pity, but I feel sorry for him this Monday morning. At least my own private life is private.

'Ey Tim, A SAY TIM,' shouts Ray across the cabin, 'they go through a lot o straw at that ridin stables don't they?'

'What tu mean?'

'I've seen your pick-up parked theer, ont last three Setday mornins, nah.'

Tim turns the colour of one of his favourite beetroot sandwiches.

But Ray shows no mercy, 'Ar yer courtin or what?'

'It don o dor bidnedd.'

'Eh?'

Tim taps his nose to indicate, 'keep your nose out.'

'A bet thas found a lass who likes to ride eh, Tim?'

Ray crackles. Ray's laugh is like a baby's frothy gurgle, fed through a bank of Marshall amps at a rock gig. As it goes on it electronically distorts, to become the scrunchy sound of cellophane being torn off a pack of 3-ply fillis, before it fades into the crackly static of a radio between stations.

Foxie makes a rare moderating intervention, 'Leave him alone. Well done, Tim.'

But Ray cannot resist the opportunity to give advice. 'Tim, a say TIM, al help yer. You've got to know ow to 'andle women, ow to talk to em. That's all they want see, some nice talk. Sooth em. A said to our lass yesterday,

Yer makin a fuss ovver nowt love. Dry yer eyes nah. It's nowt really, soothin see, Tim. A said, *it's nowt burra Satday neet chip pan fire, we've ad em befoor.*'

Ray leans forward from his seat. As if to lend an air of confidentiality. A nice touch, had there not been another four of us in the room. 'I give er me hankie then I said, *I ave been listenin. I remembered to purra wet towel on it this time.* Notice Tim ow am showing theer, ow av been payin attention to er. Then you comfort em; *we'll soon stick some new ceiling tiles up an yer kitchen'll be as reyt as rain.*'

'If they fret, like she did, what you do is to pat their arm and gently reason wi'em. *A know love, burrit's Sunday. We nivver miss avin Yorkshire puddins on a Sunday.*'

'Then look her in the eyes, an speakin softly, as if she were one o yer chickens Tim, show er ow much faith y'ave in er. *Come on nah love, you'll get this cleaned up in no time. And you waint half cheer up when them puddin's go in.*'

Tim, wide eyed, picks up an eye roll and a wink from Colin.

'Just one moor thing. Don't forget to finish off bi tellin er you love her. Don't be embarrassed abart it, Tim. A said, *O' course a love yer. That's why, I'm poppin down t'club so as not to gerr in yer way. I'll see y'in an hour love.*'

Tim is wise enough not to respond to Ray, except with a non-committal, all purpose, 'Oh aye.'

More cabin dust descends. Most eyes fall to the floor.

More of those month-long minutes pass, and then Bert says, 'Coor, that A1 mooterway wus busy Sunday.'

'Been off somewhere, Bert?' says Colin.

'Yurss. I took the missus for a run in the car and hed lunch at the mooterway services. You can say what you fuckn like, but they does a good sausage and chips there.'

Bert comes from the generation that goes out for a recreational drive on Sundays, to admire the new motorways. In fact it may have only been so busy, because there were hundreds of motorists like him, driving to the next exit and turning round to come home again for a trip out.

'You c'd do worse than take your gal up there, Tim. All very clean. They gi you serviettes. They got nice plastic menus, with pictures, an everythin.'

OLIVIA 2

Olivia and I keep writing to each other. In late August I go with some of my pub pals, along with over twenty thousand others, to the Reading Rock Festival where I meet her. I spend only a single night in the tent, it is much more comfortable at her flat. When she loses a contact lens in the main arena, we spend half an hour looking for it in the grass assisted by the dozen people around us, I learn two things. One, this is a good way to meet people, and two, that it isn't love that makes her blink a lot.

The bands are great; Yes, with the first laser light show I've ever seen - green beams that go on for miles, Supertramp, Wishbone Ash, Dr Feelgood, Thin Lizzy, Hawkwind, and the Heavy Metal Kids.

While the Reading Festival is fairly well organised, it lacks the shambly peace and love vibe of the older festivals like Glastonbury and the Isle of Wight. So straight after Reading finishes, we drive over to the Watchfield Free Festival, where Hawkwind perform again, this time on the back of a flatbed lorry, no 1970's rock festival being worthy of the name unless Hawkwind perform *Silver Machine*.

We follow our day at Watchfield with an overnight stay with Hank and Susannah in Oxford. Olivia loves the whole festival thing, and she is really pleased to meet two *gen-u-ine* laid back ex-hippies.

Olivia had been seeking more than just her contact lens and rudiments of natural history. She doesn't know what she wants, but she knows it has to be different to what has gone before. That's not a bad starting point for a change.

We pack our things and I remember the toothbrushes from the bathroom. I stare at them as I pee; resting together on a little shelf by some dried flowers, hers with stepped bristles in three colours, mine a Boots economy. On the way back for my train there are hints that our little affair has run its course, Olivia having made some decision about going to Israel to work on a kibbutz, and find herself.

It has been good. We have criss-crossed the country, south and north, and both experienced something of life outside of our usual sphere. It gives me confidence, that I can have more satisfying relationships with women and that I am right to hold out for something better. A couple of amicable letters later, it is over.

Later I learn that Olivia asked Susannah if she could come over and talk. Susannah telling her, 'You can come visit anytime *with Graham,* but understand that we are primarily his friends, and you would not be welcome without him.'

So Olivia has gone, but Hank and Suze are still in my life, and on my side.

OCTOBER CHRYSANTHS

Colin and Ray are walking ahead of me towards the small unheated greenhouse in the nursery garden where the potted late *Chrysanthemums* grow. As Ray reaches the doorway he swings his hand dramatically, before flopping it pathetically to his side. 'Chh, look at this Col. Brokken stems, even some flowers hangin dahn.'

'Bird damage?'

'Fuckin bomb damage more like. Its weer Bert has been collectin flowers for t'Manor Hall. There's one here been pulled clean out o't ground.' Ray looks disheartened as only he can, his jowls almost touching the top of his bib and brace overall. 'All that work eh? Rootin cuttins, potting em on, hardening em off, planting art, stakin, disbudding, t'ave their flower stems snapped off by im. This ones torn dahn to t'base. Bound to get diseased nah, so that's one stool less for next year.'

Ray is as cross as I've seen him. 'Get thi pipe lit up, Col. We'll ave a minute before we start tidying this lot up.'

We stand looking around in the thin autumn sunshine, while Colin lights up and I offer Ray a polo mint.

Colin says, 'Did you see that wildlife documentary last night?'

Ray doesn't respond, so I answer, 'No Colin, I was out. Was it good?'

'Marvellous. They showed us a seal colony on a rocky island, all peaceful. Hundreds of glossy mother seals laid there with youngsters suckling. Suddenly, this great bull seal came out of the sea to go to his place, and he's hauling himself over the rocks and the seals as well, crushing anything that didn't get out of his way in time.'

Colin stops to press a finger into his pipe bowl, and snap his lighter again, sucking the flame down into the tobacco. 'I said to Elaine, that's our head gardener right there.'

I push the barrow of chicken netting and posts on up the garden and unload it while Colin and Ray tidy up the chrysanths. Our main job of the day is putting rabbit fencing down the wooded side of the nursery garden. A trench nine inch deep is needed to prevent rabbits tunnelling under to eat the Sweet Williams and Bert's vegetables.

Later, Ray wanders off to find staples, leaving Colin and I to put the last posts in.

'So you reckon it is just digging holes and filling them back in again then, Colin?'

'That's about it, lad. Sometimes for fence posts, sometimes a plant, or a rock. We dig out, stick something in, then fill it again.'

'To think I'd been reading gardening books.'

'Oh it's not just gardening.'

'What?'

'It's pretty much life really. Out, in, out, in. Until *we're* planted in a hole ourselves, and that's it.'

CHRISTMAS 1975

It's an after-the-party Monday morning sort of winter sky. Like a dirty bowl full of greasy washing up water, grey suds of clouds hide a squashed lemon quarter of sun. Bearable because there is only half a week left to work now until Christmas. We walk about with barrows all morning tidying up anything we can. 'Buggering about,' Colin calls it.

Here's a rare sighting of the college joiner, Reg. He has a workshop two doors down from our cabin. He is the same vintage as Colin and Ray, a time served craftsman with a keen eye. He has the enviable job of working alone, coming and going as he pleases to his workshop of tools and timber. He occasionally joins us for five minutes in the cabin and has the measure of us all.

Ray and Colin are crossing the yard after a pre-lunch wash as Reg steps out of his workshop to stretch and straighten his back. He sees Ray carrying his jacket over his shoulder with one finger and patting the quiff of his freshly combed and parted hair. Colin is alongside; trilbied, pullovered as well as cardiganed, and dangling his unlit pipe. Their pace is slow and relaxed.

'Bloody hell, it's Danny Kaye and Bing Crosby,' says Reg, referencing the old 1950's film *White Christmas*.

Like Colin, Reg also rents out a corner of his mouth to a tobacco company and pulls on a pipe all day. He has that same tranquil air of a man at peace with the world, who savours his conversations. He especially likes to indulge in what Colin calls 'a bit of daft' now and again. He comes and goes all day with frames, shelves, his joiner's tool bag and timber creations.

'Ey you'll not get us singin,' says Ray.

Colin says, 'Nay. There's only Foxie here who's dreamin of a white Christmas. He gets overtime for grit spreadin.'

'What d'yer mean?' Shouts Foxie dimly from the cabin after hearing his name and laughter in close proximity. 'Ey that's a good film is that.'

I'm still feeling a bit vague because I just got back from three lovely days with Susannah, Hank and the children, in Oxford. Funny thing was, when I was there, I wondered if I had imagined Linklater College as it seemed so far away. Now it seems like Oxford was the dream.

Hank, looking back to his student days, said 'Oxford, is a beautiful place to fall in love.'

It made me think, what is this industrial hometown of mine being the perfect background for, in my life right now? Not, falling in love that's for sure. I'm thankful that I'm welcome to go back to Oxford anytime. Coming back home on the train for Christmas is a wonderful feeling.

Later, I'm in the Fettlers Arms having a drink with a bloke who works away. He's back home for Christmas, that lovely phrase again. I remember seeing him in his green uniform, getting the bus to the grammar, when I was coming back from my paper round. He's obviously a lot cleverer than me. He's in selling or advertising, or something like that.

He's telling me about his work's Christmas party. Or as he calls it, 'Way hey The Annual Shindig.' Apparently it must be spoken of from the corner of the mouth. Listen to what I'm missing.

'All the girls from the typing pool were there in low cut dresses, the deputy boss was asleep in a corner decorated with tinsel like a Christmas tree. Messenger boys were dragging on cigars and lots of booze was going down. People's inhibitions were being lowered, along with some clothes, especially in a cleaner's cupboard we called the *shag-booth*. Someone threw up over the office's rubber plant and there was bad behaviour all around. Well, it's only once a year, Christmas. It's for the kids really isn't it? Are you having another one?'

Later still. I've heard the story half a dozen times, as each new person joins us around the table. I'm past thinking it's impressive anymore. It's like the repeated tales at work, and I tune out just the same. John Lennon is playing on the juke box, and in a lull I hear, "another year over and what have you done?" It's as if he is speaking just to me. The words cut through the buzz of beery conversation and bonhomie and haunt me, like Dickens' spirits, all Christmas.

In 14 months at Linklater what have I learnt? Almost nothing. Maybe I am just floating along? But life is easy, and there have been lots of distractions; good music, the

Rolling Stones at Earls Court, canoeing, Olivia, and the Reading Festival too.

For the future I have walks to plan and I'm pretty free really. In the Fettlers, there's talk of more night club trips to Sheffield. I must try and look on the bright side; maybe love, and the girl of my dreams, are just around the corner.

TREE TRUTHS

The bar towel is over the John Smith's hand pump when Ben walks into the Fettlers. I have resorted to half a lager in the face of this sad situation.

'Sorry Ben, they're putting a new barrel on. *Normal service will be resumed shortly* as they say on the telly. Can I get you a lager?'

'That's alright, I'll wait.' He looks around at the pub which is looking very bare after the Christmas trimmings have been taken down. I indicate a table and we move across to it. 'New carpet?' says Ben.

'No it's the same one.'

The Fettlers' carpet is weird. No one *doesn't* notice it. Swirly patterns that, even when you're sober, can jump up at you like a soft dog. The degree of movement you perceive in it, relates to your level of intoxication. Very drunk people have been known to refuse to cross it, exiting via the tap room instead. But I don't mention any of this as I have something serious I want to ask Ben about.

As he takes off his coat and scarf I say, 'Haven't seen you for ages on your own. Before the lads arrive and work-talk is banned, tell me about those new trees at Linklater. I was down there today, most are still alive. Did you say they were paid for by donations?'

'Yes several were bought in memory of past students and staff. Did you hear about the students who died in a car crash?'

'No.'

Ben picks up a beer mat, and with his finger and thumb in the centre begins to turn it around by tapping each corner on the table edge. 'It was terrible. Gavin and Alice were in love, travelling home for the weekend. They were a bright and talented couple, the best kind of students, very idealistic and determined to change the world. Their parents paid for a tree each in tribute to them.'

'What a lovely thing to do.'

He looks up at me with a sad forced smile, 'They, like all the contributors, imagined that one day their trees would stand in a large magnificent space in the college. Just like the old beech, oak and lime do, around the main axes of the campus now.' He squeezes the beermat's sides until it bows.

'Oh God. They're barely in the college grounds at all. Have you seen them?'

Ben breaths a heavy sigh. 'Yes.' There's a long pause as if another death has occurred. 'I let them all down. I did all I could.' The beermat snaps into two. 'There were meetings, and I was appointed to liaise with the Head Gardener. Staff meetings discussed possible sites for planting, but Bert clearly resented the interference. "These is my grounds," he kept repeating.'

I recognise with embarrassment Bert's angry voice, summoned like an evil genie into my local's best room. 'Oh Ben, I'm so sorry. We didn't know any of this. We just planted them where he told us, hidden away at the back of the principal's house. They couldn't be further away from the main paths.'

'No it's OK, I understand. You had to do as you were told.'

'What a bastard.'

'Yes.'

And in that moment, the Ben I'd got to know disappeared. Replaced by this hunched and broken, tidied up hippie with his hair hanging forward over his face. 'Occasionally, you meet someone like him, someone that you cannot get through to. They will not compromise on their views, however small and ill-informed those views may be. You begin to think that education is futile.'

'You'd think he'd be pleased to get more trees in the grounds.'

'I was warned he is a difficult man. The advice to negotiate with him was fanciful, to say the least. Arbitration in Vietnam would've been easier. You know the outcome.'

'I can't argue with my head gardener.'

'It seems no one can. My card has been marked. The chance of us getting an ecological garden or even a nature trail in the grounds now is infinitesimally small. It is impossible to win an argument with that man.'

What have I done? Ben is always so cheery and bright. I wish I'd never asked about the trees now. I glimpse Chris and Dave through the window almost at the pub's porch.

But then Ben looks up into my face, as if to ensure all of my attention, and says so seriously, 'Note well, Graham. My advice to you is to avoid crossing him. He is spiteful and peevish and will destroy anyone he perceives to be a threat to his authority.'

I exhale, not realising I'd been holding my breath. 'Noted, Ben. Here come the lads, and the beers back on. I'm buying you a drink, it's the least I can do.'

ZANY ZELDA'S

Here we are four lads from the Fettlers Arms. We're overdressed like professional footballers, and being looked up and down by two gorillas, outside Wappy Zelda's on a goose pimply February night.

"Not smart enough," is a regular reason for refusing admission at Sheffield nightclubs. Of course that's smart in the sense of formal clothes. Now they *could* mean *not smart enough* in the intelligence sense, but why else would we be here? Queuing to have our gladrags gawped at by bouncers, and paying to listen to music that we could hear for free from a pub juke box, all while we stand to drink their overpriced beer. We must be stupid. Anyway, we're in now, let's not spoil it, this is meant to be a treat, and there are some attractions.

Down in the sweaty basement, where the air is sweetened with aftershave and cigarette smoke, dances a classy looking woman in a cream slinky dress. There is something especially appealing about this blonde, she's a summer day's dream, like a cornet on the beach. Maybe it's the perfect ice cream cone taper of those legs that makes me think that. She stands out from all the couples and groups because she is so attractive, and yet she is accompanied only by her handbag. Glittering ceiling lights float above her, just as she seems to float above the shining dance floor. Smooth looking men with blow dried hair, large-collared shirts and flares come and go, occasionally one flaps towards her and dances alongside before leaving her to her sublime solo moves.

Emboldened by the beer, I wonder if *she* is the woman I've been waiting for? Has *she* been holding out for *me*, the quiet guy in the checked suit and turquoise kipper tie, to gather his courage?

Two or three pints later and I'm thinking, *she is SO beautiful, go on, ask her*. I'm also thinking *stay right where you are*. My head can be like this. Staying would be easy enough on this flypaper carpet sticky from drink spills. But then the DJ has just put on Cockney Rebel and I know that this is the moment we've both been waiting for, when I will step into her life.

'Dave, mind my glass.'

I walk over elbows and knees bouncing, as much as my platform shoes will allow, to the jaunty beat. Steve Harley sings, 'Come up and see me make me smile...'

I bob alongside. She is a rainbow goddess in the changing disco lights. I shout above the record, 'Do you mind if I dance with you?'

I know I have made an impression, because she stops dancing. She sensuously lifts her hair away from her mouth with a single finger. She gives me an ambiguous short measure of a smile, but then with a clarity that cuts through the music like a fire alarm says, 'Fuck. Off.'

Before I feel the blush I turn, and to what seems now like mocking accompaniment, I dance my way back to my beer. But my bounce has gone and my elbows are merely twitching, as Steve sings, 'there's nothing left all gone and run away...'

Oh but she'd looked so perfect. I tell myself, *it's alright, it's just a silly game,* but really I wonder if I will ever get over her. Will I ever find love? Or even approach a woman again?

'Thanks, Dave.'

'How did you er...?'

'Oh, she's er, got a boyfriend. Is it about time to get the taxi home now?'

And now it's one in the morning. I'm cold in my thin suit, and my ears ring as my little brain adjusts to the mushroom coloured quiet of the taxi. The windows run with rain, and streetlights reflect in the blobs. There are glimpses of sparks, fire, and hot orange metal out there as we pass the steelworks of Tinsley and Templeborough, but here inside the taxi, sleepy heads sway, and nothing interesting happens. Like the whole evening. Like every night out with the boys.

It might be just the strange hour and the drink, but in my head, I have questions. What are we all doing here? We all have work in a few hours; pit-workshop, bank counter, railway goods yard and for me, the numbing monotony of the cabin and more weeding.

Why do the people who have least money, spend it trying to ape the rich? I've blown a week's wage on a single night out. Until now I've gone along with it all. But here's a thought, what if the *goddess* was real and she was right? What if, I *should* fuck off? Quit all this beer, club, and clothes crap. What if, she meant leave this place, where no one enjoys their work, where people "pass the time," and where ignorance is prized? Perhaps it is time to leave home again, *for good*? There must be another way to live.

'Bessemer Street?' says our Asian taxi driver.

'Yes,' I say, nudging the others awake.

'You leave here?'

'Definitely. Yes. I will.'

'Oh sorry, *live* here? Yes we do. Just drop us here by the Fettlers Arms.'

BORDER OF SANITY

Gardening can be a violent business; all morning we've worked through the herbaceous border's dead winter stems with our heads down, stabbing, slashing and piercing like a medieval army demolishing the brown pikestaffs and lances of golden rod, phlox and Michaelmas daisies. The soil surface mirroring what is going on underneath as centipedes hunt and kill, worms fumble about and springtails leap in soil voids that must seem their entire world.

We're all back in the cabin changing out of our boots for lunch, when I spot something in the dirt. I give it only a second of attention before I cross the yard to wash my hands.

I return to the boarded asylum, in time to hear Ray's voice rise at the end of one of his allotment tales. 'He said, "Useful little cabbages anyroad." You what, Percy? I said, thems not fuckin cabbages, they're me sprouts.'

Bert turns the pages of his *Daily Express* and begins some rant, about foreign cars or foreign something. I sit down, my eyes searching for the puzzle in the dirt. Got it. I'm staring at a lozenge shaped piece of soil, freshly dropped from a Wellington boot tread. Intriguingly it has a highlight to it, visible only to me against the dusty underchair darkness at Ray's feet. A sparkle that shouts, 'I don't belong here.' It's a welcome diversion from the pre-lunch imprisonment, which today is some kind of hatred interlude for Bert. His bitterness knows no end.

He despises so much, that there must be nothing left in the world for him to love.

We return from lunch, and the soil lozenge has moved. It's nearer to me now. Bert returns to steward our stupidity. I can see a pink pearly surface showing in the soil. A feminine presence among the boredom, belching and beer boasting.

Bert, fresh from the BBC news bulletin, complains about talk of car seat belts being made compulsory, and what a waste of time working with the 'Frenchies' on Concorde is, and time slowly passes. I pretend to read my book about someone's interesting life, but I'm thinking about my own. Especially my farm year. Will that be the highlight of my life when I look back? As National service was for my father. A special period of feeling alive before drudgery took over?

Bert looks at his watch, and puts it back in his pocket. I *hate* the way he does that. How did he get nominated as the timekeeper of my life? The piece of soil now looks like a coffin, with a waxy corpse face. A miniature of my body in a box. Bert looks at his watch again.

Everyday this man takes an hour glass with my own ground dust in it and upturns it on the bench. I am forced to sit looking at it. My precious life is trickling through the glassy isthmus.

This is an injustice, this exposure to Bert's hatred and his satanic timewasting. Like blood and guts on the slaughterhouse floor, it is so normal, yet it is madness.

Under the rule of this tyrant, I have no choice but to accept that, this is the way things are done here.

Bert looks out and says nothing as the sudden sound of airbrakes is followed by chatter, talking and laughter as lively students back from a visit disembark from their coach. The sound is so bright and vibrant but quickly dissipates.

No one is going to come along to help me. There is no hero, or magic beans, no beautiful heroine for whom my love will be enough, no secret door to find, no revelatory dream, or time warp to slip through, nothing is going to suddenly happen to transform all this unfairness. All I have is my feeling of things not being right, an inkling that life could be better than this. The vaguest notion that my life might improve if I could make the right decision. Henry on the farm used to say, *If things don't change they'll stay as they are*. Which of all these voices, within and around me, are right? Can any of them be trusted?

Bert's watch reappears, 'Reight,' he says, 'git back to the border.'

On the way out I stoop and pick up the lozenge, crushing it between my fingers to release its treasure as I cross the stable yard. It's a drilled bead from a bracelet or necklace, beautifully incongruous and with its own story to tell.

This is not the entire world it's just Linklater I remind myself, as I roll the bead in my fingers and wonder if one day, I will have a story to tell, one about an escape from the border of insanity.

TEA MOMENT

I need a break. I've used up some of my leave to have a week walking in Derbyshire alone. There are days of frost and snow and rain but I continue from one Youth hostel to the next along gritstone, through black peat, and down limestone dales. I chat to hostel wardens and other hostellers, when I am not the sole visitor. I settle into it and find I rather enjoy my own company. It is so rare to be alone for so long in my South Yorkshire life that the realisation comes as a pleasant surprise.

I have been enjoying learning on my day release course, so much so that I have applied to a bigger college to do a full time course in horticulture. I haven't told anyone else about this yet. It's all very uncertain. I'm beginning to think that my current job doesn't have to be forever.

I record all my walks in an old school exercise book. It's never as interesting as the walking books l read, but I enjoy doing it and looking back on the routes. On this walk I've started to write about my thoughts and reflect on the day's hike. It's almost becoming a diary, a place where I can be myself, try to sort things out, or sometimes just dump stuff to get it out of my head.

In contrast to life in a crowded terrace house, and my workplace, my walk is full of peace. I'm seeing for the first time that I'm not quite the same as other people. I don't have to be part of these weird places if I don't want to be. I am strong and capable. I've organised this trip and booked the accommodation and navigated my own way along new routes. I've been lost a couple of times, and got myself back again, and it's been no big deal.

In Bakewell, close to the end of my walk, I do something new. I read a menu in a window twice, and walk up and down a few times. It is pouring with rain. This is a very hard thing for me to do, and I know it probably doesn't sound much to you. I've checked my money carefully, I can afford a pot of tea and a piece of cake. And then, bold as brass I do it. I enter a tea shop.

On an Oxford visit once, Hank and Susannah took me for a cream tea in the village of Woodstock after we'd walked around the park of Blenheim Palace, it felt special, and rather nice. In Bakewell though, I have to fight something in myself to enter. Do garden labourers use tea shops? I sit here in my boots, baggy jumper and peat stained denims, my coat dripping onto the floor, while my rucksack is tucked under the table like a dog. I look around at the antique curios, and try to use the tiny cake fork to slow down the cake's disappearance in to my hungry mouth. There are other better dressed customers, chatting and clearly feeling much more entitled to be here than I am.

I am grateful that no one stares at this long-haired 19 year old trying to mark an important occasion as unselfconsciously as possible. The occasion being the start of a new relationship with himself, represented by crossing a teashop threshold alone. How invisible the personal milestones of others can be.

MOWER BREAKDOWN

Bert speaks in a different way to everyone else.

I arrive in the stable yard this morning to find Colin's Escort pulled up outside the cabin door. The boot is open, and Bert stands admiring Colin's newest oil painting which is laid on a blanket. It's another meticulous one commissioned by a regular customer. This one is a hunting scene with horses, red coats and a pack of hounds gathered outside a pub. Colin has told me privately that he doesn't need to work here for the money. He does it for the exercise and to get out amongst people. Each of his paintings make ten times his weekly gardener's pay.

As I approach I overhear Bert say in his gentlest voice, 'They hed oil painting right the way up the stairs they did, Orses, flahrs, an ladies. An genulmen, in tall hats. Bootiful that is Colun. Bootiful.'

Perhaps my mistake was letting Bert know I wanted to learn about gardening. He blocks me every time, 'You don't need to know that,' he says, as if am some kind of threat to him.

What he has taught me is that if someone takes against you, it's only a matter of time before you begin to dislike them. He's been no different with me since I started going on day release to the Tech, for a City and Guilds course. I hoped he might see I was keen and help me, but he disapproves of, "fuckn cawludge courses". Although as we work for the local authority he can't stop me going. No one at Linklater mentions the Tech, or asks me what I learn, but I did once say to Colin that the machinery lectures are very good, and I wonder if Foxie was within earshot. That would explain today's outburst.

In spring last year a new mower arrived, exclusively for Tim's use. I was given Tim's old one, while mine went up the ramp into the engineer's trailer for disposal.

'You better look after it,' said Bert to me, 'without no fuckn tinkerin.' I don't know what he thinks I might do to it, customise it by adding flower power stickers or something to fit into his long haired view of me?

And now a year later after a long slow walk, I push the heavy mower into the yard, and he immediately appears from the direction of the greenhouse. His jacket is off, and he's wearing that polo shirt the colour of week-old faded grass clippings. His flabby pale arms swing from side to side, as if trying to make himself move faster. His cheeks inflate and deflate. He looks angry.

'It's broken down, Bert. I think it might be a carburettor problem, it lost power, as if the engine was trying to run with the choke out.'

'You ain't bin messin with it av you?'

'No.'

'You better fuckin not 'ave.'

'I know from the motorbike that if the carburettor jets get…'

'You don't know fuckin nothing. Do you ear me?'

'Yes Bert, I hear you.'

'Git that blue roughcut out an finish off wi that.'

Bert goes off back to his greenhouse to tend his prejudices, and repot his long held opinions.

The maintenance of ignorance in your staff is greatly helped by never giving anything the correct name. I will later learn that a 'roughcut' is known by the rest of the world as a rotary mower. Just as I will also learn that the Dahlia variety names here are virtually fiction, having been so frequently rewritten over the years. Kenba (Kenora) and Hammer Bridge (Hamari Bride), never appearing in any catalogue. On a rare day when you think you are learning something at Linklater, you're probably learning it wrongly.

As Foxie likes to say to us all periodically, 'You know noffink.' And he at least, is correct.

FIONA

For the last four years I have walked alongside the privet hedges to Fiona's house many times to beg her company. My feet crunching and squeaking on fresh snow, or springing hopefully on summer's evenings, half running with my collar turned up in the rain, or my feet cracking the frozen slush over bright sweet wrappers trapped beneath. Left into Stone Lane, and right into Polly Avenue under the orange streetlights. My shadow leaping forward as I walk away from one lamp post, and then shrinking back to nothing as I approached the next one. My uncertain courage doing exactly the same. Often, regardless of season, she is suffering from a cold and scented with her regular perfume Vick's Menthol Chest Rub. Would I ever be able to release this beautiful deer from behind the hedges of her parents' home?

I have tempted her out now and again, and mostly we just walk. Occasionally we ended up in my parents' front room where I tried various records on the stereogram to gauge her interest. I run through the quieter end of my LP collection seeking her approval; John Lennon's *Imagine,* Pink Floyd's *Dark Side of the Moon,* Joni Mitchell, James Taylor and Diana Ross. 'It's alright,' her highest praise. On current affairs she is very diplomatic. Vietnam, Lennon's peace vigil, Ulster or the moon landings, the answer is the same, 'I don't know.'

We went to a party once. A blurry photo was taken and for some reason, inspired perhaps by the alleged sexual freedoms of the time that we read about in our parents' Daily Mirrors and glimpsed on album covers, she momentarily placed her hand upon my knee. This our greatest ever intimacy, flashbulb lit, and recorded for all time by a Kodak Instamatic, gives an entirely wrong impression of how we were together.

What great weight oppressed her, I will never know. If only we could have really spoken. I tried to share my limited knowledge of the world with her; music, people, plans and life outside of our hometown. But it was all without avail. Despite my efforts to blow on those dark embers, there was no evidence of fire. The wonder is, that I kept trying for so long.

But shyness can be an affliction. A constant rehearsal for not existing at all. My farm year had begun to alleviate mine and I thought that I could help her. Fiona's eyes that had such depth, had another quality too. I recognised something dark in there.

Even if I have this right, it's still not easy. When two shy unpractised communicators speak, the words that might begin a soul's thawing may not come out right, or may even be perceived as a threat to the familiar frozen state. I recall an interaction that may well have been our last:

I'm in the front room kneeling before her, picking up crumpled tissues that have spilled from her handbag in her search for a new pack of Kleenex. Her nose is cute with its usual rosy blush.

'I like your hair,' I say.

I think she might be impressed that I have noticed, 'Oh,' she says.

I'm curious about the style. 'What's it called?' I ask.

'Page boy.'

'S'nice.' I wish now I'd stopped right there, but I said, 'It reminds me of a mushroom.'

She momentarily stares, narrows her big eyes and drops her mouth into a small scowl.

Oops. I've obviously said the wrong thing. How can I make my intended compliment clear?

Then I heard my words just fall out by themselves, 'I really like *mushrooms*.' And it's just left like that. A conversation suspended.

'I'll, er, take you home shall I?'

I help her on with her coat, and we walk down the street and around the corner in the usual silence.

I pause in the sodium light and face her. 'Look Fiona, I do like your hair. And. I like you.' She is keen to keep walking, so I blurt out just for good measure, 'and I really like mushrooms.'

Unacknowledged, I imagine those words are still there. Hanging hesitantly in the air on Polly Avenue about the height of a privet hedge.

MY MUSIC

When you think about it, we get no choice about the era we live in. Yet lots of us attach ourselves to our contemporary music. It can seem like it's everything. The music of your time doesn't have to be all you hear though, with recorded music you can go back or sideways into other cultures. We had a lucky escape really, we could've been born into the time of Victorian parlour ballads.

Colin at work, was young when dance bands like Victor Silvester's and the Palm Court orchestra were around. He loved it and his parents didn't. Maybe that's all that matters for some people. I listened to a program on Radio 2 about the dance band days and it had some great tunes that really rock, or actually 'swing,' as they said then. Try listening to Benny Goodman's *Sing Sing Sing* and sitting still, it's impossible. The crooners, as some of those 1930's singers like Bert Ambrose with their new microphones were called, were reviled as degenerate by some critics. Perhaps every generation thinks they're defiant.

Of course it was all short back and sides back then, hardly The Who or Deep Purple, but there was something of the same spirit of rebellion. Our next door neighbour lent me some of his LP's, he loves The Shadows and Buddy Holly from the early 1960's. Maybe all music is connected when you look into it. In the *New Musical Express* interviews, everyone has influences, and I like to check some of them out by borrowing LP's from the library. Classical, blues, early rock and roll, jazz it's all there.

I sit and listen to James Taylor sing about country roads, finding friends, Carolina and lonely cowboys and there is some connection I feel that I can't understand. John Lennon, despite all his money, connects too. To see a band live though is the best. Ian Gillan's screeching wail in Deep Purple's *Child in Time* is wonderful, as is Wilko Johnson in Dr Feelgood when he does that robotic strut across the stage chopping out tight little guitar sounds to cheers from the audience, while the lead singer blows his dark soul through a harmonica.

Back on records; Diana Ross and Joni Mitchell melt my heart and make my mind drift faraway, Bessie Smith thrills me with a special sadness, I bask in Californian sunshine when I put the Beach Boys on, Bonzo Dog make me laugh, ska and reggae make me dance and Dvorak's *New World Symphony* flushes me with an optimism I have no right to feel.

Tubular Bells has a strange allure, I read in the NME that it has a lot of dissonance which repeats and repeats so that it actually becomes pleasant to the ear. Like work then, where I hear the same old stories and do the same old jobs, and yet it has stopped being annoying and become strangely comfortable. Isn't that odd?

You have to discriminate though. Some song lyrics are poetry, some are trash. Some of the rock stars are egomaniacs with a warped view of the world and especially of women. I think some of these people never had sisters or female friends at school to teach them important things. That's rock n' roll for you though, where *outrageous* is thought to equal *entertaining*.

You have to think for yourself, there's bad stuff around like drugs, which people who take them will try to tell you are wonderful. It's a bit like on TV, where all females are under 25 and mostly semi-naked all the time. I think Julie Birchill in the NME says it's *wish fulfilment* on the part of the male writers and TV programme makers. Just as you have to be open to music, you have to be aware of other ways of seeing things too, and decide for yourself.

I'm a bit cynical about the pop charts and try to seek out what seems genuine, but all the time we're subject to the forces of peer pressure and advertising. The moment we think we are so aware and so independent from these forces, might be the moment when some other thing has us under its influence.

Here's something else I like about music; you can feel part of something bigger, meeting kindred spirits who love it too, without necessarily understanding why. In the pub we go on about great tunes and live guitar solos that make your ears hurt, and sensational catchy riffs, along with other ideas we pick up from the NME. But I'm not a musician, just a fan. It's all magic to me.

Julie and Nigel enjoy pop music, and although I'm less keen on Mud and Abba, we all want to see Roy Wood's Wizzard play Sheffield City Hall. His song, 'Flowers in the Rain' was the first music played on Radio 1.

I love rock concerts at the Sheffield City Hall. The atmosphere beforehand is great. I love being among all these young people and great clothes; big flares and waistcoats, short dresses, denim and lots and lots of hair. From the circle you have a great view of the band's gear and can look down at the audience milling about and chatting. Sometimes a call goes up from a fan looking for a friend, and others join in calling the name. Occasionally someone calls out a silly name, and that gets repeated too, eventually the whole auditorium rings to rising shouts of 'Wally.' I love that the crowd are having fun like this, even before the support band is announced.

So here I am at the Wizzard gig. I spot Julie with Nigel looking for their seats in the stalls, and I stand up to call her name loudly and enthusiastically and wave both hands in the customary way, 'JULIE.' I assume it will be the first of many names called. But there's a problem. Maybe the Wizzard audience are not regular concert goers. Because, despite waiting for a man to come on stage in a multi-coloured wig, wearing make-up that looked like two emaciated sooty sparrows have smacked into his face, no one, absolutely no one, is going to join in with any kind of silliness. No other names are called. Instead, the buzz of conversation completely stops and what seems like hundreds of pairs of eyes turn to look at me standing up in the circle, as if to say, *What a Weirdo*. I sit down and wish I could afford a souvenir programme to stick my head in until the silence passes.

Importantly music takes me away from here. It is my education as well as my entertainment. It plays between my ears even when I'm miles away from my records. I need music to feel alive. In the case of 'Time' by Pink Floyd, on a borrowed album of *Dark Side of the Moon,* it can also bear prescient messages I don't consciously hear, about time passing while we hang on in quiet desperation waiting for someone to show us the way.

MAY 1976

It's the first week of May in the nursery garden. The morning is cool and bright with a misty, pale pink glow. It is time to plant the *Chrysanthemums* we grew from cuttings.

It is official; on all the Chrysanth tasks, Ray is in charge. Despite this, he still works hard to impress us with the legitimacy of this rare example of Bert delegating his authority.

Ray must imagine he is astounding us with his tales of first prize cards won for flower showing. His winning ways, with both incurved and reflex petalled blooms, so subtle and artful that even Frankie Bannetson, 'The National Chrysanth Judge from London' was impressed.

Frankie allegedly said, 'By eck Ray, thy vases tek me breath away, how does tha do it year after year eh?'

Ray's head swings to either side as if checking that no one is overhearing, 'A said, a can tell you Frankie, an a teld im. It's in the shapin, yer've got to tweezer art any petals not perfectly in line. A said, y'see Frankie, a 'Peter Rowe' bloom for showin should be almost a perfect fuckin globe. Like a young woman's breast, you should be able to cup it…'

Colin does one of his timely interruptions, 'Ray, how far apart d'you want the rows for these Shoesmith ones?'

The supports are rusted angle iron posts, with cross wires of old telephone and electric cables in cracked and broken sheathing. They are installed with precision, and some brute force.

Colin carefully places the tip of a piece of angle iron and calls out, 'Here Tim. A SAY, TIM. Get your hands out of your pockets, it'll still be there don't worry. A SAID, IT'LL STILL BE THERE. And bring that big hammer over here. Right. When I nod my head you hit it.' Colin's words, as always for Tim, loaded with a gentle mischief.

Later, Tim brings up another barrowful of young potted plants from the cold frame. Colin is kneeling and sorting them according to variety and then passing them to me for laying out in position. Colin looks up at Tim and rolls his eyes.

'What up?' says Tim.

Colin takes out his pipe in order to mouth clearly to Tim, 'Ey, has that barrow still got a wheel on it?'

Tim pointedly looks under the barrow, 'Yep' he says, smiling.

Colin stabs his pipe with mock aggression and says, 'Then why have you got me stretching two yards to lift these plants out?' And then with fake rage, 'Fetch the puckin thing over here.'

While Tim and Ray are at the cold frame it is quiet enough for a robin to fly in and pick up tiny worms from close by. I push in my trowel to watch it and say to Colin, 'We were talking about observing last week.'

'We were, yes.'

'I walked by some pylons at the weekend. They made a noise in the rain, like a fizzing sound. They made me think of Bert.'

'Were they low voltage?'

'Ha. No, it was the shape. They were those, asymmetric pylons, one shoulder up and one down just like him.'

'Don't waste your time thinking about him.'

I stack the discarded empty pots. 'You're right, I know, I shouldn't. But why does he dislike me so much, Colin?'

'I don't know lad. But you'll not change him.' Colin taps his pipe bowl against an angle iron post. 'Some folk are just like that. You can't put it where it ain't.'

Later, in a rare quiet moment of peace before lunchtime, I'm alone, scrubbing the soil stains from my hands with a nailbrush dabbed in Vim, under the single cold water tap. I'm stood in the partitioned off toilet in the corner of the stable building, looking at how the old vertical wooden boards have projecting metal strips between them, and I'm thinking how beasts even more powerful than Foxie have kicked against these reinforced walls in vain.

Sticking a paper towel to each hand, I pan around the familiar storage area; worn floor bricks that dish down in the doorway, rusting mangers in each corner, the machinery stall; working machines at the front, broken ones at the back, compost stall; bags of John Innes, chemicals and fertiliser, a heap of straw for protecting the *Dahlia* tubers in winter and the stink of hoof and horn, and bonemeal. Another stall has all the hand tools; ancient wooden hay rakes, spring rakes, Dutch hoes, forks, spades, shovels and a long humping row of wheelbarrows that, like the people, seem to have been here for ever. Actually it's hard to imagine anyone here ever leaving, or being anywhere else. But what about me?

Colin's voice calling from outside brings me back, 'Come on lad, 'urry up, or the greedy buggers will have eaten the lot.'

We begin to walk as he asks, 'What you been doing?'

'Just giving the old stables a coat of *look-at*.'

He laughs at this use of one of his own expressions as we speed up the road, trying to catch the crocodile of gardeners in front. Colin's decorating jobs were given, in turn; a coat of look-at, a coat of wash-down, a coat of sandpaper, and then a coat of dust-brush before painting commenced.

I like to hear Colin talk about his trade; working in gold leaf - 'Don't tear it lad, I'll take it by the piece', sign writing - 'every letter needs its own space', old techniques like wood-graining doors, scumbling and the work he did in London and abroad for the Beverley sisters 'Joy, Teddie and Babs, lovely people'.

We catch up the gang just as they're entering the back door of the dining hall, 'Funny thing is, about my decorating days,' says Colin, 'one day you just suddenly realise, it's all behind you.'

HOPE IS ALWAYS THERE

Sunday Bill and I are on a circular walk, from the village of Hope in Derbyshire, on a windy Saturday. We've had lunch on top of Win Hill and enough fresh air to lift us well away from daily cares.

'Everybody needs heroes,' says Bill. His is the boss at work. She gets her staff on the shifts they prefer, supervises Bill's learning programme and chats to him every day. Wow.

'My hero? Are rock stars allowed? No, then perhaps Blind Bill at work. Delivering the papers around the village and college. He has a way of reflecting back people's kindness. I can almost forgive him for bring Bert his *Daily Express*.'

Sunday Bill is a refreshing breeze himself. We play our game of articulacy where anything goes. Our secret sport of walking and talking, that's freeing me from shackles I don't even know I have.

'Hey what about this Bill. I had a conversation with a man in a pub who said I shouldn't go to full-time college.'

'Why?'

'Because it's, "selling out on the working man. You are one of us," he said. What does that mean, Bill?'

'Is he implying that you'll leave the working class in going there?'

'It doesn't seem like that to me. I mean I've put in three years of farm and garden labouring, and it's getting me nowhere. I don't even earn enough to take a girl out and pay for her. Is this how it has to be?' I stop walking to finger out a small stone from the top of my boot. 'Anyway it's not really about the money, I just want to be me.'

'Where does he work?'

'The NCB. He's probably on three times my pay. There *has* to be more to life than this.'

'It's your life.'

'I know.'

More fresh air passes through us.

'Hang on a minute, Graham, I need to stop and put another layer on.'

I laugh. 'You know I was thinking the same.'

We fiddle with rucksack buckles and cords, holding our coats between our knees while we pull on woollies.

'This probably sounds daft Bill, but I think it's hard for me to make decisions. As if the idea of changing something actually hurts. It's risky, it might all go wrong. Full-time college could be like school, I might not be up to it.'

Bill zips up his coat slowly, as if it gives him great satisfaction, 'Decisions *are* hard. But sometimes, you'll never know unless you try something out.'

'An old schoolmate used to say our town was a shit hole. But after coming back to it, I think it's not the place that's wrong, but some of the people in it. Ones who say in their different ways, "no to everything," or, "stay here and stay as you are." Some of us need a bit more help than that.'

'Who was this bloke in the pub anyway?'

'Good point. He was an old mate of my dad's with a beer belly straining his shirt buttons. He said my dad was a great craftsman. The best builder he ever worked with.'

'But your dad supports you going to college?'

'I'd never ask him for career advice, since he stopped me going to the grammar school. Maybe that would have been betraying my 'class' too? Why not just stop children getting an education at all?'

Our chats are broken by long silences. We pause along the broad footpath every few minutes to enjoy the views up the Hope and Edale valleys in one direction and across the Ladybower Reservoir in the other.

Is *enjoy* the right word? It is real and unreal in the same moment. How are we, and all of this, here? Among an infinite variety of greens and browns, vast distances and closeness. Surrounded by these science fiction plants; cotton grass and heavy sphagnum, bright bilberries and heather with stems like miniature Christmas trees. There are huge rocks plonked down, and otherworldly bleats from invisible sheep.

We look out across cubic miles of air, clinging mist in the hollows and a broad 'U' shaped valley cut by a glacier an incomprehensible amount of time ago. So many things we cannot know that it's a view to make you uneasy and fill you with awe. A view that grips you and says, *this is your reckoning, do you realise just how small and insignificant you and your troubles are?* You could sit entranced by it until the toothless chill of hypothermia bites you to a drowsy death, or keep it all at bay by talking, or focussing on your blisters, or the next Mars Bar. Or, you can do the decent thing, accept this transfixion, and solemnly vow to come back again. All this on a Saturday afternoon while just over there, behind a few hills, is Sheffield and shops and the life that you used to have before you stopped time itself to look at this view. Which, yes, I am enjoying.

'And just think,' says Bill, 'over there, beyond the tower blocks and the cooling towers, they'll be uncovering the pumps in the Fettlers Arms in four and a half hours.'

A ridge walk and a lunch stop later, we're dropping down off the fells and thinking about home.

'Going back to your choice of hero or heroine, Bill. Your boss sounds very good.'

'Isn't yours like that?'

'Mine? Can someone *enjoy* despising things? I think he does; women, foreigners, students, anything he doesn't understand, and that is a lot.'

'I don't know anyone like that.'

'The worst thing is that it gets to you eventually. The other month Tim and I were raking twigs blown down from nests at the top of this outcrop, all the while being mocked by the caw-cawing of rooks from above us. Tim is really observant, and he pointed out a male bullfinch. I said, Just look at that colour.'

Tim said, "E's just ad a respray." We both had a laugh about that.

Then I spotted our boss. 'That old bird could do with a respray too,' I said.

Tim replied, "No, it wants scrapping, failed MOT."

'It's funny how you see things differently from a new angle. I'd looked down from the edge of the outcrop to see our boss, Bert, in his greasy felt cap standing in the longer grass where we'd left the daffodils to grow, their yellowing leaves were strewn about like roman numerals. From up there, he looked small and ridiculous. The irregular shape of the daff patch looked like a scrotum, and his stooping form a wilted phallus with a shadow behind. As if he was the gnomon on a novelty bad-taste sundial!

He is our boss and yet Tim and I laughed at him. And I know that sounds horrible, but it felt really good, as if we were acknowledging the truth. I don't want to hate him. But no one has any respect for him. He's the opposite of your boss.'

'Maybe he's done you a favour though.'

'I don't think he is capable of that.'

'He is leading you to a solution.'

'How?'

'You realise now, that you really want to learn about plants and gardening.'

'Yes.'

'Well if he was like Adam the Gardener, or Arthur Billet, some decent old bloke sharing all his garden wisdom with you, what would you do then?'

'I suppose I'd just carry on working there, learning more. But it's not like that at all, Bill.'

'Exactly. So what will you do?'

'Oh I see. Well, I need to leave if I want to learn, get a place at college to study horticulture.'

'See? A solution, thanks to Mr Bert.'

'Oh yes, but, it's not that easy.'

'Is that a *Yes But*?'

We laugh together. On our last walk Bill told me about a book he read called *Games People Play*, about something called Transactional Analysis. One of the games was 'Yes but...' which some people say whenever a solution is offered to them. I wish I knew more people who read psychology books like Bill.

FIONA CONNECTION

It's a buoyant May morning and I'm out with Colin and Ray trimming lawn edges. We're on the long windy path that bumps down the steps, past the brash crescent of bedding under the outcrop, by the lipstick tints of the Old Manor rose beds, and in and out of the spotty shade of trees all the way to the dining room.

We're using the tool which Ray says ought to be kept under lock and key. The lawns used to run up to the path's flush kerb stones. This made an edge that only required the curved blade of the half-moon tool to be slid down it once a year to keep it neat. But Bert decrees that the grass edge must be cut back, and an inch of turf removed every year. This results in the lawns shrinking. They develop gutters around them like bowling greens, which then need to be hoed regularly, and at the first hint of summer drought the grass edge will brown rapidly. Education isn't all books and algebra is it? Sometimes it's just using your eyes, listening to reason, and then figuring it out for yourself. Wish I could look into the future, and reason out what I should do as easily though.

We soon fall into a way of working as you do; the older men edging up one each side of the path and me following along collecting the trimmings and tidying. They chat amicably, and slowly disappear around the curves while I follow on with a wheelbarrow, brush, shovel and my own thoughts for company. One of the pleasures of manual work is that your head is free, when you occasionally get the quiet to enjoy it. There is always something to think about.

I'm thinking of Fiona, and questioning what keeps taking me back to her. She is the girl with eyes the colour of mature mushroom gills, and the timid spirit of a silverfish on the morning hearth, that vanishes in the presence of light. I recall the sweetness and the pain of our last failed evening together. I know that it's time to give up with her. After last summer's relationship with Olivia, I have seen how it can be, how communication can be so natural. Even so, my mind replays the walk to and from Fiona's house. I see her downcast eyes, and then the light of her smile leak out, when I happen on the right thing to say. Just what is it all about?

My shovel scritches on the tarmac as I brush and shovel, brush and shovel, breaking off to hand weed a seedling, or chop out the odd dandelion clinging to the kerb joints. I clear both sides of the path two yards at a time, it's the only way to feel I'm making progress. As I sweep, and the debris diminishes, there's always that last bit you can't get on the shovel. Colin always says, 'Kick it abart till you lose it, lad,' something he was told as an apprentice.

My mind is elsewhere, kicking about memories that I can't get on the shovel and don't want to lose. It is walking back by the privet down Polly Avenue, following the vapour trail of camphor and menthol that has arisen from the forbidden territory of Fiona's chest. Then it hits me. A weird connection. The memory of that piquant smell springs a word loose in my head, *creosote*.

Why? Who knows how our minds work? I don't. There's nothing bashful or modest about creosote. Is it the dark brown colour, the colour of her hair? Allotment holders swear by creosote as a cure all for everything; poultry lice, carrot fly to common colds, they buy it from the boatyard. It couldn't cure shyness, surely? My nose is full of the imagined smell, but my mind's eye is seeing the great brown bow of a barge, drawn up on the rollers under the boatyard roof, by the canal. Is there some kind of chemical link between Vic's Vapour Rub and timber preservative? Has my mind cracked from the monotony of manual work, am I going mad?

I'll keep mulling it over anyway. Think. Fiona. I see her eyelids, like those patisserie shop canopies in the French text books at school, shading the sweetness. Then a song, 'It May be Winter Outside (But in My Heart It's Spring)' Perhaps we danced to that song in a fug of menthol once, but that's not it though. The walk to her house, and back, keeps returning, the hope and the disappointment. Out and back, the smell, the walk, there and back. Suddenly I'm on the canal towpath to Pete Seacroft's house five years ago. Something is the same. There's an olfactory connection to something deeper. The creosote smell of the canal. The menacing slop-slop of rainbow water against the steel edges. The walk that scared me for all those years as a kid, before I taught myself to swim. But something else there, something important, is the same. Fiona. Canal towpath. No, I never walked down the towpath with her.

I pause to feed the wheelbarrow an unbroken long piece of turf before wheeling it onto the grass, to allow two chatting students through. My eyes are on the path as they pass.

Got it. It's that *feeling*. How I felt on that walk to Pete's, is how I feel with Fiona. I think it's perhaps what she feels too. My shyness and her shyness combined, make for an overwhelming amount of it. It's *fear*. I was frightened by the canal, and she is frightened. Yes. That's it. Is this what shyness is? The downcast eyes from years of avoiding something? The look that I related to at some basic level. The fear of things happening? Is that what I am slowly overcoming in my life, reticence and fear? And is this why I am still here at Linklater?

Well dear sweet Fiona, I can't help you anymore. Truth is, I can barely help myself. But I'm going to try.

I'm so engrossed in my thoughts, that I barely notice that I'm catching up Colin and Ray, they're stood chatting. It's time to come back to earth.

'Tha'll know her, Col. Rita. Rita Chapel. From Bigley.'

Colin shakes his head, 'Was she related to Bill Chappell the butcher in Bleawell?'

'Noww. Chapel worn't her real name.'

'Why did they call her that then?'

'She had nipples like chapel hat pegs.'

Colin nods barely noticeably. With a look of relief on his face he turns to me. 'Now Graham, look what you've been missing.'

BERT'S HOLIDAY

Friday 5.00pm. This is unusual, Bert, as big and intimidating as ever, stands in the doorframe as I get up to leave. The cabin darkens with its main source of light blocked. Then, as if he has rehearsed it, he begins to wag his finger at me, even before he speaks, 'Do as zactly as I writ on there.' He points to his sheet of holiday instructions lying on the bench where Ray oiled some edging shears yesterday. The paper is already soaking up drops of pale yellow Three-in-One. Then he points back at my face, 'And *nothun* fuckn else.' He hasn't said this to anyone else.

'Ok Bert' I say gravely.

Nearly two weeks later, I'm pushing a stiff brush along the hot tarmac alone, and thinking about Bert coming back. The man who believes the only way to learn about gardening is to do it. But he is also the man who says things like, 'Them blacks in Rhodesia is trouble, all foreigners is the same.'

Bert is a brutal fool who insist on obedience. And maybe, I'm too good at being obedient. The fact is, he is wrong about almost everything. It's hard to believe that he and Ben Jones live in the same world never mind work for the same college. I'm finishing the Friday sweep up alone, as Colin and Ray have gone to water the greenhouse and nursery. They have to water three times a day in this heat. Foxie and Tim are off today.

Can it be wrong to learn from a book? Because it is according to Bert. Surely it's only learning from someone else's experience after all. I pull the barrow into the shade of the ha-ha next to the old leaf mould pile, out of the hot sunshine to think about this. I hear again in my head Bert's voice saying, 'Do as zactly as I writ on there, and *nothun* fuckn else.' There's no understanding him, look how he dislikes Ben Jones. But then Bert seems to loathe me in the same way. He wields his power like a big stick demanding obedience, just as others have; parents, and my farm boss who couldn't bring himself to speak to me. With Bert, it's shouting, reprimands and distrust.

My head is hot, but my feet are cooling in the moisture held by the dead leaves, as I look out at the shimmering heat. When I had the interview at the horticultural college, I went to look in the library and spoke to the librarian. She smiled at me from behind a pile of books and said, 'We're here to help you to learn.' I don't know why recalling that now makes me feel funny inside; sort of shivery, relieved and emotional, as if an ambulance just pulled up at the scene of an accident. Is it the notion of anyone trying to help me? I refocus on the trees overhanging the ha-ha, enjoying their kindly cool greenness. I tip out the road dust from the wheelbarrow. I know what I will do.

I push the curly leaf litter to one side of the leaf mould pile, and shovel the chocolatey shreds of humus until the wheelbarrow is fully loaded, carefully re-covering the denuded mound with dead leaves. I leave my tools against the wall, and take a deep breath before pushing the barrow out into the bright light. I wheel it the long way around the back of the library, where there's less chance of being seen, and up the hill all the way to the rear door of Biology. Where I tap on the glass.

I'm scorching from the heat and the tension in the air. I'm a desperado on the run, a criminal delivering stolen goods. I'm guilty as hell. I could hang for this. Bert would certainly kill me. Then I feel it, an icy touch down my spine followed by another on my side. It's only sweat, but it feels like something much worse; the cold chill of betrayal, or a devil's finger of delight at my disobedience.

A technician in shirt and tie, under an open white lab coat, unlocks the door and I ask to see Mr Jones. He looks me up and down as I stand there in my big boots, shorts and T-shirt and smiles weakly at the wheelbarrow, before walking away to get him. My heart feels as big, and as red, and as blue, as the poster on the laboratory wall. My chest is pounding and fluttering with the drum solo going on inside, and sweat drips from my forehead down my nose onto the bone dry paving flag at my feet, from where I watch it evaporate as the flag is so hot. *Where is Ben? Come on. Someone might see me. This feels like the most dangerous thing I've ever done in my life.*

Ben appears smiling, but he doesn't speak. He point along the lab's side and opens a French window further along. I move a stone to the threshold with my boot and wheel the barrow over it, my eyes are slow to adjust to the low light level indoors, I follow Ben through the cool laboratory and outside again to a quadrangle. I put down the barrow and sigh with relief because I can see that Bert has no access to this place.

'Welcome to the inner sanctum, Graham.'

'Where do you want this, Ben? Best baccer, Ray calls it.'

Ben grins, 'It looks perfect. Can you tip it here? We'll use it to mulch our acid border.'

He explains to me how all the local native plants grow on limestone but acid loving plants, like the ones I see out on the moors, need a different soil. He gets around this by using containers or raised beds further away from the groundwater and by adding lots of peat and humus to them.

'We water this bed only with rainwater, which is naturally slightly acid. That's why limestone is gradually weathered away by rain.'

'Yes, like the limestone pavement at Malham.'

'You know about that?'

'Clints and grikes. I did Geology 'O' level, although I failed the exam.'

I can't imagine Ben failing anything, he knows so much. He shows me some acid soil plants like *Potentilla palustris*, growing in a bucket with dark red flowers, for a native plant it's very beautiful. All the plants have neat labels on them, and he explains how *palustris* tells you it's a species from a marshy place. There's loads more about names and habitats, but soon my brain is bursting because he tells me more about plants in 10 minutes than I learned from Bert in 2 years.

'So species fit in specific habitats?' I ask.

'Some do yes. But some are cosmopolitan, they can move or thrive in a variety of habitats.'

I can't believe it sometimes with Ben. One minute he can be chatting with Ray or Foxie, or the lads in the Fettlers Arms enjoying what they say and being so attentive, so at home with them. And then he can talk like this with me about almost anything and be so inspiring.

'Talking of habitats, I'd better get back to the cabin for afternoon break, where I belong.'

'No, Graham.'

'Sorry?'

'You're not a plant rooted to one place. Animals belong where they choose. You have crossed the rubicon now.'

'With a barrow of leafmould?'

'Indeed.'

I pick up the warm tubes of the wheelbarrow handles and turn it to go, 'Look Ben, you must not *ever* tell Bert that I was here, or that I brought you leaf mould.'

Ben picks up a hosepipe end and move to the wall tap, 'Don't worry, if Bert ever asks about the missing leaf mould I'll say I took it. It will be our secret. Let's rinse out the barrow, remove the traces of evidence.'

'Don't say that. It sounds like a crime has been committed.'

Ben walks with me back through the cool lab, and I pause on the threshold, 'Before I return to Bert's territory, can I just ask you one more thing?'

'Of course.'

I move onto the parched grass and snatch something sticking up. 'What's this called?'

'It's a flowering culm of perennial ryegrass, *Lolium perenne*.'

'Huh, you know, he never gives anything the right name. Bert calls them long ends.'

Ben doesn't answer, but raises both eyebrows and inclines his head slightly. I know exactly what he's saying.

I walk back via the ha-ha to collect the shovel and brush. It's as if I've rewound a tape to an earlier point where I paused in the shade. I dust the barrow's insides with road sweeping and return for break time. Everything is the same, but everything is different. I'm on a different planet that has everything I know still in the same place. It's like the farm and Fenley again, routine work and the intelligence of Hank and Susannah, existing side by side each day.

My tea is already poured when I arrive in the cabin.

'You know, I think we might bugger off a few minutes early today,' says Ray.

BERT'S BACK

I pop back to the stables for some stakes for the *Dahlias*. Foxie is under the tractor draining the sump. Bert is leant on the door jamb doing that special voice he uses for speaking to Foxie, 'An that's where they found me and took me to the big house.'

'Can you pass me that rag, Bert,' says Foxie.

Bert pushes the raggy ball of an old cabin tea towel with his foot, 'I never even knew 'er name.'

I carry the stakes and more string back to Colin and tell him about my big decision. 'I've got my notice in my pocket, Colin.'

'You've decided then.'

'Yep.'

I use a fork to stir holes, so Colin can push in stakes for the bigger dahlias at the back of the border. He taps them home with a spade as I hold each stake while gently bending the gaudy flowers aside.

'You'd better tell Lurch first. Hang back in the yard and tell him on your own, just in case he pops.'

'I'll be mowing after break, so I'll tell him before lunch.'

'You've probably got to go to Admin anyway.'

INSIDE THE CITADEL

Mr Peregrine supervises non-teaching staff as remotely as possible from his study in the Old Manor. I change out of my work boots and wash my hands before I go to see him. One of the kindly faced bursars, who gives us our weekly pay, directs me through the unfamiliar building. Despite the fierce August heatwave outside, within the limestone walls of Old Manor the wood panelled and polished corridors are cool, as if the air is coming from a deeper more ancient and superior source.

He opens the door and looks at me in a slightly puzzled way. His lips are thin, straight and bluey-red, as if he's been eating cherries.

'Mr Peregrine, I've been told to bring you this.' I say.

He takes the envelope from me. 'Come in,' he says, turning immediately and walking stiffly back to his chair. He pinches the creases of his twill trousers and sits down to his desk, behind a heavy old black Bakelite telephone.

Looking like a man staying outwardly calm despite the severest provocation, he slits the envelope, opens out the letter, and drops it onto a large blotter. He doesn't invite me to sit, so I stand, looking down at my best writing on the neatly creased Basildon Bond paper. On his desk, my letter looks very small. The phone rings.

After a morning behind the lawnmower, the silence and the little noises in his office are striking. It is so like a sound studio in there that just before he speaks you can hear his tongue leave its seat in the bottom of his mouth with a damp click. The phone's ring is a trembly bell sound from a past era. He picks up the receiver and listens, pushing my letter away, as he looks up into a corner. Unsure where to look, I stare again at my letter, now lying with one half hinged off the blotter's surface. It reminds me of the dihedral angle in the aeroplane models of my childhood, the angle of the wings so critical for successful flight.

Ex-army Captain Ronald Peregrine is rumoured to have worked for MI5, before becoming General Manager of the college. Obviously an important man of sound judgement, 'Yes. No. No.' is all he says. With a flash of gold cufflink the receiver is replaced, making a soft 'tuh' sound.

He puts on his glasses to scan my letter, then takes them off again to speak. His eyes meet mine properly for the first time, and despite their warm brown colour, they have the contemptuous empty look of a bronze statue in a park. I think I am prepared for his response, routine indifference, or maybe polite congratulations.

But instead he narrows his eyes and his mouth, as if he's just bitten his lip, and in an incredulous tone he spits the words, 'People like you don't give up a job to go to college, don't just hand in their notice.'

He swallows and the words float overhead, as if trailed on a banner by a silent aeroplane. While he seems to be waiting for a sound technician's thumbs-up, the first four words tattoo themselves onto the inside of my skull and connect up to something hidden, deep inside me, that I won't understand for a very long time.

I don't give it much thought at the time. Perhaps decades of working in security, learning to suspect the worst of human nature every day, can do this to you. Or maybe he just doesn't like anyone with long hair?

Afterwards I will think of many possible responses, but in the moment I politely ask him to confirm my notice is satisfactory and is accepted. I leave to return to the company of sunshine, birdsong and for now, 'people like me.'

SUBSTITUTE

Bert says, 'This is Jack. He's replacin Graham.'

We all look up in disbelief, at a figure almost filling the door frame. Broad with stooped shoulders, his head turns around the cabin without his eyes actually looking anywhere.

'How do.' says Ray.

Colin nods.

Foxie stares.

'This ere's Ray, Kennedy, an Colun, that's Tim, and Graham.

Jack dips his head in a clumsy nod, and moves to sit down awkwardly on the only free chair, without speaking. He lets out a sigh of apparent satisfaction, as if instantly at ease with the cabin and his new situation.

First days somewhere new are difficult. Over his first morning I see everyone try to talk to him. But to this civility, as well as to Colin's witticisms and Ray's stories, Jack responds only, 'Whuh?'

Before lunch, in the cabin alone with him I say, 'If I can help Jack, just say.'

His eyelids are drooping as if I'm keeping him awake.

He pulls out a biscuit tin of sandwiches from a bag under his chair. 'You might not need all that,' I say, 'they give us a cooked lunch at 12.25 prompt, after the cleaners and the handymen have had theirs.'

He doesn't look at me, or speak, but stares off to one side, pulling the tin tightly in to himself as if I might try to steal it.

A few days later, as we wait for Tim and Colin with our hoes by the stable stores, he asks me, 'Oos that?'

'That's Foxie, talking to Bert. He does all the tractor work, his first name's Kennedy, but don't call him that, only Bert calls him that.'

He mutters 'Kennedy', and closes his mouth to blow air noisily. It's the biggest sound I've heard him make so far.

Tim emerges and walks across the yard to the cabin for secateurs.

Jack narrows his quartzy eyes and says, 'An what's up wi 'im?'

'Tim? Nothing. He's deaf that's all. He's a grand lad.'

'Huh,' Jack says, and kicks his boot's toecap against the blade of his hoe.

Towards the end of his second week, it is looking as if it may take some time for Jack to integrate, because he doesn't seem to like chatting. He also chain smokes cigarettes. An unpleasant habit, which strangely, despite being an avid collector of unpleasant habits, Foxie loathes. It also unsettles Ray, because he only gave up smoking about five years ago after a doctor's warning.

I can only think that Bert, after the disappointment that I have been, has chosen someone he reckons will definitely not aspire to leave for 'cawludge' after only two years, regardless of whether they will fit in.

NEW WHEELS

Frederick Alderson's book *England by Bicycle* has been a favourite bedtime read. He retired from work and cycled around, staying in bed and breakfasts. Obviously I can't afford to do that, although I love the idea.

Last winter, I used my restored bike to cycle 10 miles to the day release course at the technical college. With new wheels, repainted frame and new mudguards it looked a treat. Someone else thought so too; the person who hacksawed through its chain to release it from the bike shed. The police never found it.

Now the second bicycle I have been rebuilding is finished. It's my father's old one from the 1950's. It was very lightweight, but I've had to replace both wheels with steel ones as the alloy ones are so expensive. I've been doing little trips on it, as well as putting on my pumps to run a three mile route to improve my fitness. I've been cycling to work on it too.

I will take my motorbike back to the shop tomorrow, they've offered me a decent price, which will fund my trip and give me some money to start college in September. I have also bought a good lock and a heavyweight chain.

STORY FOR TIM

On my last day, my oversized replacement has a pre-arranged day off. I hope for his sake, that he's got a job interview for something better. Tim and I are sent to weed and deadhead the brightly coloured rectangles of summer bedding plants by the Manor, amid the scorched grass. The geranium and French marigold scents rise in the August heat, and I take a liberty in Jack's absence.

I have something to explain to Tim, which I do in the deliberately patronising and slow tone that *he* uses in his mock training sessions, and I exaggeratedly mime the actions.

'Tim. You - must - be - kind - to - my - replacement,' (I hunch my shoulders to make myself taller and make serious face). He's - been - made - by - Bert, (I inflate my cheeks, lift one shoulder, push hands together as if shaping clay). He's - been - made - very - big, (tall hand) - because - he - is - not - as - strong - as - me, (I shake my head while touching my bicep). Bert, (inflate cheeks, lift shoulder) - loves - him (I cradle a baby in arms and flutter my eyelids) - like - a - son - because - he - reminds - him - of - himself, (I inflate cheeks, lift a shoulder and do a silly smile in a hand mirror) - when - he - was - younger (hand palm down as if patting a child's head).'

I pause until Tim has uncurled himself, and tell him with my straightest face that he shouldn't be laughing, *this is not funny*. I continue, 'He's built Jack using parts from all the mowers you've broken, and some odds and ends from Reg the joiner (I hold a large pipe bowl), and old clothes from the handymen, (I open a stepladder and use it to change a lightbulb).'

'He's been working late at night on Jack.'

I mime Bert's long suffering wife in hair rollers, coyly lifting the hem of her nightie and saying sweetly, 'Come to bed, Bert.'

Bert replies (loud and intense), 'No I gotta finish this Marjorie, that fuckn Graham he go Friday.'

Ted carries on, measuring, sawing and welding. I wag a forefinger to warn Tim that, *'no wrestling* is allowed with Jack. This is because he is so weak, his arms and legs can easily just break off.' I tap my arm and making it swing from the elbow.

This might be a bit mean of me, but Jack has not yet endeared himself to anyone, except Bert, who has started to take him to one side to chat, as he does with Foxie.

On the way back to the cabin for morning break, I imitate the robot Jack from my story, but contrive to fall over. Remaining face down on the dry grass I keep my arms and legs moving like a clockwork toy. Tim enjoys all this so much that I have to repeat the entire story, with actions.

LEAVING LINKLATER

Bert is gazing out into the afternoon's fly buzzing brightness through the half open cabin door. As always, he is listening to our conversation, and nosing at who is walking past. He sways and suddenly leans. For the final time, he has choked the life out of the last half hour of my working day, and I solemnly witness the ritual checking of the pocket watch, where he draws it onto his fat fingers and drops his head down with a straining grunt. 'Reight' he eventually says, standing up, 'it's time.'

I'm next up, 'Bye Bert,' I say neutrally, 'and thanks for the reference.'

This is the barely legible handwritten note where he tells my prospective new employer that in my two years at Linklater College I have been sober and honest and that he would not hesitate to recommend me for a simular [sic] position elsewhere. Its tone seems positive, even though it appears to condemn me to a life of garden labouring.

Bert has something to say. In a declaiming voice of blessing he says, 'Well...A wish y'all the fuckn best but you won't learn nothin at cawludge.' Then resuming his more usual mutter he adds, 'It's no way to learn about fuckn gardenin that's what I say.'

'Bye,' I reply politely.

The others are much warmer, and as we walk down to the car park together in the hot sunshine, there are back slaps and good wishes all round.

Foxie shakes my hand surprisingly gently. Ray tells me I'm a good lad. I shake Tim's big hand and tell him he'll be alright. "Long ends" and plantain heads nod in agreement above the beige desert of the dying lawns.

Lastly I say, 'Well that's it. I've done it now, Colin.'

And he says, 'You'll be fine. Remember, try and live a bit every day, lad.'

'I will, Colin.'

He offers his hand and we shake. I'm having a problem letting go. I may have a bit of dust in my eye.

Just don't look back,' Colin says.

I know that like Blind Bill, I've been feeling my way to this exit for some time, but it's still strange to see their cars pull out and watch them all do that low key wave, just like any other day. And for a moment I just stand there knowing this this an important occasion, the end of something. Although like all endings, it is just a beginning of something else.

I roll homewards past the outcrop, down Low Meadow road between the trees and ponds, and pass the power station's cooling towers for the last time singing a line of Deep Purple over and over at the top of my voice, 'Maybe I'll find on the way down the line that I'm free, free to be me.'

EPILOGUE

Two weeks later I had cycled a long way from Yorkshire. I'd enjoyed the way regional accents merge into each other, village by village, all the way to West Sussex. At the day's end I felt as always, thoroughly at home in my tent, enjoying the September sunset and the way the low sun emphasized the South Downs' undulations. My socks hung on the guy line, my bicycle leant against a post behind which a hedge swayed as birds flew in to roost. I was in the middle of my travel adventure before college, and I felt more at ease than at any other time in my life up to then.

In a youth hostel the previous night, I'd looked up the psalm from the Linklater Manor doorway, but found another one I liked more; Psalm 129, 'They have greatly oppressed me from my youth…but they have not gained the victory over me.' It briefly made me think back to my old eyeless Teddy bear, witness to my early years, and sole survivor of my childhood things when I returned from the farm.

'Well we thought you'd gone for good,' mother said, in her offhand way.

And I thought also of Farmer Thurpley, who might well have stuck his head out of the Land Rover's window and said something similar; 'John-nie, I think the boy's gorn for good,' had Hank not intervened that Easter.

And my head gardener, Bert? I tried not to think about him at all.

Soon I'd visit Ben in Cornwall for a pint, and hear *his* native accent spoken. A few days later I'd see Hank and Susannah in Oxford, then Johnny at the farm. I'd see Julie in October as she'd asked me to be godfather to her first child. I had also arranged to go on holiday with Tim the following summer, if he wasn't married to 'Tarah' (Sarah) by then.

Apart from sending postcards to Colin and Ray, I didn't think of Linklater much at all. But a year later, I visited Colin at home, and between admiring his recent paintings - 'Peace' roses, and a lone horse drinking, I spoke of my struggle with the course. As I left he said, 'Stick it out. Do it for us lad. Do it for Ray and for me.' And I did.

Years passed. Occasionally still, I get a dreamy image of a large clay plant pot in the Linklater greenhouse. It has dark green and yellow-green algae on it with white salt stains. I can feel the terracotta, warm in my hand, but then as I turn it, I see that the pot is badly cracked and only held together by the tight piece of wire under its rim. It's fit only for breaking up and being used as crocks, but it still has an odd sort of beauty to it.

While I followed Colin's advice about not looking back for quite some time, decades later I learnt that while we can't change our past, we *can* try to understand it better. It is our history after all.

Meanwhile in the late summer of 1976 I felt so lucky to be liberated from work. I'd left a lot of people behind in the last few years. I was cycling through countryside every day, enjoying my own thoughts and a new kind of freedom. Cows mooed to and fro, grain was harvested, and old crops were ploughed under to feed the roots of new seedlings.

That windless night, before I cycled to catch the Isle of Wight ferry, was idyllic. The future, all mine to decide. I put down my diary, and lay back to watch the bats flitter like velvety guardian angels over me, in the light of the full moon. I freed the knot of the tent flap, and drifted off to a blissful sleep. Unaware that some of those people I thought I'd left behind would be with me my whole lifetime.

ACKNOWLEDGEMENTS

I would like to thank the following people who have inspired and encouraged me towards making this book a reality; Lizzi Linklater, Dannie Hancock, Guy Mankowski, Barry Calder, Sophie Coulombeau, Doreen Gurrey, Paul Dodgson, Sharon Richards, Bridget Holding and John Lamont. Any mistakes are entirely my own.

This book would not have been possible without the patient support of my wife Carole, and the feedback from members of both the Pen 2 Paper and the Bootham Writers groups

ABOUT THE AUTHOR

Graham Clift worked in a variety of plant related jobs and eventually experienced both Further and Higher education. He joined the Civil Service and worked with farmers and growers before settling in North Yorkshire. After retiring through ill health, major surgery allowed him to return to the land (an allotment). He writes to try to make sense of his life. This is his first book.

If you have enjoyed reading this book, please consider leaving a review on Amazon.

Printed in Great Britain
by Amazon

55757887R00231